P9-EMP-013

Bio
Rub   Levy, Shawn.
       The last playboy:
       The high life of
       Porfirio Rubirosa

OCT 1 0 2007	
OCT 2 9 2007	

THE LAST PLAYBOY

ALSO BY SHAWN LEVY

Ready, Steady, Go!:
The Smashing Rise and Giddy Fall of Swinging London

Rat Pack Confidential: Frank, Dean, Sammy, Peter, Joey,
and the Last Great Showbiz Party

King of Comedy: The Life and Art of Jerry Lewis

THE LAST PL

AYBOY

THE

HIGH LIFE

OF

PORFIRIO

RUBIROSA

SHAWN LEVY

Fourth Estate
An Imprint of HarperCollinsPublishers

HarperCollins books may be purchased for educational, business, or sales promotional use. For information, please write: Special Markets Department, HarperCollins Publishers, 10 East 53rd Street, New York, NY 10022.

FIRST EDITION

Designed by Jessica Shatan Heslin

Title page photograph © Bettmann/CORBIS

Printed on acid-free paper

Library of Congress Cataloging-in-Publication Data has been applied for.

ISBN-10: 0-00-717059-9   ISBN-13: 978-0-00-717059-3

05   06   07   08   09   BVG/RRD   10   9   8   7   6   5   4   3   2   1

FOR VINCENT, ANTHONY, AND PAULA,

WITHOUT WHOM THERE WOULDN'T BE MUCH POINT

CONTENTS

THE LAST PLAYBOY

This, he reckoned, must be what they called a joint.

Normally in New York he didn't go into joints. The Plaza, El Morocco, the Stork Club, the Copa, "21": That was the sort of thing he liked. He was in the city so rarely, he was only interested in the best of it.

In Paris, of course, he knew such places, cafés and bars and clubs where you might meet a killer or somebody with an interesting business idea or a woman who would change your life— or maybe just a few minutes of it. But this, this had something of the savor of a café back home, one of the places along El Conde— an air of abandon and indulgence and danger. It was dark, spare, ominous. He liked it.

Besides, the best places were, how to say it, a little chilly right now. All this talk: newspapers and the television and people on the street and the ones they called "the right people." The snobs and the writers hated one another, but to him they seemed very much the same. . . .

He had nothing to fear, nothing to hide, nothing to be ashamed about. But he didn't need the headache of answering questions and being stared at by gossips and trying to figure out who would talk to him and who wouldn't.

This place would do just fine, then: convenient, quiet, anonymous.

He had agreed to meet the newspaperman because he needed to get his own story out and he was assured by friends that he could trust the fellow. Earl Wilson he was called: owl-faced, a little thick in the waist, an easy laugher, a good listener.

Right now, he needed someone to listen—and then go and tell it in the way he wanted it told. All around New York the most horrible things were being said: He was a threat to his new wife; he was only interested in her money; he was some kind of villain or crook or gigolo. People knew nothing about them: He had known Barbara for years; she was charming, vibrant, delicate, cultured, creative; why shouldn't he truly love her? And in Las Vegas, that madwoman with her press conferences and her eye patch and her ridiculous lies about what he had said to her and what he felt. No wonder people were giving him funny looks.

No, his own voice had to be heard, and for that he needed someone neutral, someone who would tell the truth about him: Earl Wilson, his new best friend.

They sat at midnight in a booth in the back of the Midston House bar on East Thirty-eighth Street, one freezing night, one of the last of 1953. They drank scotch—*scotches*—and he nibbled from the bowl of popcorn the waitress had put on the table when they sat down. "My bachelor dinner," he joked.

Some pleasantries, and then the questions.

This was Barbara's fifth wedding and his fourth. Why would anyone expect it to work out?

"Wonderful Barbara brought something new and different into my life," he said, "and I will not be like her other husbands. I will make her happy at last."

Next, Wilson wanted to know, like they all did, about the money: Barbara was said to have $100 million; was he after it?

"Riches to me don't count," he said sweetly. "I don't need anybody's money. I have plenty of my own. We will be married like civilized people under the law of separate property. What property she has is hers and what property I have is mine."

He didn't, of course, mention the prenuptial contract he had signed that very afternoon: $2.5 million on the barrelhead, plus future considerations, of which he also had plenty of his own. Let the great reporter find some things out on his own. . . .

"Is she ill?" Wilson asked.

"Ill?"—a laugh, with a little scorn in it, which he caught almost as quickly as he'd shown it. "Not at all, she's the healthiest woman—it's fantastic! Yes, she was in Doctors Hospital, but only to rest. And now, my God, what a vitality! She's so strong that when she shakes hands I say, 'My God, where did you get all that weight?' "

"But I thought she was slender from loss of weight. . . ."

"Oh, no. I don't like skinny girls—and she's all right!"

They laughed a little and Wilson wrote.

And what about this business in Las Vegas, Zsa Zsa claiming he had asked her to marry him and that he had hit her when she refused him?

Now he was impatient.

"Zsa Zsa is just trying to get publicity out of Barbara and me, and I don't think it's ladylike."

The writer kept his eyes on his notepad, scribbling, silent.

The man seated across the table remembered who he was—a public figure, a glamorous consort, a world-famous lover, an intimate to power and wealth and sensation. He could breeze through it. He would have to get the smile just right. . . .

"Barbara is such an intelligent girl," he continued. "She understands human nature so well; she'll know it's all ridiculous. She's one of the most intelligent women anybody ever met."

They returned to small talk: who would attend from the bride's family, where would they honeymoon, where would they live.

And then, nicely buzzing, he rose and excused himself.

Tomorrow was going to be a big day.

How did they say it in English?

Like a zoo. . . .

ONE

IN THE LAND OF

TÍGUERISMO

When he sat down and tried to remember it all, in the '60s, near the end of his life, he began, naturally, with his child-hood, as he could retrieve it: a series of brief scenes, like film clips, set in his intoxicating, perilous homeland—ran-dom moments, yet with a cumulative impact that shaped him irrationally, subliminally, imparting to him tastes and biases that he never lost. A man of the world, he forever defined himself by reference to a specific place. . . .

Rifle fire; early morning; a child springs up in bed. "At most," he remembered later, "I was three years old."

Not long after, in the dead of another night, the child startles awake once again, panicked to find himself alone. "I was in the habit of sleeping with a cat." He leaves his bed to seek his feline bedmate, and is shocked to find strangers everywhere. "The house was filled with armed men asleep in the hallways."

And maybe a year later still, a mounted rider approaches. "Without getting off his horse, he took me in his great big hands and pulled me up to its neck, in front of him. One click of his tongue, and we were off! 'Careful Pedro, careful! He's so little!' shouted my mother. My father laughed. The night was gentle and sweet. I had the horse's mane gripped in my hands. I heard his hard breathing. I wished the corral would never end."

Gunshots; soldiers; a strongman; a horse; a shouting woman; the thrill of speed; the danger; the Cibao Valley of the Dominican Republic in its Wild West phase, circa 1913: the earliest flashes of memory in the mind of Porfirio Rubirosa.

=====

In the early twentieth century, when a little boy was being imprinted by these memories, the Dominican Republic was, as it had been for centuries prior, a place where fortunes might be made and dominions might be established—but only after painful struggles that were not always won by the most honorable combatant. It was a place that tended to favor unfavorable outcomes. Indeed, despite the noble charge and historic pedigree of the first white men who stumbled on it, the first European to settle the island and live out his days there was, in all likelihood, a rat.

Just after midnight on Christmas Day, 1492, a Spanish caravel gently foundered onto a coral reef beside the large island that its passengers had dubbed *Española*—Hispaniola in English—the sixth landmass it had encountered in the dozen weeks since departing the Canary Islands.

By dawn, the ship had broken up and sunk.

At that moment, Christopher Columbus had a complete fiasco on his hands.

A nondescript Genoese merchant sailor who made his home in Portugal, Columbus had sufficiently gulled the queen of Spain with his outlandish theories about a sea route to Asia that she arranged a backdoor loan for his enterprise from her husband's treasury. Isabella invested enough in his pipe dream for Columbus to acquire supplies, a crew, and three ships—the largest of which, the *Santa María*, had just become the first in several centuries of fabled Caribbean wrecks.

Gold Columbus reckoned he would find, and jewels and spices and a path to the riches of the other side of the world that would make trade with the hostile Moors unnecessary. But to date, he had gleaned significantly less than his own weight in treasure, and with the *Santa María* sunk, he was down to two ships for the trip home.

So he formed a landing party (which included at least one stowaway rat, whose bones—distinct from those of native species—would be discovered by archeologists centuries later), and he went ashore. There he shook hands with the leader of the native Tainos, accepted a few gifts, and founded a colony, named La Navidad in honor of its Christmas Day discovery. He looked around for a mountain of gold and, seeing none, packed up the *Niña* and *Pinta* and went home.

Ten months later, having raised enough capital to fund a fleet of seventeen ships, he returned, intent on exploiting the fonts of gold he believed the island nestled. In January 1494, he founded a second settlement, named La Isabela for his patroness, and used it as a base from which to explore the interior of the island.

Specifically, Columbus was curious about the Cibao, a highland valley that meandered eastward along a river from the northern coast through two mountain ranges and met the sea again in swamplands in the east. On his previous trip, he'd been told that the valley was home to fields where chunks of gold as large as a man's head lay about just waiting to be gathered. He forayed inland and found the valley—he labeled it La Vega, "the open plain"—but there was no gold. He was nevertheless impressed: The soil was rich, the climate mild, the river navigable, the mountain ranges, particularly to the south, formidable. If he had been a settler and not a buccaneer, he might have colonized the place for ranching and farming. But his priority was raw wealth. He moved on.

Columbus would make two more trips to Hispaniola, still looking for gold, still luckless. He and his men would found the city of Santo Domingo on the southern coast, a deep harbor from which Spain would rule the Caribbean and the Americas. In the coming centuries, the island, genocidally cleansed of natives, would be a keystone of the Spanish slave trade and an important colony of plantations. The Cibao would yield real wealth—fortunes based in coffee, cattle, sugarcane, tobacco—but nobody would ever again venture there in search of treasure.

Indeed, those who did choose to settle there were often lucky just to keep their heads. For hundreds of years after Columbus, the island, despite its import as a staging ground, would be overrun by a continual string of colonial and civil wars and the never-ending scourges of disease, poverty, rapine, and neglect.

Hispaniola fell into ruin in large part because it was, uniquely, colonized by two European powers. The Spanish contented themselves with dominating the eastern side until the French established a foothold in the west in the mid-seventeenth century. The island, long neglected by Spain in favor of colonies that yielded more in the way of obvious riches, suddenly seemed a valuable commodity, a point of contention. Back and forth forces of the two rivals fought, trying bootlessly to vanquish one another until the island was split by treaty in 1697 into two nations: Haiti and Santo Domingo. The plantations of Haiti, under French guidance, prospered, while Santo Domingo lapsed into a tropical torpor more typical of Spanish rule: Slaves bought their freedom and married with Europeans; infrastructure, never the strong suit of Spanish colonialism, was neglected; the economy declined into stagnation. When the Haitian slave rebellion led by Toussaint L'Ouverture spilled eastward over the border in 1801, there was little resistance. Under a rampage of murder, rape, and butchery, Santo Domingo simply fell into French hands for twenty bloody years.

Then a hero arose: Juan Pablo Duarte, a homegrown nationalist who sought freedom not only from the Haitians but from Spain. Starting as a governor of the Cibao, he routed the Haitians and the Spanish, but he failed to bring true unity to the nation. From the expulsion of the Haitian forces in 1844 through the expulsion of the Spanish in 1865 and onward toward the new century, the Dominican Republic, as it had been renamed, was ruled by chaos. Presidents came and went in brief, nasty succession; unrest and poverty were epidemic; and a species of tribal warfare ground on. There were puppet heads of state, bloodthirsty chieftains, coups and battles and massacres and ambushes and ceaseless conflicts. It seemed the destiny of the country always to roil.

=======

Into this quagmire, in San Francisco de Macorís, a small city of the swampy eastern portion of the Cibao, Pedro Maria Rubirosa was born in 1878. The Rubirosas were an educated family, with a tradition of public service. But in this wild era, public service meant choosing a side in the never-ending civil wars. Although he was well schooled, by the time he was in his teens, Pedrito Rubirosa was riding with bands of soldiers. And by the time he was in his twenties, he was leading them.

Half a century later, his son regarded a tintype of his father from these days: "In the photograph in my hands, my father already shines like an adult. With his strong cheekbones, his powerful head, his thick moustache, his gaze falls arrogantly from a height of five-foot-ten. He doesn't seem at all an adolescent: he is a man by deed and right. They called him Don Pedro."

Don Pedro, his son related, "was always in a campaign. It was the time of basements stocked with rifles and houses filled with soldiers. In effect, my father negotiated a ceaseless labyrinth of skirmishes, assaults, forays, and guerilla attacks." And through a combination of personal qualities and historical accidents, he became, in the military algebra of the era, a general. In this context, mind, a general wasn't a professional soldier promoted after of a long career of battle and governance. He was, rather, the smartest, luckiest, boldest in his troop, responsible for arming, feeding, and housing his men, and for strategizing and liaising with the other bands of soldiers with which they were allied. It was a position earned as much with guts as brains. "A general who didn't march in front of his men didn't exercise great dominion over them," Don Pedro's son said. "This explains why Dominican officers rarely died in bed of old age, like their European colleagues, and why rapid promotions permitted a youngster of 20 to become a general."

But there was another quality to Don Pedro, even more important than his daring or his brains or the poor luck of his senior colleagues. As his son put it, "One had to be a tiger to command a group of tigers."

Tiger: *tigre* in Spanish, *tíguere* in the local argot, in which the word came to represent the essential defining characteristic of the Dominican alpha male. The Dominican *tíguere* was, like the ideal male in all Latin cultures, profoundly masculine—*macho,* in the Castilian—but had dimensions unique, perhaps, to the Creole culture of Hispaniola. He was handsome, graceful, strong, and well-presented, possessed of a deep-seated vanity that allowed him the luxury of niceties of character and appearance that might otherwise hint at femininity. He could move with sensuality or violence; he was fast, fearless, fortunate. A *tíguere* emerged well from nearly any situation that confronted him, twisted any misfortune to an asset, spun a happy ending of some sort out of the most outrageously poor circumstance; he was able, being feline, to climb to unlikely heights and, should he fall, always landed, being feline, on his feet. The *tíguere* bore the savor of low origins and high aspirations, as well as a certain ruthless ambition that barred no means of achieving his ends: violence, treachery, lies, shamelessness, daring, and, especially, the use of women as tools of social mobility. A *tíguere* always married to advantage.

If there was an element of the outlaw or the delinquent in the *tíguere,* if only in his early days, he could hope to transcend it and reach the highest rungs of society—indeed, it was widely understood in Dominican life that an element of *tíguerismo* was essential to most success. To some degree, the Dominican male, if he was true to his blood and his culture, could be permitted virtually any impudence or trespass whatever. Adultery, theft, tyranny, violence, bellicose savagery, social cruelty, excesses of libido and appetite and greed: All could be ascribed to—and forgiven as—*tíguerismo.*

Pedro Maria Rubirosa clearly fulfilled the role of *tíguere* as a warrior and man of action. But he did so as well as a lover of women. "My father was a handsome man," the son remembered. "His form was lithe, his eyes brilliant; he shone with every aspect of a gentleman. Women admired him."

Among those admirers was a girl from his hometown, Ana Ariza Almanzar, granddaughter of a Spanish general who had fought in Cuba. At the dawn of the new century, Don Pedro took this well-bred young woman as his wife.

They began their family with tragedy, losing at least one child before 1902; then a daughter, Ana, managed to survive the perils of tropical infancy. Three years later came a son, Cesar. The *tíguere* now had a male heir to boast of and to train.

It was a flush time for Don Pedro. The tyrant Ulises Heureaux, who had ruled the Dominican Republic with a ruthless hand for two decades, had been assassinated in the summer of 1899, and a period of relative calm had descended. Don Pedro's daring, loyalty, and intelligence had recommended him to the new government, and he was appointed as governor of a string of small cities—first San Francisco de Macorís, then the coastal city of Samaná, then El Seibo, each posting finding him assigned farther from home as the warrior-politicians of the Cibao peacefully extended their influence.

In El Seibo, where he arrived in 1906, Don Pedro allowed himself the pleasure of other women. (Ana, her son would offer by way of explanation, "got fat after her first children arrived.") With a local woman and her cousin he fathered four children *en la calle*, as the saying went: "in the street": bastards.

He acknowledged them, though only one took his name. And then his duties called him back to San Francisco de Macorís, where the last of his legitimate children was born, on January 22, 1909. They named him Porfirio.

It was such a sparkling name: Porfirio Rubirosa Ariza (the Ariza a technicality, following the Spanish convention of retaining the matronym for legal purposes).

The surname was, of course, a given, and it meant "red rose."

The Christian name, however, was something of a fancy, not a family name like that of the baby's sister or an obviously historical name like that of his brother. There were some obscure antecedents: an ascetic

Saint Porphyry of Gaza; Porphyry of Tyre, a mathematician and philosopher of Phoenicia, noted to this day for his treatises on vegetarianism and named after the purple dye for which his home city was famous (at root, the word "porphyry" refers to a shade of purple that naturally occurs in feldspar crystals). But Don Pedro and Ana probably had in mind Porfirio Díaz, the autocratic president of Mexico under whose hand that nation modernized itself into the envy of the Caribbean—a strongman whose career, like Caesar's, would be worth emulating.

Ironically, soon after the baby was baptized, the great Díaz found himself falling into a struggle to maintain his rule—just as Don Pedro once again found himself commanding men in the field when yet another civil war broke out in the Dominican Republic in 1911. This was the campaign that formed the young Porfirio's first memories: the rifle shots at dawn, the soldiers sleeping throughout the house, the cat that crept away in the night.

The boy would grow to remember, too, a fearful, devout Doña Ana: "My mother, who was very pious, lived at prayer . . . I remember her often curled up in the darkest corner of the house, praying." Doña Ana Ariza Rubirosa may have seemed a pushover: born to a family of soldiers, married to a soldier, countenancing her husband's infidelities, burying herself in counsel with the Virgin of Altagracia, draped demurely in black, growing plump. But there was steel in her as well. Take the way she saw to the woman who was making time with Don Pedro and then ran, unopposed, for the presidency of the ladies' club of San Francisco de Macorís. On the day of the vote, with all the notable women of the city assembled and prepared to anoint their new leader, the outgoing president announced that she was so sure that they all approved of her successor that the election would be conducted by acclamation. "No," came a voice. All heads turned to face the speaker, Doña Ana. "This woman is my husband's lover," she declared. "Under these conditions, I don't think it's possible to make her our president." Shock; murmurs; a hasty conference of officials; and a new presidential candidate was impressed and elected. Ana got in her carriage, according to her son, "and returned home without saying a single word to my father about the scandalous scene she'd made. And he, after being told about the incident a few minutes later, also remained silent."

Perhaps the scandal she'd created with her outburst was too great; perhaps Ana feared in time of civil war for the safety of her children ("Careful Pedro, careful! He's so little!"); perhaps Don Pedro, in his mid-thirties, had grown too comfortable, too encumbered, too secure to lead troops; perhaps his intellect was recognized by his colleagues as more useful to them than his bravery; perhaps he was in flight from enemies. For whatever reason, in 1914, soon after Doña Ana's bold gambit, the Rubirosas found themselves sailing away from their bellicose, agitated little country. Don Pedro had been named to serve in the Dominican legation in St. Thomas, the Virgin Islands.

At the age of five, Porfirio Rubirosa had begun his lifetime of wandering.

TWO

CONTINENTAL

SEASONING

I n a one-room schoolhouse—a large hut, really—the teacher
bent down to address his new pupil, who spoke neither French
nor English, and handed him a small violin. It was time for the
school orchestra to practice, and everyone took part.

But this slim little boy didn't know how to play. He took his
instrument and dutifully joined his classmates, who included
his older brother and sister. He stood in the back. The others, following the teacher's directions, began to saw away at their music.
The boy began to cry.

The teacher spoke to him kindly: "Act as if you can play, that's
enough."

And the child, mollified, did just that.

And he thought to himself, "Is the world of grown-ups, perhaps,
a world in which appearances are all that matters?"

St. Thomas, where Porfirio Rubirosa learned how *not* to play
the violin, was an Antillean idyll for Don Pedro's family. For less
than a year they lived in a small house in the middle of a sugarcane plantation while Don Pedro saw to his ministerial duties.

Back home, the situation was still dangerously unstable: Haiti too had fallen into turmoil, and the United States, to which the Dominican treasury owed a sum it couldn't possibly repay, had taken a more active interest in the rising chaos on the island. Fewer than twenty years earlier the Yankees had driven Spain out of Cuba; now events in Europe—where a continent-wide war had been set off—made the securing of the Caribbean a matter of increasing import in their eyes.

From St. Thomas it was impossible for Don Pedro to read the subtleties of the power struggle back home. So he chose, in a sense, to turn away from it. In 1915, he accepted another diplomatic appointment, one that would have an indelible impact on himself and his family. He would represent his country at its embassy in France.

This new charge meant more than just uprooting his wife and children. Don Pedro was being sent to the most prestigious posting in the world by a government he couldn't be sure would exist from week to week and at a time when his new home was itself embroiled in war. Even as he could anticipate with zest a new life in Europe, the onetime warrior of the Cibao sobered at the weight of the prospect. And Porfirio, sensitized by his musical experience to the language of appearances in the adult world, noticed the metamorphosis. "My father had changed," he recalled later. "No longer did he wear a pistol in his belt or a saber between his shoulder blades. He was now Chief of a diplomatic mission."

And not just any diplomatic mission, of course, but Paris—the capital of the world insofar as it had one. "We have perhaps forgotten," Don Pedro's son would write, "that before the war of 1914, the prestige of France throughout Latin America was immense. From the other side of the Atlantic, France seemed the ideal marriage of the style of the *ancien régime* with the dynamism of revolution."

Getting there was a fantastic adventure. The family sailed on the *Antonio Lopez* to Gibraltar, where they were greeted not with flags and salutes but with gunfire; British authorities suspected that among the ship's passengers was a German spy disguised in frock and wig. Again the young boy's imagination was fired by the strange simulations of the grown-up world: "The mustached warriors of the Caribbean had been succeeded by Europe and spies dressed as women!" After a search, the *Antonio Lopez* was permitted to disgorge its passengers. The Rubirosas headed north by train. Ana and Cesar were left in Barcelona, the nearest important Spanish-speaking city to Paris, to continue their schooling. Porfirio continued on with his parents.

The city to which Don Pedro had been posted was a wonder to his son. There were strange new creature comforts, like the kidskin coat he wore as a redoubt to the astonishing cold. There were the impressive signs of war: cannons encircling the Arc de Triomphe, soldiers in the streets and the cafés. And there were glamorous sensations of the sort never seen in San Francisco de Macorís. On the first full day the family spent in the city, Don Pedro took his son to a cinema, where the boy sat in awe watching the great star Pearl White in *The Mysteries of New York,* a movie serial filled with barbaric cruelties, thrilling chases, impossible situations miraculously escaped from, and a fiendish villain, the Clutching Hand, who preyed on the beautiful heroine for occult reasons only he fathomed. One image would linger in the youngster's mind for decades: Pearl White trapped in a tube that slowly filled with water, threatening to drown her.

The family made its home first in temporary quarters on Boulevard Saint Germain and then within shouting distance of the Arc de Triomphe at 6 Avenue Mac-Mahon, an address that would exert a nostalgic pull on Porfirio throughout the decades in which he would live in Paris. The house sat in the true symbolic center of the city, which perhaps accounted for the number of times the Rubirosas found themselves collaterally involved in aerial bombardment by German planes, which regularly cut through the sky, flaunting their black-and-white crosses. Most French families fled underground at the sound of enemy aircraft, but Don Pedro reasoned that this would be a terrible hideaway, a lair of death by crushing or suffocation or slow starvation. Rather, he insisted that they stay above stairs, where they endured the occasional air raids and the accompanying thunder of bombs with stoicism the English would have admired: Don Pedro reading his newspaper, Porfirio playing with toys, Doña Ana saying her rosary. Only after the house suffered a truly astonishing concussion one afternoon when a bomb hit the nearby Avenue de la Grande Armée did the brave *tíguere* rethink his policy and direct his family to belowgrounds safety.

These close calls exerted an accumulative toll, and the Rubirosas soon moved to the coastal city of Royan, less than two hundred miles north of Spain on the Atlantic coast. There, Cesar and Ana rejoined the family and Don Pedro received some shocking news: The civil war back home had so escalated that marines from the United States had occupied the Dominican Republic.

Don Pedro had foreseen as much, according to Porfirio. "My father," he remembered, "realized that this constant civil war would only lead to catastrophe—the loss of national independence or dictatorship." But preparing for such a blow didn't lessen its impact, turning Don Pedro permanently from a man of action into a man of words, ideas, and policies. "Suddenly," Porfirio noted, "with the decisiveness that characterized him, he changed into a quiet man and began to study, with the help of a professor who came to the house, the worlds of economics, politics, international relations and languages." He was particularly taken with the law, and built a small library in his house of the imposing legal volumes published by Dalloz. It was, in his son's eyes, a poignant metamorphosis: "In my childhood, I never saw my father without a Smith and Wesson at his side; in my adolescence, in turn, I never saw him without a Dalloz under his arm."

=====

Despite the example of his father's study, young Porfirio realized that he wasn't cut from quite the same material. "Books didn't find in me a very faithful friend," he confessed, "nor did the professors find a conscientious student. The only things that interested me were sports, girls, adventures, celebrities—in short, life."

Once the family was back in Paris after the end of the war, Porfirio—who watched the victory parade along the Champs-Élysées from the prime vantage of the roof on Avenue Mac-Mahon—attended a string of schools, making no impression in any of them save as a goalkeeper in soccer, a skill that he maintained into his twenties. He was enrolled in some of France's finest seats of youthful learning: l'Institut Maintenon, l'École Pascal, and the lycée Janson-de-Sailly, all in Paris, and l'École des Roches in Verneuil-sur-Avre, some sixty-five miles east by train. Nothing took. He lived only for the spectacles of Parisian life, for thrills and novelties and chums and escape . . . and to get out of his short pants.

Almost more than his first shave or sexual experience, the privilege to wear long pants on a daily basis was a symbol of achieving manhood for a young teenager of the era—a sartorial bar mitzvah for the Little Lord Fauntleroy set. At school, Porfirio had become chummy with a Chilean boy, Pancho Morel, and a boy named Jit Singh, youngest son of the maharaja of Karpathula. They were younger than Porfirio, but they didn't have the protective Doña Ana as their mothers and had not only begun wearing trousers but had worn them into nightclubs in Montmartre, lording their mature adventures over their bare-kneed Dominican pal. He seethed.

Finally, when her son was sixteen, the painstaking Doña Ana allowed him the dignity of long pants. And as soon as he buckled his belt, he was off. From the first night he steeled his nerve and sauntered into a Montmartre nightclub, Porfirio Rubirosa was at home.

"I had a racing heart and boiling blood and a delicious impatience throughout my body," he confessed later. "I remember the doorman, the music that came in waves, the diffused light that imparted mystery to the faces. . . . More than 30 years have passed since that night, and I still see the wet lips opening on white teeth and the eyes that shone like lights, and I hear the laughs that merged into one single strident trumpet blare."

He wandered home at dawn, drunk on the atmosphere and the possibilities—as well as the libations. His parents had been up all night, worried sick, more grateful for his safety than angered at his presumption. Porfirio was chastened, and resolved privately never to frighten them again. But presently he realized that, truly, he felt only the slightest bit contrite: "I am, and will always be, a man of pleasure."

And why not? Fate and history had brought him to come of age in one of the great seats of pleasure the world would ever know. "Those who didn't know Paris in the '20s," he declared with certainty decades later, "don't know what a nightclub is." The interwar demimonde into which he flung himself was the stuff of legend. The Montmartre of the 1920s was no longer the bohemia of starving artists that it had been before the Great War; Pablo Picasso and his adherents had moved across the Seine to Montparnasse and founded a new enclave that would soon draw the Lost Generation of American writers and free spirits. In their wake, the neighborhood that sported such venerable outposts of debauchery as the Moulin Rouge, Le Chat Noir, and the Folies Bergère as well as such lower-rent cousins as Tabarin, Monaco, La Perruche, Zelli's, Chez Florence, and Le Grand Duc, had become increasingly associated with a blend of criminality and pleasure that lacked the éclat of arty bohemianism. It was no longer an aesthetic wonderland but rather a carnival world of low life lived hard—no place for innocents.

And yet its denizens looked favorably on this ambitious Dominican boy. Latin men were, at the time, enjoying a unique cachet. The tango craze that had begun before the war was booming and had, indeed, been amplified by other musical fads imported from the Caribbean and South America, including the Dominican merengue. Latin musicians and idle young Latin men were everywhere, and they drew to their hangouts a clientele of slumming locals, many of them women; from afternoon on into the early morning hours, the clubs of Montmartre hosted a stream of Parisian matrons led provocatively around dance floors by younger Latin men who were paid for their time: *gigolos* (from the French word for a loose-moraled dancing girl, *gigolette*). These hired guns of the boites were glamorous in a sinister fashion that gave additional luster to their reputation as men employed for pleasure.* None other than the great Rudolph Valentino, who died of a perforated ulcer during the days of Porfirio's induction into Parisian night life, had voyaged to America from Italy as a tango specialist and was said to have made his first living in New York as a gigolo. A young Latin man couldn't help but admire and aspire.

But crazes, of course, are designed to fade. And although the Latin

* In England and America, they came to be known as lounge lizards.

vogue was wearing out, Porfirio was still in luck. The new fascination in the Parisian demimonde was with American hot jazz and black musicians, singers, and dancers. The area of Montmartre below the Butte was the Parisian Harlem, teeming with African-American expatriates and dotted with hotels, bars, cafés, and nightclubs that catered to them. Once again, a boy from the Caribbean, of mixed blood, with café au lait skin and hair described as somewhere between wavy and kinky, would blend easily into such an environment, acquiring a liberal education in sensation and reckless living that would, obviously, ingrain itself in his spirit far more deeply than anything going on at school.

In this sexy, dangerous world, the game young Porfirio more than fit in, he was a hit. But his love affair with Parisian night life would prove, at least for the time being, a dalliance. Once again, in 1926, Don Pedro's work called for the family to move. Another tottering government had been established in Santo Domingo—this one installed by the Americans, who had pulled out their troops to allow the locals a chance. The new regime assigned Don Pedro to its embassy in London; Porfirio would be schooled relatively nearby, in Calais.

As evinced by his decision to move the boy closer to where he himself would be, Don Pedro had some concerns about this boy who seemed more dancer than warrior. Porfirio was thin, wasp-waisted, coltish. And although he had an undeniable knack for sports, there were no obvious bulges of muscle on him, nor had his mettle ever been truly tested. Don Pedro arranged for him to be tutored in boxing. "The man of action still lived beneath the diplomat's clothes," he later explained, "and he wanted a solid son with quick fists."

Porfirio did no better in his studies at his new school than he had at any of the others. But the boxing was another matter. Springy and quick, he was a natural. And even better, the gym was located in a louche part of town where the young man's eyes were caught one afternoon by a sign reading Piccadilly Bar.

He went in. He ordered a drink. He made small talk. He had a good time. He came back. "I quickly became a regular," he later boasted, "celebrated for my youth, my free way with money, my Dominican nationality, a taste for strong cocktails and a strong hunger for the ladies." As in Paris, his race got him noticed and his cool, breezy, agreeable manner made him popular.

The taste of notoriety went to his head. He soon felt sufficiently full of himself to accept the challenge of a fight against a local champion named Dagbert. On the big night—the humming crowd, the smoke-filled room—a sense of grandeur infused the young fighter. For a round or so, he used his training, his wile, his wits to keep Dagbert safely at bay. Then he reckoned he could grab the advantage and got cute. Dagbert saw an opening and pasted him squarely. "I got hit right in the Adam's apple," he remembered. "I couldn't breathe, I was suffocating, but I was saved by the bell. But by the end of the rest period, I still hadn't recovered. Despite the shouting, I quit the fight. The thrills of the Piccadilly were less dangerous."

It was the last proper boxing match in which he would ever take part, and, indeed, he quit his formal training soon after. But he didn't quit leaving campus for lessons. He simply told the authorities at school that he was off to the gym and made a beeline instead for the Piccadilly, where he delved deeper into his cups until finally he was found dead drunk one evening by his scandalized schoolmaster. It was a terminal offense: He would not be permitted to return to the school after the summer holidays.

—————

That was just as well, because by then Dominican politics had yet once more yanked at Don Pedro, pulling him from London back to Santo Domingo, where a seemingly stable government had been installed and was working toward elections. Don Pedro, now a seasoned international diplomat and legal mind, was thought more valuable at home than in foreign courts. He returned home and, with the chimerical hope that his wayward youngest son would straighten himself out in his absence, left Porfirio in France to finish his baccalaureate studies.

The freedom provided by his parents' absence was absolutely intoxicating. Porfirio passed most of that summer partying in Biarritz with his wealthy schoolmates. "The images that come to my mind," he recalled "are pictures of a brilliant sea beneath the sun, sports cars tearing through little towns, *thés dansantes* with women who acted like girls. Everything was the pretext for a dare: swimming, drinking, racing, love. Naturally, when we returned to Paris, we tried to extend the crazy atmosphere of our vacations. This was made easier for me because of my father's absence."

Don Pedro hired a tutor—"friendliness personified" as Porfirio remembered him euphemistically—but the boy was a confirmed debauchee by this point, as he gladly confessed. "I only opened the books that appealed to me, and those weren't many. The only geography I was interested in was the geography of Paris's night life." He naturally failed to graduate.

And then he went home to Santo Domingo: "a brutal break from what I referred to at this time as 'the life.' "

The exact details of his removal from Paris would prove a blur. The grown-up Porfirio would claim that he had been living with the family of his Chilean schoolmaster Pancho Morel and, upon failing his baccalaureate, received a telegram from Don Pedro ordering him to Bordeaux, where transit home had been booked for him on the *Carimare*. He claimed the boat docked in the Dominican port of Puerta Plata and that he traveled by car from there southward through the Cibao to join his family in Santo Domingo.

But another account emerged from a witness less disposed to putting a pretty shine on things. Leovigildo Cuello was a doctor who lived in Santiago, the chief city of the Cibao, and was friendly with Don Pedro. His widow, Carolina Mainardi di Cuello, would remember years later that a frightened, hungry, filthy Porfirio showed up at her doorstep unannounced and unexpected one day in 1928. His clothes were spotted with engine oil, and he had a fantastic story to tell: Having been cut off by his parents for his excesses and failings, he had spent several months in Paris living hand to mouth as a member of a Gypsy dance troupe that busked for money; summoned home, he stowed away in the engine room of the *Carimare*—hence his disheveled state—and needed some help to make his way to his family. The Cuellos cleaned and fed and clothed him and, despite his entreaty "please don't let my father know," phoned Don Pedro, who was visiting nearby San Francisco de Macorís and came to Santiago to fetch him.

It was hardly the happiest of reunions.

"I was wrong to leave you alone in Paris," Don Pedro declared. "I took you for a man, and you're just a ruffian." He announced that he would bring his prodigal youngest son to Santo Domingo where a "double dose of studies" would be administered to him by a brace of teachers: a tutor for his baccalaureate exam, and a new member of the family—his sister's fiancé, the attorney Gilberto Sánchez Lustrino—to prepare him for law school.

That was disappointing news. But it wasn't nearly so deflating as Porfirio's impression of the man who delivered it: "My father, in one year, had aged a great deal. Once so tall, he was doubled over. His cheeks had fallen. And his gaze was filled with a profound sadness." At barely fifty, Don Pedro was falling into moral despair and was further cursed by a weak heart. He managed to engage himself in the affairs of the capital, but the process taxed him, to his son's concern: "My father's aspect worsened more each day. Nothing is sadder than the sickness and aging of a man who has asked much of his body and received it."

To his surprise, Porfirio found Santo Domingo an agreeable successor to Paris.

For one thing, even though he'd left the island some fourteen years earlier, he felt its stir still in his blood. "I wasn't more than a baby when I left my homeland," he reflected, "but the echoes of infancy, on top of the stories told me by my parents, exerted an extraordinary force."

The family lived in a three-story house on the corner of Calle Arzobispo Meriño and Calle Emiliano Tejera, in the midst of the city's colonial zone. It was not the capital of the world, that was plain. In lieu of grand boulevards there were narrow streets whose gutters teemed with garbage that was hosed toward the sea several times a day. The great monuments of Columbus's era—cathedrals, convents, hospitals, palaces—lay in untended ruin. Rather than nightclubs, there were impromptu dances in plazas or in private homes, from which music and light would spill out onto dark cobblestone streets in magnetic pools. The jeweled, befurred, painted, perfumed women who gave Paris such an erotic charge were replaced by *damas* straitjacketed by a nearly medieval propriety and their daughters, repressed into crippling shyness. Instead of the dizzying savor of modernity, there was a stolid adherence to old ways. The latest cars, clothes, music, ways of living: completely unheard-of.

And yet that didn't mean there wasn't some semblance of "the life" to be found. There was an agreeably languid pace to the Caribbean—the siestas and paseos and macho camaraderie. Porfirio was naturally drawn to the groups of raucous young men who gathered on street corners, in plazas, and in parks. A friend who met him at that time, Pedro Rene Contin Aybar, remembered Rubi as "tall, of good build, with an energetic face, thick lips, curly hair, an intense gaze and an agreeably deep baritone voice." His acceptance among this new crowd was facilitated by his exotic pedigree as a Dominican raised in Paris: "I had a lot to tell them. They envied my free comportment, of course. And after the free life I had known, I took a certain wicked delight in scandalizing this closed society a little bit."

At the head of a fast bunch, he whored, he drank, he showed off his sporting and terpsichorean skills—he was noted for something called an apache dance—and his small talent with the ukulele. It was the era when the merengue, the indigenous folk music of Hispaniola, blossomed into a jazz-influenced sound suited to the dance hall; some of the most infectious music ever produced in the Caribbean was being played nightly, live on stage for Rubi and his chums, and they adored it.

In the midst of this, Rubi evinced an entrepreneurial streak, establishing a boxing ring in the small plaza in front of the church of San Lázaro, in a lower-class neighborhood of the capital; admission to the fights, which featured such local phenoms as Kid GoGo and Kid 22–22, was a few pennies.

And he put his natural audacity and European sophistication to comic use among his chums. There was the day, for instance, when they were all standing on a corner of Santo Domingo's busiest shopping street, El Conde, making mock-heroic protestations of chivalric devotion to passing girls who, in the manner of the day, wouldn't even make eye contact with boys to whom they weren't related. Porfirio approached one and took the bold initiative of snatching a notebook from her hand. The startled girl shrieked and ran off to a nearby tavern, only to emerge a few minutes later with her uncle, a local bully known as Suso García. He walked up to the boys on the corner and demanded to know which of them had so affronted his niece. Porfirio allowed that it was he, and the belligerent fellow came rushing at him. But with the footwork he'd learned in Calais, he sidestepped the attack and countered with a solid right hand to the big man's chin, sending him reeling backward to trip over a curbstone.

As García gathered himself and wandered off, dazed and ashamed, Porfirio accepted his friends' acclaim with sarcastic pomp. ("I preened," he recalled.) But a minute or so later, García was back, this time wielding a knife and demanding satisfaction. Porfirio agreed to a duel, and the two set off down El Conde in search of a blade of equal size and weight. Failing that, García suggested they find a pair of matching pistols; again, the younger man agreed. As they walked along, García made small talk, and asked Porfirio who he was.

"I am the son of General Rubirosa."

The bully stopped walking. "In that case," he declared, "I cannot fight you. I served under your father."

The episode became a local legend, spun in some versions with elaborate detail. But there was a bitter private irony to it: Don Pedro's name might still have been big enough to ward off an angry man with a knife, but his body was failing. In 1930, just before the national elections, he moved to San Francisco de Macorís, ostensibly to run as a congressional deputy for the district but quite obviously to die in the tranquility of his birthplace.

He moved into the house of his father-in-law, a strange old bird who'd been an important local lawyer until he was accused, in 1895, of having embezzled public funds; he was proven innocent, but he was so offended that his fellow townspeople should doubt him that he became a hermit, isolating himself in his house. "He never left his study or library and he refused to see anyone besides his family and clients," remembered Porfirio. "He never again put a foot in the street, and the only journey he made out of the house was in the hearse that carried him to the cemetery." Don Pedro wasn't quite so eccentric, but he was just as surely retreating from the world.

The gravity of his father's condition impressed Porfirio, who left Santo Domingo for Don Pedro's side and applied himself sufficiently to his studies to pass his baccalaureate and find work teaching French in a local school. He kept up his soccer, he took up competitive swimming, he traded lessons on the ukulele for guitar lessons from his cousin Evita.

And he sat patiently as Don Pedro, his voice weakened, told stories of his warrior days and shared his worries over the seemingly permanent chaos of Dominican governance. Indeed, even as Santo Domingo prepared for what was being billed as a free election, a rebellion against the government was brewing in—where else?—the Cibao.

Don Pedro knew the minds of both the government and the rebels. He had been offered positions of responsibility by both, refusing in each case because he saw the country's salvation in neither. In particular, he had strong fears about the leader of the National Police, a cunning and unlikely arriviste who had diabolically made Don Pedro the offer of ruling the country after a coup. As he sat with his son reading a newspaper account of the brewing rebellion, Don Pedro pointed a feeble finger at a name in a headline and said, as his son recalled, "Here is the heart of the plot. The one in charge, in the shadows, pulling the strings, who has all the trump cards, is Trujillo."

THREE

THE BENEFACTOR AND
THE CHILD BRIDE

His uniforms were always immaculate, as were, when he could finally afford them, his hundreds of suits.

His manner careered unpredictably from obsequious to civil to icy.

His appetites for drink, dance, pomp, and sex were colossal.

His capacity for focused work seemed infinite.

He was a finicky eater.

With his thin little mustache, he looked a cross of Charlie Chaplin's Monsieur Verdoux and a bullfrog, always with his hair slicked back, always standing erect to the fullness of his five feet seven inches, always tending slightly toward plumpness (as a boy, he was mocked as *Chapito:* "little fatty").

He had a massive ego that sat perilously on a foundation of dubious self-confidence.

He remembered everything and forgave nothing, though he might wait years to avenge a grudge.

He wasn't above physically torturing his enemies and throwing their corpses to the sharks, but he had at his disposal more insidious schemes that involved anonymous gossip, public shunning, and other shames that cut deeper, perhaps, than any punishment his goons might mete out.

His scheming and brutality and cunning and shamelessness and greed and nepotism and cruelty and gall and paranoia and righteousness and delusions of grandeur verged on the superhuman.

He was one of the most ruthless and reprehensible *caudillos,* or strongmen, ever to hold sway in the Western Hemisphere—and one of the most enduring.

He was Rafael Leonidas Trujillo Molina, and he formed an unholy bond with Porfirio Rubirosa that would crucially shape the latter's life.

=====

Trujillo was born in October 1891, the third of eleven children of a poor family from San Cristóbal, a provincial capital in the dusty south of the island. The town began as a gold rush camp, then settled into a long, hard haul as one of the island's many centers for processing sugarcane. It was never an illustrious spot, but for several decades of the twentieth century, it was known by federal decree as the Meritorious City, simply because it was the birthplace of this one man.

By his sixteenth birthday, with only a grammar school education, Trujillo was working full-time as a telegraph operator—and perhaps doing a little cattle rustling on the side, though records of his activities in that sphere would one day disappear. (Likewise, he was convicted of forgery and at another time suspected of embezzlement, but in neither case could it be shown on paper after he'd established his domain over the nation and its historical records.)

By his twenty-second birthday Trujillo was married to a country girl named Aminta Ledesma who was pregnant with a baby daughter who would die at age one and, like her father's criminal record, be erased from later accounts of his life. A second daughter, with a grander future, came the following year. They named her Flor de Oro—"golden flower" in English, "Anacaona" (the name of a warrior chieftainess of the Jaragua tribe) in the native Taino.

Trujillo first engaged with the hair-raising brand of Dominican politics in the mid-1910s, when he joined an unsuccessful rebellion against one of the nation's fleeting governments and had to live on the run in the jungle until finally, ragged and starving and underfed and missing a few teeth, he threw himself on the mercy of the authorities. Granted amnesty, he came back home and turned to crime, as a member of a gang called the Forty-four. And then he found honest work in a sugar refinery, first as a clerk and then, providentially, as a security guard.

It was no rent-a-cop position. In the lawless Dominican Republic of the era, the *policía* of a thriving private business constituted, in many cases, the only local authority of any standing. These forces were charged with keeping the peace and guarding their bosses' property from theft, but they also fought fires in the cane fields, protected payrolls, made sure workers didn't defect to rival operations, and mounted and supervised such profitable side businesses as bars, brothels, and weekly cockfights.

It was a position that called for a calculating mind composed of equal parts soldier, accountant, psychologist, and mafioso. Trujillo was perfect for it.

He liked the work so well, in fact, that he decided to become a career soldier, applying at the end of 1918 to join the National Police, the only military force open to a Dominican during the American occupation. His letter requesting induction was a combination of bootlicking, braggadocio, and bald-faced lies: "I wish to state that I do not possess the vices of drinking or smoking, and that I have not been convicted in any court or been involved in minor misdemeanors."

He was accepted, enrolling as a second lieutenant in January 1919. Within three years, he had attended an officers training school and been promoted to captain. The Yankees liked him: "I consider this officer one of the best in the service," wrote one evaluating officer. And he continued to advance, sometimes in shadowy fashion. In 1924, the major under whom he served was killed by a jealous husband; most onlookers assumed that the offended party was put onto the scent of his wife's affair by Trujillo, who eventually replaced the dead man in rank and duties. By the end of that year, with the North American marines having returned home, Major Trujillo was third in the chain of command of a military force that was virtually unopposed in ruling the land.

All that remained now was to take over.

But before he could ascend to full power, there was a domestic matter to resolve: namely, the peasant girl he had married, hardly a fitting wife for a man of his status. Sexually, Aminta had long since been replaced by a string of women, one of whom, Bienvenida Ricart, Trujillo had singled out as a likely next wife. Divorce by mutual consent was, curiously, legal in the almost homogeneously Catholic Dominican Republic at the time, and in September 1925 the Trujillos' marriage was dissolved by civil decree. Trujillo was ordered to pay alimony, to provide Aminta with a house, and, to his frustration, to leave Flor de Oro to live with her mother—a detail he would revisit.

A full two years later, serving at the rank of brigadier general, he married Bienvenida. But by then yet another concubine had taken a special place in his heart: María Martínez, who in 1929 would trump her rivals by producing a male heir, Rafael Leonidas Trujillo Martínez, a boy stamped for life with the nickname Ramfis, derived from his father's love of Verdi's dynastic opera *Aida*. Through the coming years, just as he navigated with Machiavellian deliberation the political waters of the nation, so would Trujillo manipulate these women, regularly discarding a lower-class mate for a higher as a means of fashioning his image and his fate: a proper *tíguere*.

He proved as decisive and ruthless in public life as in private. In the next two years, he moved gradually, in the shadows, to solidify a power base from which he might seize control of the country. In 1928, the National Police was transformed by law into a proper National Army, and Trujillo was named its chief. But he had additional resources at his disposal—thuggish gangs that enforced his wishes and maintained a cordon sanitaire of plausible deniability between his official position and the more brutal imposition of his will.

He patiently bided the ineffective presidency of Horacio Vásquez, the military man whose ascent back in 1924 had convinced the North American occupiers that the country could see to itself. As Vásquez's health failed and his government weakened toward collapse, various groups jockeyed to replace him. Each knew that it would need Trujillo on its side. None, however, fathomed the deep logic of the situation as well as he or recognized that he had fancied himself the best man to rule the country.

Presidential elections were announced for 1930, and it wasn't clear that Vásquez was out of the running; many notables—including, at times, Trujillo, at least publicly—declared an interest in his reelection. But at the same time, Trujillo hatched an audacious, sinister plan to usurp the presidency. In broad outline, he would confide in an ally in each opposition party his intention to support its cause by staging a rebellion of disloyal troops in—where else?—the Cibao; when Vásquez sent him to quell the rebellion, for he could turn to no one else, Trujillo would instead take command of it, leading it into the capital and overseeing a rigged election that would put his candidate—whoever that might be—in power.

What Trujillo told almost no one was that he was his own preferred candidate, that he was going to pull his support from whichever side came closest to power when it would be too late to stop him, seizing the top spot for himself. He shared his plans with the American diplomats who monitored Dominican politics from a judicious remove while wielding the threat of a second occupation as a means of influencing the nation's affairs (the Yanks were still impressed with him, if less than enthusiastic about his plan). He also shared his plans with Don Pedro Rubirosa, who declined to take part.

The scheme was so risky that Trujillo hedged against failure by keeping a small fortune in cash at the ready should it fail and he be forced to flee. As it turned out, it went almost exactly as he'd planned. He found credulous dupes in each political camp and played them sublimely: Each man, in his own ambition to usurp the presidency, was certain he had the army's support. He fomented just the right amount of faux unrest in the Cibao; when Vásquez felt himself nervously in need of a stronger military of his own, Trujillo was promoted to minister of national defense. A little more than a week later, as the phony revolt approached the capital, Vásquez, masterfully gulled, demanded assurances of loyalty from Trujillo and, mollified, directed him to stave off the impending coup. Trujillo sent a token platoon to oppose the insurrection—with orders, of course, to join rather than stop it—and then holed himself up with a more sizable and better-armed force in the chief redoubt of Santo Domingo, the Ozama Fortress. And there he sat implacably, insisting on his loyalty to Vásquez while the besieged president was forced to resign without a shot being fired in his defense.

Trujillo allowed his coconspirators in the opposition briefly to enjoy a show of control over the nation. And he equanimously allowed the presidential election to be held, with Vásquez's party still permitted to run a candidate. But the whole thing was a dark farce. Everyone who might have taken power had been suborned by Trujillo into treason; no one could risk exposing his own deceit by stepping forward to claim the reins. Trujillo used frank acts of intimidation and violence to curb any dissent to his own puppet candidate, Rafael Estrella Ureña, and then simply strong-armed the man out of the race. The sham election was protested even before it occurred: An oversight board resigned en masse a week before the balloting. In May 1930, Trujillo was elected president by a near unanimous (and patently fabricated) majority that would have made the most megalomaniacal despot envious; in August, amid the high pomp he had felt was due him even in his days as a telegraph operator, he was inaugurated.

With epic tenacity and iron severity, Trujillo would so impose his personality on the Dominican Republic and its people that there would be no appreciable distinction between the man and the nation. Stalin, Mao, Castro, Amin, Ceausescu, Hussein, Kim Il Sung: none would have the same degree or depth of impact on the psyche of his people. In the course of time, every home in the country would boast a sign reading "God and Trujillo"—often right out on the roof in huge letters. Santo Domingo would be renamed Ciudad Trujillo; calendars would all be dated according to the Era of Trujillo, with 1930 as Year One; Pico Duarte, at ten thousand feet the highest peak in the Caribbean, would be renamed Little Trujillo—as opposed, of course, to the *big* one who sat, literally, on the throne in the National Palace; the first toast at any formal dinner, *especially* those at which he was not in attendance, would be to the health and honor of Trujillo; and he would be spoken of not as the President or the Generalísimo or the leader but, unironically, as the Benefactor.

These ritualistic incarnations of the cult of personality didn't emerge immediately after Trujillo took power. No, before the *tíguere* Trujillo could metamorphose from soldier to god, certain parties reluctant to being held in his domain would have to be made to knuckle under. In particular, there was the refined circle of bourgeois families who dominated the social and cultural life of the capital. Educated, traveled, wealthy, born to relative privilege, they looked frankly down their noses at Trujillo with his mean roots, antiquated manners, and precise mien. In 1928, still merely an ambitious officer, Trujillo had stood for election to the Club Unión, one of Santo Domingo's most elite social institutions, and was admitted because, as everybody who observed the process knew, somebody acting under his orders had tampered with the vote. That he nevertheless went ahead and joined and attended the club was the most desperate sort of social climbing; Trujillo felt the sting of having been forced to embarrass himself and filed it away for future vindication. His revenge was swift: In 1932, after filling the club with military officers, he was elected as its president, transferred the entire membership wholesale to a newly formed premises, and had the genteel old home of the Club Unión razed.

But Trujillo characteristically had another, more cunning scheme for gaining influence over the Dominican elite. If he couldn't enlist the parents, he would enlist the children. And he found a perfect candidate with whom to begin his campaign: the feckless, French-educated, popular son of the estimable and recently deceased Don Pedro Maria Rubirosa.

———

In the autumn of 1931, Porfirio was out at a drinking party with friends at the Country Club, another of Santo Domingo's swank gathering places, when he noticed Trujillo, in full, glistening uniform, presiding over a party of military officers across the room. It was an inauspicious time for the young man: Upon his death a year earlier, Don Pedro had left his son little more than the thin veil of a good reputation—for which, truly, Porfirio had no practical use—and a deathbed wish that he continue his legal education. With the household now dominated by his brother-in-law Gilberto Sánchez Lustrino, a dreary future seemed probable. Obviously the opportunity to return to Paris was negligible, and the seemingly unavoidable legal studies would clearly tear him from the sporting, leisurely life of the streets of Santo Domingo.

Sánchez Lustrino was a true Dominican bourgeois, more dedicated to shows of courtliness and refinement than Don Pedro had ever been, a born-and-bred member of that class of gentlefolk who sneered, sometimes openly, at the pretenses of the rustic new president. And, as Porfirio didn't care much for his brother-in-law, he was particularly pleased when an aide of Trujillo's came to the table that night at the Country Club and told Porfirio that the president wanted to see him.

As he approached the group of soldiers who, in contrast to his boisterous friends, sipped their drinks in tightly wound decorum, Porfirio observed that "one man dominated with his energetic mien, his dark and severe gaze, a certain hidden brutality and his impeccable uniform: Trujillo." But when he was introduced to this forbidding man, a chameleonic transformation occurred before his eyes. "I was stupefied at the change that came over him," he later recalled. "His severe expression disappeared, and he seemed very pleased to meet the son of an old friend."*

Porfirio knew that Trujillo had attempted to lure Don Pedro into the byzantine scheme by which he gained control of the country and that his father, partly because of his ill health, partly because he genuinely

* A legend would evolve that the two men met after Porfirio had captained the Dominican national polo team to a victory over Nicaragua, but Porfirio's equestrian life only truly began after he met Trujillo, and polo wasn't played in the Dominican Republic, certainly not at the international level, until the 1940s, when he was himself instrumental in introducing it.

desired that his nation's future be decided democratically, demurred. So he wasn't entirely surprised that Trujillo made mention of his grief at Don Pedro's passing: "You know, I was very pained by your father's death. Men like him are what we lack today."

Likewise, Porfirio wasn't surprised that Trujillo failed to be impressed by his choice of profession. "Students, always with their noses in books!" he snorted. "If we don't advance more quickly, it's because young men like you don't participate in this great effort."

But there was a surprise coming: Hard on that admonition, Trujillo gently suggested that Porfirio meet him at the National Palace the next morning to discuss his future, say 10 A.M. The matter agreed, the older man stood and, begging pardon, left the club, but not without a final invitation: "Sit here with your friends. Tonight you are the guests of the President!" Porfirio waved his chums over and they joined the soldiers, who slackened their rigid posture when Trujillo left and drank brandy and champagne with the young men until the early morning hours.

He returned home and prepared for his meeting, his head heavy from the night's indulgences. At the palace, he found Trujillo characteristically alert, erect, immaculate, and direct.

"Did you enjoy yourself last night?"

"Thanks to you, Mr. President."

"Very good. Now let's get to more serious matters. I am going to make you a lieutenant in my Presidential Guard."

There was no time—or, indeed, reason—for retort. Trujillo immediately sent a lackey to fetch an administrative official, to whom he announced, "I have just named Señor Rubirosa a lieutenant. I want to see him in uniform immediately. Take him to my personal tailor, my shoemaker and my gunsmith. Tonight he'll enter the military training academy."

As he was outfitted in the splendor that Trujillo demanded for himself and those closest to him, Porfirio tried to wrap his mind around the situation. "At 22," he admitted, "this was a windfall . . . I was sufficiently vain to believe that my personality and the name of my family had occasioned this treatment by the General." But he managed as well to plumb Trujillo's deeper motives. Addicted to gossip—especially as a means of dominating its subjects—Trujillo had heard about Don Pedro's popular boy-about-town and determined to use the young man's social standing for his own purposes. Porfirio understood it instinctively: "He had resolved to get the golden youth of the island involved in the reform of his army. I seemed a young man well suited for this plan because of the prestige of my father and the esteem that my Parisian education had among young men of my generation."

At heart, he understood Trujillo because the two were cut of the same material: "The General was a *tíguere*," he recollected, "crueler than any of the other *tígueres* Santo Domingo had known before. This *tíguere* was smarter than a fox." In time, their relationship would evolve into a complete symbiosis. Trujillo, capable of the most ruthless acts, would pass virtually all his life in the Dominican Republic to keep his iron fist on its affairs, would commit the most ruthless acts of violence and immorality to suit his pleasure and his power, but would always take especial care to maintain at least a show of public decency. Porfirio, who would eventually emerge as his country's most visible emissary to the outside world, habitually engaged in a more extroverted and sensational form of *tíguerismo,* based not on the ruthless wielding of fear but on suavity, dash, ambition, charm, and magnetism. He would provide the sophisticated public face of a brutal regime while Trujillo would, in turn, provide a steely foundation for his stupendous adventures—a mutuality that Trujillo seemed almost to have planned from the start.

It began when, hung over and greedy, Porfirio swallowed the bait dangled before him, allowing yet another of the older man's schemes to unfold exactly as it had been planned. "Just as Trujillo imagined," he confessed, "many young men of the Dominican upper classes followed me."

He didn't care if he was being used. Military life, contrary to expectations, appealed to him. As he would recall, "Physical efforts filled our days: calisthenics, various sports, arms training, target practice, horseback riding. For a young man like me, it was paradise." It was made for him: the smart, elaborate uniforms, the camaraderie of fellow junior officers, the freedom from the responsibility to feed or house himself or define his days.

He loved his uniforms, and he looked brilliant in them: pinch-waisted, sharp-jawed, muscular, whippy, with a tight crown of wavy hair, a broad forehead, dark almond-shaped eyes, wide cheekbones, and that café au lait complexion. He wore his hair longer than other soldiers and his boots were more suited to gentlemanly pursuits than to combat or training. If the elite society of Santo Domingo wasn't yet prepared to accept Trujillo and his military, there were certainly young ladies whose eyes, and more, would readily be caught by the spectacle of this handsome, cultured young officer. He was in his glory.

His golden impression of his new life wasn't shared at home. His brother-in-law asserted his domain over the household by refusing to allow a soldier to live under his roof. Porfirio simply moved into the barracks.

As a young soldier, he didn't necessarily comport himself according to the strict standards of self-control that were so important to Trujillo. Having been promoted to first lieutenant and named a member of Trujillo's personal staff, Porfirio was required to attend all of the deadly dull affairs of protocol of which the president was so enamored. Among these was a formal ball that would be attended by all of the civilian elite of Santo Domingo, a company by whom Porfirio was loathe to be seen in the role of aide-de-camp, a mere lackey. Ordered to attend in dress whites, he showed up instead in khakis, declaring that he hadn't been told about the day's dress code until it was too late and that his formal uniform was in the laundry. ("I still recall the look Trujillo gave me," he would say more than thirty years later.)

With the other junior officers, Porfirio was ordered to stay put behind Trujillo, but he boldly strode over to where a young woman he knew was seated, and he took a chair beside her to chat. A nervous senior officer approached.

"Are you Lieutenant Rubirosa?"

"Yes."

"The President has sent me to tell you that you may dance if you wish."

The rest of Trujillo's military corps gaped in astonishment as Porfirio enjoyed champagne and the company of the ladies for the rest of the evening. They had reckoned he'd be lambasted; instead, he had the time of his life.

That close call with the president's anger wasn't quite enough to scare Porfirio into the straight and narrow that was becoming the norm for *trujillistos,* as the most ardent followers of the president were known. In May 1932, he injured his knee in a one-car accident in San Pedro de Macorís, thirty miles east of Santo Domingo: As if he didn't care how he'd comported himself he'd been speeding. "The distinguished young military gentleman," as a fawning newspaper account referred to him, was attended in a local hospital and then transported by ambulance to the capital where he was seen by top military doctors. "The injury doesn't apparently require additional care," the report continued. "We are happy to wish him the quickest and most complete recovery."

His first smash-up!

―――――

In July, Trujillo told Porfirio that his presence would be required the following day at the harbor, where a full complement of officers and a military band would greet the arrival of a ship that was returning the president's daughter, Flor de Oro, from two years of school in France. Trujillo had special need for his audacious, French-speaking aide-de-camp at this particular reunion. "She knows Paris like you do," he explained. And then, after a pause, he added, "Well, really, not like you do, I would hope. . . ."

The seventeen-year-old girl who got off that boat was, as she would later remember, "bedazzled" by her reception. " 'El Supremo,' " as she referred to her father, "stood there in an immaculate, starched white-linen suit, flanked by shining limousines and his handpicked aides. I noticed one lieutenant instantly—handsome in a Dominican uniform that had a special flair. Even the gold buttons looked real."

It was, of course, Porfirio. And he, of course, noticed her noticing. "She was enchanting, with dreamy eyes and hair as black as night," he later recollected in the florid style that overcame him when he wrote of romance.

No words were exchanged between the French-educated youngsters as Trujillo whisked away the daughter with whom he'd had virtually no contact since infancy. For Flor, riding with her father was quite nearly like making a new acquaintance. From the time the North Americans came to occupy the country, Trujillo had left his first wife and their daughter behind. "We knew little of what he did," Flor remembered. "Three or four times a year, he'd come home, each time more and more overbearing. My proud job was to wash his military belt in the river for 25 US cents."

Aside from such childish domestic chores, the girl served another purpose for her father: Trujillo spent Flor's childhood offering different military or political bigwigs the chance to serve as his daughter's god-father, a singular honor in a Latin family. But he never made the designation official, continually jockeying for a better and more prestigious candidate until the girl was almost fifteen years old and had either to be baptized or to be refused admittance to the French boarding school her father had chosen for her. (To get a sense of Trujillo's relatively low standing at the time, the lucky winner of this sweepstakes was the family doctor; Flor, for her part, suffered the mortification of being the only baptismal candidate at that particular mass who walked on her own power to the altar rather than be carried as a babe in arms.)

When Trujillo failed to gain custody of the girl upon divorcing her mother, he moved them both to a small house in Santo Domingo and enrolled the adolescent Flor in a nearby boys' military school. But she soon found herself among the students at the Collège Féminin de Bouffémont, a short distance from Paris.

It wasn't necessarily a comfortable fit. "Naïve, thin, with legs long as a stork's, unable to speak French, I was the shy tropical bumpkin," she remembered, "the classmate of girls who included a princess of Iraq." There were luxuries: her own thoroughbred horse to replace the burro she rode back home, summer in Biarritz, winter in St. Moritz, regular trips to Paris and the opera, the theater, the museums, and the shops.

Still, she felt distant from her father; for most of her life, despite documentary evidence to the contrary, she claimed never to have heard a word from him in all her years away from home.*

Having been transformed, in her own estimation, into "that exotic hybrid, a French-speaking Dominican young lady," she returned home not sure which father she would be meeting: the one who might hand her a $100 bill and declare "buy some toys" or the one whose volcanic temper aides warned her of in advance of their meetings. "Like the humblest *dominicano*," she remembered, "I prospered and suffered under his rule and came to think of him as immortal. I had succumbed to the Dominican neurosis, a willingness to swallow anything because it came from Trujillo."

The pomp of the greeting that summer morning at the port of Santo Domingo must therefore have reassured her, along with her father's suggestion that she plan a coming-out party for herself, a major social event in a capital that had fallen increasingly under Trujillo's sway in all its activities. Among those Flor hoped would attend but didn't dare invite was that dashing lieutenant; years later she confessed, "It was love at first sight." Eager to learn more about him, she quizzed her one Dominican friend, Lina Lovatón, a tomboy athlete who had been enrolled in the Santo Domingo military school with her. Lina knew little of Porfirio, and nothing further was learned at the party, during the whole of which the aide-de-camp stood stiffly behind the president, this time in proper uniform.

Soon Trujillo announced that the family and his personal staff would pass the rest of the summer at his estate in San José de las Matas in the western foothills of the Cibao. There, the attraction between the two young people escalated, though it would not always be clear in later years how exactly or at whose instigation. Flor would forever insist that they never spoke during this period, but Porfirio would recall idle con-

* Among the surviving correspondence was a letter from Flor de Oro at Bouffémont dated October 29, 1931, in which she thanked her father for his recent telegram and declared that she was looking forward to the fulfillment of his promise to bring her home for the coming summer. He responded three weeks later with a thoughtful and tender note in which he praised her maturation and indicated that he'd heard good things about her academic progress from the headmistress of her school.

versations in French about Parisian landmarks and "the differences between the life one encountered in Europe and in the Caribbean." That these initial contacts were, at any rate, fleeting they would both agree.

More was, however, suspected. The childless Doña Bienvenida, jealous of Trujillo's attentions to this daughter of his first marriage, somehow got wind of the fledgling romance—Porfirio surmised that she overheard the two speaking French in the garden one evening—and warned her husband about the lieutenant's impertinent behavior. Without a moment's hesitation, Porfirio was reassigned to confined duty at the fortress in San Francisco de Macorís.

Again, what happened next would be in dispute: Either *she* wrote *him* to say that she was stricken at the thought of his departure, which assumes his story that they were already on close terms; or *he* wrote *her*, out of the blue, if her account of their merely polite relations is more accurate, to express his despair at being separated from her. (Years later, Rubi explained simply, "As in any good script, we found ways of getting letters to each other.")

Whichever, the next step was indisputably hers. Learning that she would be attending a dance in her honor in Santiago—midway, more or less, between his new post and Trujillo's ranch—she snuck off on horseback one afternoon and phoned the fortress to invite him. He accepted and, feigning a sore throat and the need to consult a specialist in the city, made his way to Santiago on the day of the dance.

She spied him first in the town plaza, fittingly enough having his boots blacked. Then at the dance, she was seated among the town's elite when he walked confidently over and asked her to dance. Defying every principle of decorum, they danced together repeatedly—"five times in a row," as she recalled—and compounded the sensation by speaking in French and then, during the open-air concert following the dance, walking slowly twice around the plaza, albeit under the vigilant eye of her chaperone.

—————

As far as Porfirio was concerned, that was it: "From that moment I was in love, and Flor was as well."

And that was it as far as Trujillo was concerned as well.

"The dance wasn't even over when Trujillo heard," Flor recalled. When she returned to San José de las Matas, she was met with a storm. Her father sent her directly to her room and began grilling his aides to find out who was responsible for the communications between Porfirio and his daughter and who was responsible for letting the banished lieutenant out of the fortress to attend a dance. Flor was terrified by the degree and intensity of his temper and cowered at the door listening as he sputtered to Doña Bienvenida, "She's gotten herself mixed up with that good-for-nothing lieutenant!"

The next day, an even more dire fate awaited Porfirio: An officer marched into his quarters and announced that he was to be immediately expelled from the army and stripped of all his gear, including, to his special pain, "my uniforms, which I loved so well."

This was a staggering blow, and he remembered it with high drama: "I was an outcast in my own country. Ignominiously dumped and rejected by the army. Marked on the forehead with the sign of infamy which no one could ignore." He entertained the thought of exile but he couldn't leave the island, he said in his most lugubrious voice, because "to leave would be to lose Flor. And to lose Flor would be to die. But to stay would also be to die."

This was no exaggeration: Trujillo was entirely capable of having his onetime protégé eliminated and, in fact, he dispatched a team of hit men that very afternoon from his goon squad, who roamed the country in ominous red Packards doing the despot's bidding.

Had he been stationed in any other city, Porfirio might not have survived the day. But San Francisco de Macorís was, of course, his birthplace, as well as the hereditary seat of both sides of his family. "My uncles and my grandfather united in counsel," he recalled. "My uncle Oscar gave me a well-oiled pistol. A truck was obtained. It took me to a cocoa plantation owned by one of my uncles, Pancho Ariza, about 10 kilometers away." For more than a week, he hid in an outbuilding on the farm, "staring into space, ruminating on this cascade of catastrophes."

He was alone in neither his anguish nor his isolation. Before bolting to his hideout, he sent off a note to Flor describing his situation. The emissary who delivered it was tied by Trujillo to a tree and thrashed, while Flor watched in horror. She locked herself away from this frightening tyrant, refusing to speak with him, refusing meals, and writing letter after unsent letter to the young man who had suddenly come to dominate her dreams. Like the heroine of a pulp novel, she would love Porfirio to spite her father.

"Flor had the same strong blood in her veins as her father," Porfirio would recall. "A will of iron and an indomitable courage guided her. She was the only one who could stand up to her father, even if he was in a state of fury." When Trujillo sent an intermediary to speak with her, she replied, "Tell my father that I want to marry the man I love, and I will marry him. Otherwise I would not be worthy of being his daughter."

At least that would be how Porfirio remembered it—or maybe how he imagined it. Flor's memory was different: a cruelly imposed isolation; the ceaseless slander of the former lieutenant by her father and stepmother; a strange limbo, like being a nonperson.

In his hideaway, Porfirio grew impatient and decided, on instinct, that danger had passed. "It has always been one of my chief principles," he later confessed. "I will risk everything to avoid being bored." He rode back to his uncle's home in town, shocking his family with his sudden appearance. "You don't have a lick of common sense," they admonished him.

But, in fact, the worst of it seemed to have passed. Indeed, the lull emboldened Doña Ana Rubirosa to visit Trujillo to plead for her son. As Porfirio recalled it, his mother stood up to the president by asking, "What secret mark is there against our family that Señor Trujillo cannot tolerate that a Rubirosa would dare put his eyes on his daughter?"

The meeting was barely a quarter hour along when Trujillo slapped his desk and declared, "That's enough! They will marry right away!"

———

This was like tripping over a winning lottery ticket on the street. From disgrace and near-death, Porfirio was now slated to marry into the first family of the country. Maybe he was in love, truly, or maybe he was too scared to cross Trujillo a second time by refusing Flor, or maybe he was as bold a *tíguere* as the Benefactor himself. Whichever, he had heedlessly reached for the impossible by making eyes at the president's daughter and, through charm, gall, and luck, had seized the prize. At twenty-three, he would be wealthier and closer to power than Don Pedro ever had been.

For Flor it was a stunning shock: "Five dances in a row, two circles around a park, an innocent flirtation, and I was to marry a man I scarcely knew!"

Still, marriage would liberate her, she hoped, from a man she knew all too well; as she admitted, she was "wild to leave my prison, to run like hell from Father, an instinct that was to propel me all my life."

The nuptials were planned for early December at the fateful ranch house where the abortive courtship transpired. Trujillo orchestrated all the details: the invitations, the ceremony, the party. The best man would be the U.S. ambassador, H. F. Arthur Schoenfeld, whom the groom had likely never met. The ceremony would be performed by the archbishop of Santo Domingo. Flor was sent to the capital to have a dress made; her fiancé stayed with his family in San Francisco de Macorís—and was named, if only for the sake of having a title worthy of his entry into the president's family, secretary to the Dominican legation in London.

On December 2, a caravan of trucks bearing flowers and bridesmaids wended from the capital to the wedding site. The groom was flown in on a military plane. The next day, after the civil and religious ceremonies in the town, the wedding party began late, at 4:30, on what turned out to be a rainy afternoon.

In the photographs of their wedding day, the newlyweds look frightened and tiny, despite their finery and the attendant pomp. Rubi stands with shoulders thrust back and tiny waist forward, a pompadour stiff on his head and a grin set in the baby fat of his cheeks. Flor is a head shorter, with wide-set eyes and a toothy smile; she holds a hand protectively across her breast, cradling her bouquet. They might be a prom couple on their first date.

As the photo attests, the wedding wasn't a completely comfortable experience for the groom, who hadn't once laid eyes on his prospective father-in-law since before being sent away for flirting with Flor. "During the ceremony," he recalled, "I saw Trujillo again for the first time. Instead of his happy air, he was cold and quiet." Nor was the bride entirely at ease, recalling that "Father hadn't spoken to me since my engagement."

But it was a lavish celebration nonetheless, with music, champagne, food, dignitaries, and a trove of gifts, which the bride said "would have filled a house." (Conspicuously absent was the bride's mother, still shunned by Trujillo as if dead.) By 7 P.M., the newlyweds were headed to Santo Domingo in one of their presents from the Benefactor, a cream-colored, chauffeur-driven Packard with their initials embossed in real gold on the doors.

Two days later, the capital's most prestigious newspaper, *Listín Diario,* carried an account of the wedding written by someone whom the editors referred to as "an esteemed and distinguished friend of ours." The author was, in fact, Trujillo, who would employ this and other newspapers throughout the tenure of his reign to carry, pseudonymously, compositions of his own, often using them to undermine or frankly smear someone who had fallen out of his favor. He could be vicious and snide in his writings, but this time, his tone was florid and precious:

> Distinguished personalities of the country added to the glow of the nuptial ceremony . . . beneath the cool pines of the marvelous setting of San José de las Matas, an ambiance rich in exquisiteness. . . . The bride, who is a flower because of her perfumed name and because of the charms that flower within her, lit up a precious wedding dress. . . . It was one of the most aristocratic weddings ever recorded in the social annals of the Republic. The genteel couple have united their pulsing hearts in emotion. They have our most sincere and cordial wishes for their personal journey and their eternal happiness.

According to the report, the couple would live in "a handsome chalet within the bounds of the presidential mansion in the aristocratic and comely 'faubourg' of Gascue" in Santo Domingo—another gift from Trujillo.

But it was to a temporary home they retired that evening, their first as husband and wife and another experience that they would remember differently.

"When we left for our honeymoon," Porfirio remembered, "I felt like the happiest of all men."

Flor, on the other hand, was a nervous wreck. However much she had talked with her mother, her stepmother, or her older friends, she was entirely unprepared for the night's activities. She wore a pink negligee into the bedroom and was startled into apoplexy by the sight of her husband's erection. "I ran all around the house, and Porfirio chased me," she remembered.

Somehow she talked him out of consummating the marriage that night, but she couldn't keep him at bay forever. She let him have his way, however awfully. "I didn't like it because I bled so much, and my clothes were ruined," she confessed. "In time, he began to make love to me in different ways, but when it was over my insides hurt a lot. He was such a handsome boy and so charming that I let him do whatever he wanted. But he took so long to ejaculate that by the end I was a little bored."

Et voilà the maiden marital bed of a man who would become famous as one of the great lovers of his time.

FOUR

A DREDGE AND A
BOTCH AND A BUST-UP

I t was, by all objective standards, easy street.

In a house facing the sea in Ciudad Trujillo, the newlyweds lived in true splendor. Both had multiple servants; in addition to a valet and a masseuse, Porfirio employed a sparring partner—Kid GoGo, from back in his San Lázaro boxing promotion days—with whom he exercised daily in a ring he'd had erected in a spare room.

But the shadow of Trujillo obscured their horizon, and they were unable ever to forget the source of their good fortune. Flor recalled that their presence was required every day for lunch in the presidential mansion—"plain fare, rice and beans, no drinks, no cigarettes, no small talk: it was a bit like two slaves dining with the master."

Along with all the gifts, Porfirio was given real work to do. Having decided against dispatching the couple to London, Trujillo appointed his son-in-law undersecretary to the president in April 1933, and then, the following July, undersecretary of foreign relations. In that post, Porfirio took charge of some genuinely sensitive responsibilities, such as communicating with Gerardo Machado y Morales, the Cuban president who'd been exiled to the United States after a coup in August; several rounds of correspondence between the two, with Porfirio gently dissuading the elder man from attempting to enlist Trujillo's help in regaining his position, would survive. When foreign dignitaries came to the capital, Flor and Porfirio, the stylish, French-speaking face of the modern Dominican Republic, were trotted out to meet the visitors. A Haitian newspaper columnist was so charmed that he praised them as the "best-dressed, best-educated, most popular couple in town"; Trujillo, cross at having failed to be mentioned himself in a similar light, found in these compliments a slight, which he avenged by adopting a calculated iciness toward the couple.

There was phony work as well. In May 1933, Porfirio, who had never taken a course in business and had never had a bank account in his own name, was named president of the Compañía de Seguros San Rafael, an insurance firm established by Trujillo—like the other leading companies in virtually every field of Dominican commerce—as a false front for his private monopolization of the nation's economy. The entire Trujillo family—the president's many brothers and sisters, countless nieces and nephews and cousins—would be enriched through the years via such schemes. And not only blood relatives but in-laws and the relations of in-laws; Flor said of Porfirio's kin, who'd so scorned the sight of him in his uniform barely a year earlier, "His family didn't much cotton to Trujillo, but after the wedding they suddenly got big positions in the government."

A lot of Dominican men would have been satisfied with this routine: the sinecures, the luxurious home, the servants, the prestige, the $50,000 bank account (controlled by Trujillo and in Flor's name, but still). Not Porfirio. He was living within easy walking distance of his old haunts, the bars and brothels and clubs where he'd idled before he joined the army. He settled into a double life, half the time an obedient son-in-law, half a notorious rake participating in marathon drinking-

and-whoring bouts: *parrandas*. When news of this behavior filtered back home, as it inevitably would, there were dustups with Flor. At least once Porfirio went so far as to hit her; she ran off to the palace, interrupting a meeting to tell her father of her husband's violence; summoned by Trujillo, Porfirio mollified him by declaring that he'd struck her for failing to respect him under his own roof, a provocation with which any true *tíguere* would sympathize.

Even as he forgave that trespass, Trujillo harbored little warmth for his son-in-law. "I think that at bottom he never forgave me for marrying his daughter," Porfirio surmised. "That his daughter could love someone other than him seemed impossible to him." The president's withering remoteness, coupled with Porfirio's own restless inability to settle into the life of a bureaucrat, impelled him to ask for reinstatement to the Army, where he'd so enjoyed the life of vigor and male camaraderie. Trujillo consented, posting him at the rank of captain, assigning him no specific duties, and doing little to couch his disgust at Porfirio's apparent contentment with his new station.

The source of the president's contempt was, in Porfirio's view, obvious: Little Ramfis had been commissioned as a senior officer in the Army the previous year; as Porfirio put it, "What sort of son-in-law would be content to be captain when [Trujillo's] own five-year-old son was already a colonel?" (A letter from Robert L. Ripley's "Believe It or Not" offices in New York would arrive on Trujillo's desk in February 1936, seeking confirmation of Ramfis's position in the Army and asking whether he wore full uniform and collected the appropriate salary for his rank. By that time, the young soldier had been seen beside his father at several official functions wearing elaborate military uniforms and partaking of champagne toasts.)

But Porfirio endured the Benefactor's scorn because he simply wanted to be his own man. Without responsibilities as a soldier, he could look for private opportunities around the city. "I had very little to do," he recalled, "and I wanted to learn about business." But, as he should have known from his brief stint at the insurance company, nobody did business in Ciudad Trujillo without doing business with Trujillo. And it was a uniquely bold and crafty businessman indeed who could make a success at that.

======

Félix Benítez Rexach wore his hair to his shoulders, wasn't too particular about washing or combing it, and habitually topped it with battered straw hats. His clothes weren't much more presentable: He could show up at official functions in torn and muddy outfits as if oblivious entirely to protocol. He looked for all the world like a hobo, but it was a calculated guise. He was actually a millionaire engineer willing to stand up to gangsters and governments to see his business interests come to fruition. Born in Puerto Rico, he traveled widely and grew especially fond of France, where he owned homes in Paris and on the Riviera. There was suspicious talk about his sexuality, but he had two wives, the second being the onetime Parisian flower girl Gaby Montbre, who had a sort-of musical career as La Môme Moineau (literally, "the bratty sparrow"), a chanteuse in the vein of Edith Piaf. There was suspicious talk as well about his engineering credentials, but he had built himself a yacht from his own design (his wife would become more famous for being photographed by French magazines on its decks in sailing clothes than for her singing), and he had successfully overseen the creation of deepwater harbors in Puerto Rico, where he had additional interests in the resort hotel business.

Benítez Rexach showed up in Ciudad Trujillo in 1934 when Trujillo's government announced plans to enlarge the harbor at the mouth of the Ozama River; until then, the largest ships arriving in the capital had to anchor a short distance out at sea and have their passengers and cargo ferried ashore. The project would require the use of a massive shipboard dredge—and whoever successfully completed the job could hope on doing further business with Trujillo at other ports around the country.

Benítez Rexach read all the implications of the situation, including the nepotistic nature of Dominican political and business affairs, and he sought a pry hole that would get him into the president's good graces. He found one in Trujillo's tomcatting son-in-law. He dangled his wife as bait in front of Porfirio, cynically affording him ample opportunity to sample her favors. (Flor knew about the affair and so, she claimed, did the whole city, including her father.) To tie the knot tighter, Benítez Rexach suggested a business partnership: If Porfirio acquired a dredge, and Benítez Rexach knew of one available in New Orleans, then the engineer would rent it for the duration of the job; they drew up an agreement.

For Benítez Rexach, it was politics: cozen the son-in-law to get to the real power. But for Porfirio and Flor, it was a lifeline—and a gamble. "Neither of us had much business sense," Flor recalled. She and her husband "were alike in so many ways, neither of us really good-looking, both mixed-up Dominicans, in love with the high life, hungry for what money could buy, but unable to earn an honest living on our own." Success in the harbor project, however, would mean autonomy from Trujillo's money and influence. The risk was worth it.

The first obstacle would be getting the capital necessary to buy the dredge. Flor's father still controlled the $50,000 dowry; would he be willing to open the purse for the project? Willing wasn't exactly the word. "I don't have much faith in second-hand machinery or in this investment," the president told his daughter even as he agreed to her request. Rubi sent an emissary, cash in hand, to buy the dredge, a vessel called the *Tenth of February*, and bring it back to Ciudad Trujillo.

While he was risking his fortune and good name, such as they were, in this scheme, Porfirio was also upholding his share of the bargain he'd struck with Benítez Rexach, establishing a connection between the engineer and Trujillo. Eventually, the two men so bonded that an intermediary was unnecessary; Benítez Rexach sufficiently impressed Trujillo, in fact, that he was routinely forgiven the effrontery of strolling into the immaculate palace in his grubbiest condition and eventually enjoyed brief appointments from the president in the diplomatic service in France and Puerto Rico.

With these two in cahoots, it was only a matter of time before Porfirio was frozen out. The blindside was delivered with an assassin's cunning. By the time the *Tenth of February* was in Ciudad Trujillo and ready to dig, Benítez Rexach had acquired a brand-new dredge of his own for the job and had convinced Trujillo of the superiority of his vessel to Porfirio's. But Porfirio had the engineer's signed promise to use his equipment, and he demanded that it at least be tested. In the coming weeks, Benítez Rexach submitted the *Tenth of February* to trials but sabotaged them at every turn: He claimed that the dredge wouldn't function properly in the tropical weather; he insisted that it first be tried in the most ill-suited portion of the harbor; he whispered to Trujillo that its gas-powered engine might ignite and blow up the whole port.

Porfirio, suffering one of his father-in-law's periodic silent treatments, couldn't get a hearing. He could see that he was being shut out of the operation, and he was realistic enough to wish only to recoup the lease money he'd been promised so as to repay Trujillo for the dredge. Even that much Benítez Rexach refused, and so Porfirio took decisive action. In his full captain's uniform, complete with sidearms, he rode a launch out to the work site in the harbor and accosted the engineer. "I leapt at him, grabbed him by the collar and shook him like a carpet," Porfirio remembered. " 'Thief! If you continue waging war against me and don't pay me right now what you owe me, I will destroy you!' He was terrified. He collapsed. He promised everything I wanted."

But as soon as Porfirio left, Benítez Rexach raced to tell Trujillo that he would have to quit working on the harbor improvements for fear that Porfirio would kill him. Trujillo offered reassurance: "Four officers of my guard will accompany you and let Captain Rubirosa know what it will cost him if he touches one hair on your head." The operation continued without further hindrance while the *Tenth of February* sat unused and worthless. As a Dominican businessman—indeed, as a Dominican *man*—Porfirio was toast.

It would be hard to imagine a worse fall: from golden aide-de-camp to anointed heir to broke, disgraced nonperson in less than three years. With whatever money they could scrounge, Porfirio and Flor decided to leave the country and look for less dreary prospects in the United States. In the winter of 1934–35, they moved to New York City. Trujillo, perhaps to let them tumble further into his debt, let them go.

<hr>

This was, in most ways, madness. In Ciudad Trujillo, even on the outs with the Benefactor, they had connections, prestige, resources. In New

York, for which they didn't even have the proper winter clothing, they were broke, they didn't speak the language, and they were anonymous refugees living in a cheap Broadway hotel and, later, in Greenwich Village, where at least one associate would later remember Porfirio working, briefly, as a waiter.

"It was a nightmare," Flor remembered. Her husband, as he had back home, "disappeared to play poker with Cuban gangster types while I waited in that dingy hotel room, watching the Broadway signs blink on and off."

There was no money: "When he won, we ate; when he lost, we starved."

And he had other interests: "He would come home at 6 a.m., his pockets stuffed with matchbooks scribbled with the phone numbers of women."

They fought: "Angry, brutal, he shoved and hit me when we argued."

It was utterly foolish to think of New York as a going prospect. They could count on no help from the consulate, which obviously answered to her father. There was a Dominican presence in the Latin American community in the north of Manhattan, but most of that contingent was made up of people who had fled Trujillo and were actively plotting his replacement—again, a dead end. The only significant contact they had was a mixture of comedy and menace: three cousins of Porfirio's, sons of Don Pedro's sister, who had been raised in the city since boyhood and had spent most of their grown years engaged in petty crime and worse. "When I saw 'West Side Story' I was reminded of them," Flor recalled. "Good-for-nothings who had never worked."

Among them was Luis de la Fuente Rubirosa, aka Chichi, who had been in trouble with the law since boyhood. In 1925, he had been arrested for burglary and sentenced to a spell at the New York Reformatory for Boys. In 1932, he was tried for assault and robbery and acquitted. He was short, maybe five-foot-six, with jug ears and a pinched face and sharp cheekbones, a wiry, dangerous little creep, plain and simple, with nothing to offer his cousin and his wife in the way of truly promising possibilities.

New York was coming to seem even more disastrous than Ciudad

Trujillo. And then the most unexpected lifeline appeared: a telegram from the Benefactor announcing that Porfirio had been elected—*elected!*—to the national congress and that both he and Flor were required back home. Unable to explain what was happening, they were equally unable to resist.

———

Trujillo's congress was a dog-and-pony show that fooled no one. The deputies were required upon taking office to submit signed and undated letters of resignation so that the president could remove them at any time for any cause; it wasn't unusual for a man to return from lunch to attend the afternoon session only to find out that he had, without knowing it, quit his post during the recess. And when they did sit, the legislators were utterly impotent. "In every session," Porfirio remembered, "the President read aloud a proposed law and we adopted it with a show of hands. There was never any question of discussing it."

A nation conditioned by centuries of rebellion and despotism wasn't especially outraged by this pantomime of a government. And Trujillo was modernizing the Dominican Republic in a way that no previous tyrant had: paying off its staggering national debt to the United States, paving roads, building an electrical grid, and so forth. Soon after he took power, the island suffered a devastating hurricane that virtually bowled it back to the Stone Age; the speed of repairs and, indeed, improvements under Trujillo's firm hand made him a hero in the eyes of his countrymen.

As a result, Trujillo had no shortage of stooges who could fill the seats of this cardboard congress, so it wasn't at all clear to Porfirio why he was so urgently needed. But in April 1935, he was called in to see the president—who suddenly seemed very happy to see his son-in-law—and given a delicate assignment. When he got home, he told Flor that he would be going back to New York the next day on official business.

On April 16, Porfirio disembarked from the S.S. *Camao* in New York and checked into the St. Moritz Hotel on Central Park South. Along

with his personal effects, he had a suitcase containing $7,000 in cash.*
A few days later, he toted that suitcase to the Dominican consulate on
Fifth Avenue, where he met with a small group that included his cousin
Chichi. On April 27, he left for Miami; from there he sailed for San
Pedro de Macorís, his spare suitcase filled this time with new dresses
and other gifts for Flor.

The following day, a Sunday, a group of Dominican dissidents met in
Manhattan to discuss their plans for unseating Trujillo. Among them
was Dr. Angel Morales, the most recognized Dominican statesman in
the world. In the years before Trujillo's assumption of power, Morales
had served his country as minister of the interior, minister of foreign affairs, minister to Italy, minister to France (he was once Don Pedro Rubirosa's boss), and minister to the United States. In the mid-1920s, he
had been elected vice president of the League of Nations. In 1930, he
had run in the rigged election that gave Trujillo the presidency; when
he lost, he fled to New York for his life and was declared a traitor; all
his property in the Dominican Republic was confiscated by the new
government.

As an alternative to Trujillo, Morales had supporters not only in the
Dominican exile community but in the U.S. government and among private parties in North America who sought to foster change in the island
nation. But he so feared Trujillo's ruthlessness and reach that he lived
in New York like a hunted man. He shared a Manhattan rooming house
flat with Sergio Bencosme, a general's son who had served Trujillo's rivals as a congressional deputy and minister of defense. The two lived
on the proceeds from a small coffee importing business. And they tip-
toed around the city in mortal trepidation: Morales was said to be hes-
itant to eat anywhere save at his landlady's table for fear of being
poisoned or attacked.

His fears were justified that Sunday night. When the dissident meeting broke up, Morales, in a rare feeling of well-being, went to dine out
with friends. Bencosme returned to their apartment on the seventh floor

*Figure $100,000 in 2005.

of a Washington Heights walk-up and a supper cooked by Mrs. Carmen Higgs, their thirty-year-old Latina landlady.

At about 8 P.M., there was a knock at the door. Mrs. Higgs, who shared her lodgers' fears, asked who was there.

"Open this door," came the harsh reply.

She cracked the door to have a look, and a short, wiry man in a brown suit and brown hat pushed in past her, brandishing a .45 caliber pistol. Mrs. Higgs screamed and leapt back into the kitchen; fearing a robbery, she removed her engagement ring and wedding band and tossed them into a coffeepot that was percolating on the stove. The gunman looked into the kitchen and then moved down the hall, first into the living room and then into an adjoining bedroom.

Bencosme, shaving for dinner, his face covered in lather, heard the commotion, came toward the front door, and peered into the living room. Finding it empty, he went on to the kitchen to see what the screaming was about. From the rear of the apartment came a shout— "Die, Morales!"—and two shots struck Bencosme in the back; the bullets passed through his body and lodged in a bureau. The gunman ran through the hall—over the body and past Mrs. Higgs—and down the six flights of stairs into the street. Bencosme, staggering and in agony, made his way to the apartment of a neighbor who had a telephone and rang for help.

When police and ambulance drivers arrived, they couldn't at first make out what happened. Mrs. Higgs was so frightened that she couldn't bring forth any English and insisted that she'd been robbed until a detective found her jewelry brewing with the coffee. Bencosme, barely conscious by the time he was taken off to Knickerbocker Hospital, muttered that he was a political refugee. Only when Morales returned home at midnight to find the chaotic scene did a reasonable theory of the case emerge: Somebody had tried to kill *him* and had mistakenly shot Bencosme.

On Monday, forty known Trujillo supporters from among Manhattan's Dominican community were rounded up and questioned by detectives of the so-called alien squad at the West 152nd Street station, but no arrests were made. On Tuesday morning, Bencosme succumbed to his wounds and died in the hospital, leaving behind a widow and two children in Ciudad Trujillo. Finally, Mrs. Higgs sat in a station house and looked at mug shots of Dominicans with histories of criminal violence. She looked at a 1932 booking photo and declared that the man pictured in it was the killer.

It was, of course, Chichi de la Fuente Rubirosa.

After going before a grand jury to present the known facts of the case, many of which derived from Morales's own contacts and investigation, the New York County District Attorney's Office filed an indictment *in absentia* for murder against Chichi on February 18, 1936. According to the charges, "Captain Porfirio Rubirosa" had been in New York immediately prior to the shooting and Chichi was, nearly a year after the shooting, living in Ciudad Trujillo as a lieutenant in the Dominican army despite his total lack of military training. Chichi's extradition was sought through the State Department, but little hope was held out that the accused killer would be sent back to New York.

Back in Ciudad Trujillo, Flor knew nothing about the events in New York—the murder wasn't exactly front-page news in the state-controlled local papers—but like everyone else in the culture of gossip that was coming to thrive under Trujillo, she heard things. She was only mildly surprised, therefore, to answer a knock at her door on a night when her husband and father were out of town to find Chichi standing there begging for help.

"I had to leave the States," he explained. "They are pursuing me."

For a while, Chichi lived with his cousin and his wife and sought work around the city; he even put in a spell on the harbor project that had driven Porfirio and Flor to leave home the year before. It wasn't a promising situation, and Porfirio didn't exactly relish it, especially as Chichi aggravated matters by hinting broadly around town that he had done Trujillo a great service and deserved to be at least a captain for his efforts.

He might as well have cut his own throat. "One evening," Flor recalled, "we came home to find him gone. Servants said 'strangers' had surrounded the house and taken him away. We never heard from Chichi or saw him again—and my husband would not comment on the affair."

(When a year or so later Flor thought she saw Chichi on the street and pointed the look-alike out to Porfirio, he snapped back, "Don't mention that name! Those kids were good-for-nothings!") When the U.S. State Department inquired as to Chichi's whereabouts, they were told alternately that no such person existed and that the fellow in question had died in a dredging accident in the harbor. But police and prosecutors in New York still wanted to talk to Porfirio—and they would be patient in waiting to do so for decades.

———

This drama did little to stabilize the marriage of Porfirio and Flor, which continued to be roiled by Trujillo. In the summer of 1935, they found themselves once again in the Benefactor's confidence. He was suffering from a severe case of urethritis and required surgery. Because of his need to maintain a show of superhuman capacity, he arranged for a French specialist to be brought secretly to perform the operation. The doctor was put up—again, on the QT—at Porfirio and Flor's home, where he conducted three operations on the president, using only local anesthetic. Trujillo was so weakened by the ordeal that rumors spread as far as Washington, D.C., that he was dying. To put an end to the gossip, he left his makeshift intensive care bed and had himself driven through the capital in a Rolls-Royce for an hour, long enough so that word of his good health would circulate. When he recovered, he returned to his own house without so much as a thank-you for his daughter and son-in-law.

At the time, Flor's own health was of concern. She had been trying to conceive a child and was told by her physician to seek the advice of a specialist in the United States, where she underwent a surgical procedure designed to address her infertility.* When she came home hope-

* The question of who was to blame for the couple's childlessness would never be answered. Neither ever had children, despite the combined twelve marriages they entered after this first. It was long rumored that Porfirio was rendered sterile by a childhood bout with the mumps, and Flor occasionally hinted that one or both of them had been rendered infertile by a venereal disease Porfirio had contracted in one of his rambles and subsequently shared with her.

ful of starting a family, she found her household had been the scene of one of Porfirio's bacchanalian *parrandas:* There were women's earrings in the swimming pool, and one of her servants confided that "all the whores in Santo Domingo have been here."

She begged her father to help her do something about this nightmare, and he offered a unique solution: In July 1936, he named Porfirio secretary of the Dominican legation in Berlin.

═══

They arrived at the height of preparations for the Nazi Olympics, an event that drew to the city a claque of idle rich scenesters from around the Continent: Porfirio's crowd exactly. With almost no work assigned to him, he kept up the equestrian skills in the city's parks, began to take a series of fencing lessons, and, in general, dove into a more luxe version of the life he had lived in Paris as a feckless teen. "Berlin suited me perfectly," he admitted blithely. "I could ride, go to clubs, drive fast and dance at the afternoon teas at the Eden."

Needless to say, those afternoon teas involved women—and not Dominican whores, either, but a breed of woman that intimidated Flor. "How could I," she wondered, "still a provincial girl in her early 20s, unworldly, badly dressed, mousy, compete with these women?" She was particularly anxious about a certain Martha: "Soignée, blazing with diamonds, she was everything I was not."

But there were other, nameless rivals. There was the time one of Porfirio's afternoon teas turned into dinner and an overnight stay. He snuck home to the Dominican embassy at dawn, quickly showered and dressed for breakfast, and made his way to his dining room where Flor and the ambassador, among others, awaited him. He sat nonchalantly and then noticed a bouquet of roses in front of his place setting. Attached was a note written in a feminine hand, a paean to a night that had seemed never to end, like midsummer's eve in Sweden. Whatever cock-and-bull story Porfirio had planned to offer vanished from his head: "My pretty German spoke of the Scandinavian summer. Breakfast proceeded like the middle of the Siberian winter. Since then, I can't see a bouquet of roses without feeling a bit of a shiver." But any chastening he felt soon dissolved, as when he had frightened his parents by spending the night out as a boy, and he presently resumed his rambles.

Official duties dotted the high life. Because of their relative worldliness, because they were relatives of the Dominican president, and because the Third Reich was courting Caribbean governments as part of its scheme of global expansion, Porfirio and Flor were granted a number of remarkable privileges. When the Olympics began, they were permitted to sit in Hitler's box at the main stadium, where they observed the Führer's caroms between childish glee at each German victory and rock stolidity when another nation's anthem was played at a medal ceremony. They were feted by Hermann Göring, who took Porfirio aside during the evening and expressed interest in obtaining a particularly handsome Dominican medal. They were invited to the annual party rally in Nuremberg, where they gazed in stupefaction at an orgy of adulation on a scale of which Trujillo, with his own budding cult of personality, could only dream.

Despite such impressive shows, both young Dominicans were shocked by the outright anti-Semitism of the regime. Flor found herself secretly aiding a Jewish girl who had been her schoolmate in France, obtaining visas for her and her husband and seeing to their getting settled in the Dominican Republic and started in the tobacco business. Porfirio was staggered one day as he rode through a park and saw a young man wearing a yellow star and being humiliated by Germans. "Racism never occurred to me," he reflected. Indeed, he had enjoyed a certain éclat for his Creole heritage, which was evident even though he was fair-skinned enough to pass for Latin as opposed to Negro. "In the Dominican Republic, blacks and whites were equals. At times they mixed. There were social differences, but in the most exclusive places one met people of color. In Paris as well, racial problems didn't exist."

But at the same time, neither of them had any inkling of how truly invidious the Reich was or would be. Dazzled, perhaps, by his good fortune to be living with money in a posh European capital, Porfirio reckoned that Hitler's great shows of force "were no more than a bluff." In retrospect he would feel some shame at his miscalculation. "I'm not a politician," he would explain. But he noted, too, that the diplomatic corps of larger and more sophisticated nations were equally gulled by the Führer. If he had been fooled, he wasn't alone.

Before he could fathom the truth of the Reich, however, he found himself transferred. Flor was so miserable living in Berlin with her rakish husband that she wrote to her father to express her displeasure:

> I have learned a little German and seen a lot of the country, and I have admired the great work of Hitler. But nevertheless I'm not happy. . . . In diplomatic circles, most of the officials are on the left. They don't invite us to their dances and I don't have the chance to meet anybody. If it isn't too much to ask, I'd like you to transfer us to Paris. . . . There, I'd have occasion to attend many conferences and get to know better the French literature that I like so well. Please let me know if you can comply with this request.

Indeed, he could, but first a royal interlude in London: On May 12, 1937, they represented the Dominican Republic at the coronation of George VI; Porfirio met the monarch in a private audience. Two days later, at the Dominican legation at 21 Avenue de Messine in Paris, the following note arrived from the undersecretary of foreign relations in Ciudad Trujillo:

> It pleases me to inform you that the most excellent Señor Presidente of the Republic has seen fit to name Mr. Porfirio Rubirosa as Secretary First Class of this legation in substitute for Gustavo J. Henriquez, who has been designated Secretary First Class in Berlin in substitution for Mr. Porfirio Rubirosa.

This was far more like it.

Paris had changed in the decade since he'd last lived there: The tangos and Dixieland in the nightclubs had been swept away by a wave of Russian music and Gypsy-flavored hot jazz; the chic hot spots were now on the Left Bank of the Seine instead of the Right. But it was intoxicating to be there, to saunter into his old haunts in search of old friends, to pass by the erstwhile family house on Avenue Mac-Mahon, to delight in the new fashions favored by women in both couture and amour. When he stowed away on the *Carimare* and left France he was a child, as Don Pedro had despairingly declared; now he was a twenty-eight-year-old man with means and liberty.

"As soon as I arrived in Paris," he remembered without shame, "invitations began pouring in. I was out every night, often alone. My wife objected . . . she could not keep up with me."

In large part, his duties at the embassy would be, as in Berlin, ceremonial. He and Flor were presented to the general commissioner of the upcoming *Exposition Internationale des Arts et Techniques dans la Vie Moderne,* and he found himself appointed to a panel of judges who would award prizes to various exhibits. It was a prestigious post. The exposition, a gigantic world's fair celebrating global modernity, took over the area around the Eiffel Tower and Palais de Trocadero throughout the summer. It was a marvel of aesthetic novelties paraded by nations on the verge of global war: Albert Speer's soaring German pavilion; Pablo Picasso's searing *Guernica* in the Spanish pavilion; a Finnish hall designed by Alvar Aalto; illuminated fountains; exhibitions dedicated to the latest advances in refrigeration and neon light. The Dominican Republic couldn't compete with those sorts of things, but they did share some exhibit space with other Caribbean nations, showing off native crafts and the work of the latest Dominican artists. Trujillo instigated dozens of letters between Paris and Ciudad Trujillo about the exposition; he was delighted to learn that the French artist and critic Alfred Lebrun "had formed an elevated new idea of the progress achieved by our country," and he sent the eminent man a box of cigars in gratitude.

The Benefactor lived for this sort of thing, and he kept Porfirio busy with the most bizarre little requests to satisfy better his comprehension of the modern world and his nation's place in it. He sent to Paris for atlases and diplomatic dictionaries; he hired a Paris-based Caribbean journalist to analyze the possibility of his being awarded a Nobel Peace Prize; he had framed photos of the legation sent to him, and signatures of foreign officials, with whom he also exchanged pens; relishing the opportunity to acquire foreign honors in exchange for those of the Dominican Republic, he ordered miniatures and reproductions of each new award he received. Porfirio served so well as the conduit for all this ephemera that he was promoted to consul in July 1937.

But at the same time that he put forward the shiny front of his daughter and son-in-law for Europe's leaders, Trujillo was revealing his most atrociously dark side back home. He had spent the first years of his rule quelling—through political machination, bribery, and, especially, brute force—all internal opposition. Now he turned his attention to Haiti. It was a natural target for him: The border between the two countries was something of a fiction, having been drawn along no clear geographical or political lines and passing through remote districts whose residents truly might not be able to say which country they lived in or who its ruler was. Moreover, Trujillo, like every Dominican, had been bred with a fear and hatred of Haiti born of centuries of conflict, and he had, like every leader of both nations, harbored dreams of uniting Hispaniola under his hand. At the very least, he wanted clear autonomy over his own portion of the island, and Haiti and its citizens always seemed to be interfering with that prospect. Throughout the early years of Trujillo's reign, Haitian encroachment on Dominican territory became burdensome in a number of ways: public health, cattle rustling, an increase in churches practicing a mixture of Catholicism and voodoo, Haitian infiltration into the Dominican sugar industry, and so forth. There had been some efforts toward a détente between Trujillo and his Haitian counterpart, Stenio Vincent. But as the grievances were felt chiefly by Dominicans, it was inevitably Trujillo who was the more vexed.

His frustration reached the tipping point in October 1937, when he gave a provocative speech about Dominican sovereignty and national purity. That very night, up and down the border and in the areas farther inland that were easily accessible to Haitian migrants, small cadres of armed men—some from the official military, others no better organized than the makeshift platoons that Don Pedro Rubirosa had once commanded—rounded up all the Haitians they could find and slaughtered them.

It was the most brutal sort of genocide. In a land where virtually everyone was of mixed blood, it was nevertheless assumed that Haitians were generally darker-skinned, meaning that many black Dominicans were swept up in the raids; a crude test of certain Spanish words that French speakers notoriously had trouble pronouncing was instituted. Have a dark enough complexion and say *perejil* ("parsley") improperly and you were dead. It went on for several days: mass murder by machete and pistol. By the time it was over, some 15,000 to 20,000 people had been killed.

It took several weeks for word of the massacre to reach the outside world, and when it did, the bloody face of the Trujillo regime first became known globally. In France, the colonial fatherland of Haiti, the events were received with special outrage; Trujillo took out subscriptions to French newspapers to keep track of what they were saying about him. For some time, Trujillo managed to keep the world at bay by explaining the genocide as a spontaneous outburst of his people, who had grown tired of being inundated with and exploited by Haitians. That charade didn't last long—the United States government, still keenly observing Dominican affairs, was particularly anxious to uncover the truth—and Trujillo finally submitted to mediation and a judgment against his government, which paid $525,000 in damages to Haiti. The reaction of the world to this ghastly event forever altered Trujillo's political prospects. He had forced his way to the presidency in 1930; he had run unopposed for reelection four years later; but after the Haitian massacre he could never again hold the office, satisfying himself rather with strictly managing Dominican political and economic life through a string of puppet presidents he installed in the National Palace. As a sop, he had himself declared generalissimo, adding an unprecedented fifth star to his epaulets and another title to the encomia by which he demanded to be addressed.

═════

While Trujillo was roiled by grisly events of his own making, his son-in-law prospered in small fashion. In August 1937, as the barbaric Haitian plot was forming, a letter arrived at the Foreign Ministry in Ciudad Trujillo from a stamp collector in Paris: He had seen in the collections of several local dealers whole sheets of uncanceled Dominican stamps and was wondering if he might buy such rarities directly from the source and avoid paying a markup to middlemen. Trujillo immediately wrote to the Parisian embassy notifying the ambassador that somebody in his charge was stealing stamps and selling them on the sly to philatelists around the city. After several weeks, a reply was sent declaring that the dealers had identified their source for this contraband as Porfirio's brother-in-law, Gilberto Sánchez Lustrino, who had, in the way of things in the Trujillo Era, turned from snobbish disparagement of the Benefactor's mean roots to groveling obsequy and parasitic dependence. In the coming years, Sánchez Lustrino would paint sycophantic word pictures of the Benefactor's greatness in prose and verse, and as editor of the ardently proregime newspaper *La Nación*. In Paris, one of several foreign postings in which he would serve, he had obviously fallen in with Porfirio, whose delicate fingerprints would be invisible on this clever but short-lived enrichment scheme. In any case, no record of punishment for the thefts found its way into the diplomatic archives.

Perhaps Porfirio wasn't guilty. But more likely his complicity was overlooked by the ambassador himself, the Benefactor's older brother Virgilio Trujillo Molina, who would fill ambassadorial posts in Europe for decades. Virgilio was always frankly resentful of his younger brother, if for no other reason than the mere notion that he was older and yet less powerful. Dependent on his sibling, like all other Dominicans, for work, money, and even life and limb, he made a habit of cultivating his own cadre of acolytes and, on occasion, hatching his own financial and political intrigues. Virgilio found a sufficiently eager ally in Porfirio, for instance, that he overlooked the younger man's infidelities against Flor, who was, after all, his niece. And he would continue to maintain friendly relations with Porfirio as the illustrious marriage of 1932 devolved into the domestic shambles of 1937.

Paris, alas, hadn't, as Flor had hoped, proved an even ground where her familiarity with the surroundings would counterbalance her husband's shamelessness. The couple had moved from the embassy to a home in Neuilly-sur-Seine, a suburb just beyond the Bois de Boulogne.

It should have been heaven. But, "unfortunately," in Porfirio's view, they were not alone: "A cousin of Flor's was with us constantly." The girl was Ligia Ruiz Trujillo de Berges, the daughter of the Benefactor's younger sister Japonesa (so nicknamed for the almond shape of her eyes). "When I went to the embassy," Porfirio recalled, "she didn't separate from Flor for even a minute; in the evenings, she went out with us. She was in all our conversations, even our arguments, and this is no good for a couple. It's possible to convince a woman of your good intentions or of the meaninglessness of a little fight; but two!"

Ligia had Flor's ear and convinced her cousin that the marriage had degenerated irredeemably. She persuaded Flor to return to Ciudad Trujillo to seek her father's help in corralling Porfirio and perhaps in making him feel sufficiently jealous or guilty or nostalgic that he would change his ways. Flor explained the trip by claiming that her father wanted her back home because of some family crisis ("She lied," Porfirio declared with misplaced umbrage) and left France. When she arrived back home, she sent word of her true intent. "I feel life between us has become impossible," he reported her to have said. "I want to see if I can live without you." Then, he claimed, she visited his mother, Doña Ana, to solicit her help in repairing the marriage. Per Porfirio's account, Flor sobbed to her mother-in-law, "Ask him to come find me. I love him. I know I've always loved him. Ask him to forgive me. Everything can go back to how it was." Doña Ana, taking pity, relayed as much to her son.

But, he said, he balked. "Everything couldn't be as it was. Nothing could ever be as it was. It's true I erred as a husband, but there's no doubt that I regretted this match. In the lives of men, as in the histories of nations, there are periods of acceleration, and I was living through one. The brake that Flor represented no longer worked. My mother's letter didn't move me."

Naturally, Flor's account of their separation would be different. The parent at whom she threw herself in her version of events was her own father, who coldly declared that he'd warned her about marrying such a wastrel and tried to mollify her with this consolation: "Don't worry, you're the one with money." As proof, he tossed her a catalog of American luxury cars and told her she could choose one for herself; she picked a fancy Buick and tried to have it sent to Paris as a gift to Porfirio, hoping it would mend the breach; her father put a stop to that plan.

Indeed, not only wouldn't Trujillo allow a car to be sent to his son-in-law, he wouldn't allow his daughter to return to him. "I'll never let you go back to that man," he announced, and he had his lawyer begin writing up the papers necessary for a divorce.*

Flor claimed that the shadow of divorce evoked a new passion in her husband: "When I wrote that I wasn't coming back, he sent letters pleading with me to return, threatening to join the French Foreign Legion if I didn't."

But Porfirio had a slightly different recollection of his impending bachelorhood: "Freedom in Paris was never disagreeable. I went out a lot."

In November 1937, the decree was declared; in January 1938, the couple were officially divorced. Separated from Trujillo's wrath by an ocean, protected by Virgilio and, perhaps, by his ability to implicate the Benefactor in the Bencosme affair, connected more to Paris than he was to his own homeland, Porfirio stayed put, chary but more or less safe and even eager. Having married the boss's daughter and returned in luxe fashion to the city of his boyhood ramblings, he was ready to take huge gulps of the world.

* Just the year before, Trujillo had passed a remarkably progressive divorce law that allowed a marriage that hadn't produced children after five years to be dissolved by mutual consent of the spouses. It was a means for him to leave Doña Bienvenida, with whom he had no children, and marry María Martínez, the mother of Ramfis. Not long after he pulled off this legislative coup and took his third wife, however, he fathered a child—technically a bastard—with his just-divorced *second* wife.

FIVE

STAR POWER

On the one hand: liberty.

On the other hand: liberty.

In divorcing Flor, Porfirio had unchained himself from an anchor, but he had also let go of a lifeline.

Yes, she behaved prematurely like an old Dominican *dama* with her petulant whining about his carousing and his other women, refusing to accept him for the type of man he was.

But: As the daughter of a powerful man, she was a direct conduit to money, security, and stature—and perhaps, given Trujillo's incendiary nature, life itself. Losing her meant unmooring himself totally from the life he'd known since boyhood, a life implicated in the political goings-on of his homeland.

He lost everything. Before long, dunning letters began arriving at the Dominican embassy in Paris—saddleries and purveyors of equestrian clothing looking for payment on items he'd bought with a line of credit he no longer commanded.

By then, at any rate, he was no longer, technically, an embassy employee. Trujillo had expelled him from the diplomatic corps in January 1938. Virgilio, the generalissimo's resentful older brother, managed to secure him a temporary appointment as consul to a legation that served Holland and Belgium jointly, but that expired by April. He held on to his diplomatic passport and was occasionally seen around Paris in embassy cars, but he was, literally, a man without a country. He wasn't about to go home to the Dominican Republic, where his prospects for work were no better than in Europe and his prospects for play considerably worse. Plus, he had already heard from his mother not to risk the trip: Trujillo wanted his head; Paris was decidedly safer.

He was certain in his own mind that Flor hadn't instigated her father's fury. Indeed, he would declare that he always harbored warm feelings for her: "After this romantic catastrophe, we stayed good friends." (They were widely said, in fact, to reignite their sex life whenever Flor, who'd apparently overcome her initial aversion to his lovemaking, was in Europe.) "And," he continued, "I followed, with friendship, her life." With friendship and, no doubt, amazement: after divorcing Porfirio, Flor would go on to take another eight husbands, including a Dominican doctor, an American doctor, a Brazilian mining baron, an American Air Force officer, a French perfumer, a Dominican singer, and a Cuban fashion designer. She had a short heyday as a diplomat in Washington, D.C., but during long periods of her life her father disowned her and even had her held under house arrest in Ciudad Trujillo. She would eventually come to dismiss her first husband with a shrug, answering interviewers who asked whether he was handsome or charming with a curt "For a Dominican."*

=====

And so what to do?

Another man might assess the situation and reckon it was time to

* She died in 1978 at Beth Israel Hospital in New York, married to a ninth husband, cut off entirely from her family.

think about settling down in France: a wife, a job, kids, a house, responsibility.

Not a *tíguere,* not with this sort of freedom, not at this time, in this place, with this thrilling sense of possibility and a titillating sense of impending catastrophe. "I was a young man in a Paris that the specter of war had heated up," he remembered. "I lived a swirling life, without cease, without the pauses that would have allowed me the chance to think and make me realize that giant steps aren't the only strides that suit a man."

He spent time at Jimmy's, a Montparnasse nightclub run by an Italian whose real name too closely resembled Mussolini's to make for good advertising and who therefore took an American name as a PR maneuver. There, the comic jazz singer Henri Salvador became a friend. Porfirio sat in with his band for late night sessions—his little skill on the guitar and enthusiasm for drums were fondly received—and led *parrandas* of the musicians and clubgoers late into the night, retiring to this or that partyer's flat for bouts of drinking and merrymaking that could last until the middle of the next day.

Of course, this sort of traveling circus required funding, and, as its ringmaster no longer enjoyed legitimate work as a diplomat, other strategies emerged. There was the familiar one of living off a woman. La Môme Moineau, the singing, yachting wife of Félix Benítez Rexach, was in Paris and available to him once again as her husband was off earning millions on his various projects in the Dominican Republic. Now, however, she had a fortune to spend on and share with her lover; he drove around the city at various times in one or another of her little fleet of luxury cars; occasionally, he would raise cash by selling off some valuable bijou from her jewel case.

This character—nightclubber, cuckolder, kept man, gigolo, scene maker, skirt chaser, dandy—was not so much a new Porfirio as an evolved one. Nearing thirty, freed of father, wife, and father-in-law—the living connections to his homeland that had thus far defined him—he was no longer an exotic, a Dominican in Paris, but, more and more, a Parisian with intriguingly Dominican roots. He had been an enthusiastic regular in the demimonde; now he was a staple of it. And, free of the constraints of decorum that adhered to him as the son of Don Pedro or the son-in-law of Trujillo, he no longer required so formal and elaborate a name as Porfirio Rubirosa. Anyone who knew him, truly knew him, in Paris after his divorce or, indeed, for the rest of his life, knew him as *Rubi*. Even more than his mellifluous given name, which he still used to dramatic effect and for official purposes, this new moniker captured his mature essence: the jauntiness, the rarity and high cost, the sparkle and the sharpness and sensuality and the bloody, cardinal allure.

Especially, perhaps, the bloody allure.

Over the years, he would—by virtue of his high living, his obscure origins, his association with Trujillo, his love of thrills and danger—almost inevitably be associated with shadowy events. Most of it was idle gossip. In some cases, such as the Bencosme murder, there were real reasons to think he was involved, albeit peripherally.

And then there was the matter of the Aldao jewels and Johnny Kohane.

For all the munificence of La Môme Moineau, Rubi wasn't satisfied with his solvency. The life to which he aspired required real capital. He needed a score. In early 1938, while he was still holding, despite Trujillo's injunctions against him, a diplomatic passport and temporary consular position, Rubi became involved in a scheme to smuggle a small fortune in jewels out of Spain. The goods in question belonged to Manuel Fernandez Aldao, proprietor of one of the most esteemed jewelry establishments of Madrid. In November 1936, when the Spanish Civil War had so turned that Madrid was under siege, Aldao had fled for safety to France and left a good deal of his wealth behind in the form of a safe filled with jewels guarded by an employee named Viega. Two years later, Aldao had need of his resources but was unable to retrieve them himself. He came into contact with Rubi, perhaps through Virgilio Trujillo, and hired him to go to Madrid and use his diplomatic pouch to transport a cache of jewels—and an inventory describing them—back to Paris.

In the time it took for the details of the operation to be worked out, another errand was added to Rubi's schedule and another conspirator to the plot: Johnny Kohane, a Polish Jew who had also fled Spain without his fortune (some $160,000 in gold, jewels, and currency, he said), was introduced to Rubirosa by Salvador Paradas, who'd replaced him at the Dominican embassy. Kohane had need of his stash, and it was agreed that he would join Rubi on the trip using a passport borrowed from the Dominican embassy chauffeur, Hubencio Matos. In February, the two would-be smugglers got into the embassy's Mercedes and drove across southern France and, through the Republican-controlled entry point of Cerbere-Portbou, into war-ravaged Spain.

A dozen days later, Rubi returned—alone.

He handed a sack of jewels over to Aldao—a smaller one than the Spaniard expected—and claimed that he'd never been given any inventory to go with it. And he told a hair-raising story about the bad luck he and Kohane had run into outside of Madrid when they were off fetching the Pole's fortune. They were set upon, he said, by armed men, he wasn't sure from which side, who chased them and shot at them, killing Kohane. He was lucky, he said, to get out of there with his own skin intact.

What could anyone say? He'd had the moxie to go get the jewels and to get back in one piece. As for Kohane, it was a war zone; he knew it was a dangerous proposition going into it. Suspicion was natural. The car in which Rubi claimed to have been ambushed evinced not a single scratch. But there was no tangible proof that the story, however far-fetched, wasn't true. Aldao paid Rubi his agreed-upon fee—a platinum-and-diamond brooch—and stewed over the matter for years.

When the situation in Spain finally settled and it was safe to cross back through France, Aldao returned home and looked into the matter of the half bag of jewels and the missing inventory. He wasn't pleased. There *had* been an inventory, and Viega *had* handed it to Rubi; a carbon copy of the original document still sat in the company safe. What the inventory showed was that the bag that left

Madrid held jewels worth some $183,000 that never made their way to Aldao in Paris. What was more, a fellow who'd been enlisted to help the Mercedes cross the border swore that he'd never received the platinum-and-diamond bracelet that Aldao had instructed Rubi to give him.

Aldao wrote Rubi in Paris several times to inquire about the missing items but was repeatedly ignored. He sent a Parisian friend to confront Rubi and, as he later declared, his emissary was rudely rebuffed: "The result of the meeting was completely negative, and he was moreover very discourteous to my friend." Finally, a few years after the fact, he wrote a letter of formal protest to Emilio A. Morel, the Dominican ambassador to Spain. It wasn't the first Morel had heard of the case— an anonymous letter had found its way to him a year or so earlier, a note, he recalled as so "crammed with inside information" that he believed its author was "a compatriot of Rubirosa's, actually a principal in the smuggling plan, who felt he had been double-crossed out of a commission from Kohane and took this method of seeking revenge." Morel dutifully sent notice of these claims against Rubi to the Secretariat of Foreign Relations in Ciudad Trujillo; not only were his inquiries sloughed off, but he, a noted Dominican poet and onetime leader of Trujillo's own political party, found himself, by virtue of making them, suddenly in the bad graces of the generalissimo. He left Madrid for New York, where he lived out his years in exile. And Aldao got nothing.

———

Rubi likely had the jewels—and all of Kohane's assets as well. His finances seemed to have worked themselves out for the decided better. He had been so skint at the start of the year that he would on occasion feign illness so as to summon friends to his house with restorative meals—the only food he could, apparently, afford. After returning from Madrid, however, he spoke of opening his own nightclub and renewed his habit of forming an impromptu club wherever he went; the genius guitarist Django Reinhardt was soon among the players in his ever-expanding, never-ending, ceaselessly moveable feast. Deauville; Biarritz; the French Riviera; and all through the Parisian night: He was ubiquitous, a star. Old friends who encountered Rubi in Paris— among them Flor de Oro and his brother Cesar, now himself a cog in Trujillo's diplomatic machine—found him exultant, even though they'd been led to expect he'd be sporting a more destitute aspect.

Perhaps news of his self-made success made it back to the Dominican Republic, perhaps he was vouched for by Virgilio Trujillo, but in the spring of 1939, the most amazing bit of fortune landed in his lap: a phone call from Ciudad Trujillo. "The President, who is beside me," said the official on the other end, "would like to know if you could see after his wife and son, who will arrive in Paris in a few weeks. You'll have to find a house of appropriate size, accompany them, show them around."

"I was so stupefied," Rubi remembered, "that I couldn't answer straightaway. At first I wondered what sort of trap it was. I couldn't see one."

He hurriedly made arrangements to receive Doña Maria and ten-year-old Ramfis and met their boat in Le Havre, where he was startled to find the president's third wife a full eight months pregnant. Rubi immediately arranged for her to be taken to a clinic where, in comfort, she gave birth to a daughter, Angelita, on June 10.*

In the weeks before and after the birth, Rubi engaged in a full charm offensive, presenting Doña Maria with gifts of jewelry (booty, no doubt, from the Aldao collection) and seeing that the awkward, friendless, un-

---

* At this stage in his life, Trujillo was sprinkling the world with progeny like a dandelion gone to seed: After Flor and Ramfis, he added Odille, the baby Doña Bienvenida bore him subsequent to their divorce; two more children by Doña Maria; and four bastard children, all acknowledged. Of these nine, the most astounding were the two he sired with Lina Lovatón, Flor's schoolmate and co-conspirator in the early stages of her affair with Rubi. In 1936, Trujillo had become enraptured with the girl and had her crowned queen of the carnival of Ciudad Trujillo to enormous fanfare; when Doña Maria grew aptly jealous, he relocated his young mistress to Miami, where she and her children lived in plush comfort.

schooled Ramfis was kept happy; the two rode horses together, and it was likely around this time that they began tinkering at polo. As Rubi recalled, the campaign was a success: "Doña Maria wrote to her husband that I was useful, attentive, charming and courteous. Was it due to the sentiment that accompanies pregnancy? Was it due to the change of nations and distance? Trujillo warmed to me."

The Benefactor had come to recognize that in Rubi he had a truly unique asset: a young, handsome, worldly, cultivated Dominican of notable suavity and negotiable loyalty. Doña Maria, who had no history with the young man, must have impressed her husband with tales of his social skills and tact. And, as Trujillo was soon to discover himself, no Dominican was as enmeshed in the manners and mores of the great European capitals than his scalawag former son-in-law.

The dictator made a grand official tour of the United States in the early part of the summer and then wrote to France to announce that he would be joining his family there. He had his yacht, the *Ramfis,* sent ahead to Cannes and then sailed to Le Havre himself aboard the *Normandie.* Rubi was at the dock to meet him. "In the place of a furious father-in-law and an autocrat exasperated by my impertinence," he recalled, "I found a friendly and agreeable man."

Trujillo wanted to see the grand sights of Paris—"the elegant Paris, without beans and rice," as Rubi remembered. But he was perhaps even more interested in the louche part of the city that his former son-in-law, unique among Dominican expatriates, could show him. "Porfirio," he pronounced, "do not leave my side. I want you to show me everything. You understand? *Everything.*" Everything included a trip to the top of the Eiffel Tower, where the generalissimo fell under the spell of a girl selling flowers and postcards (presently he courted and bedded her, Rubi remembered, "because he wanted to seduce the loftiest woman in Paris"—"loftiest," *geddit?*). The visit included nights out at Jimmy's, where the generalissimo, unusually in his cups, declared, "We need a Jimmy's in Ciudad Trujillo, but much bigger, with four orchestras, gardens and a patio open to the sea." They moved on to Biarritz, where Trujillo expressed a similar desire to re-create the local hot spots back home. And finally the entire Trujillo party relocated to Cannes and a Mediterranean cruise—all the way to Egypt, they hoped—at the launch of which the dictator whispered to his guide, "Porfirio, I am putting you in charge of this entire voyage."

But it wasn't to be. The war that Rubi hadn't foreseen when he was sitting within a few feet of its architect in a Berlin stadium began in earnest. And although the Dominican Republic was still officially neutral in the boiling European conflict, events in the Old World seemed likely to upset the balance of power in the Caribbean. Trujillo felt he had no choice but to leave Doña Maria and the children in Rubi's care and sailed home on the *Ramfis*. By the time he reached Ciudad Trujillo, Rubi had safely sent his family after him.

═══

If Trujillo felt cheated out of his grand tour, Rubi was handsomely rewarded for the part he played in orchestrating it. Back in the dictator's good graces, he was reinstated at the French and Belgian embassies as a first-class secretary.

It was a truly auspicious time to hold such a position. Trujillo, still stung by the beating his image had taken after the Haitian border massacres, had made a grand show of opening his country to refugees from the Spanish Civil War; it wasn't a huge influx, but the PR bounce was good. When he became aware of the desire of European Jews to relocate to the Western Hemisphere, he saw an opportunity to ingratiate himself with U.S. interests. Although he reckoned Judaism to be synonymous with communism, he declared that the Dominican Republic would accept one hundred thousand European Jews on its soil and demarcated a territory where they would be allowed to settle: Sosùa, a beachside village on the northern coast; a large parcel of his own land would be given over to the enterprise.

Word that Trujillo was accepting Jewish refugees led to a run on Dominican consulates and embassies in countries not yet controlled by the Nazis. A chancer like Rubi, given access to papers that could liberate anybody he favored, was sitting on a gold mine. He sold visas on a sliding scale, getting as much as $5,000 a head, and never concerned himself with how or even *if* his customers got out of France, much less all the way to the Dominican Republic. As it happened, Trujillo's offer was chiefly rhetorical: Fewer than one thousand European Jews made their way to Sosùa, and the projected Caribbean Jerusalem eventually became a resort with a little Jewish history sprinkled in.* But from the vantage of Paris, it didn't matter: Rubi did a thriving business until the Nazis took the French capital. "He got rich selling visas to Jews," shrugged his brother Cesar. "Didn't everybody?"

The business wasn't always pernicious. A Spanish journalist who feared Fascist reprisals against him managed to get a visa out of Rubi for free but had to pay him $5,000 for transport from Paris to Barcelona to Puerto Plata, where a train would take him to Ciudad Trujillo. "When I got to Puerto Plata I learned that there had never been a train from there to Ciudad Trujillo," he recalled with laughter.

And sometimes the results were profound. Take the case of Fernando Gerassi, a Turkish-born Spaniard who came to Paris in the 1920s and, as an abstract painter in the mode of Kandinsky and Klee, chummed around with such Left Bank icons as Picasso, Sartre, and Alexander Calder. By the late 1930s, Gerassi had fought for the losing side in the Spanish Civil War and found himself living back in Paris under the uncomfortable threat of German ascendancy. And then he had a chance meeting with somebody who could help. According to Gerassi's son, historian John Gerassi, the painter and Rubi met playing poker and hit it off and Rubi was able to help his new friend by hiring him as a secretary at the Dominican embassy. Then, when the Nazi threat grew more intense, he gave Gerassi a more prestigious title that resulted in safe passage out of Europe not only for him and his family but, as it turned out, for many others.

"My family was leaving Paris because the Germans were coming," the younger Gerassi recalled. "Rubirosa gave Fernando the position of

* By the mid-1990s Sosùa had become so synonymous with sex tourism and prostitution that the national police shut down every bar in the town for a year, killing both the legitimate and illegitimate economies and scattering the sex workers and their customers to other locales.

ambassador from the Dominican Republic, gave him the official stamp. Fernando, in turn, gave eight thousand passports to Spanish Republicans, Jews, whoever he could help, before the Germans caught up. My parents came to America as Dominican diplomats." Not only did Fernando Gerassi save the lives of his family and the thousands for whom he obtained visas and passports throughout 1940 and 1941, he was, when the United States entered the war, enlisted in the OSS as an operative in Latin America and then Spain. In the latter operation, Gerassi engaged in disruptions of German military traffic, abetting the Allied landing in Africa and receiving commendation and a medal from the U.S. government. "Without your actions in Spain in 1942," OSS founder William Donovan wrote to Gerassi, "the deployment of Allied troops in North Africa could not have taken place." Thousands saved, Nazis frustrated, a painter become a humanitarian hero, and all because Rubi found lucrative use in the black market for his Dominican diplomatic privileges. *It's a Wonderful Life* with an ironic coating of avarice.

It wasn't long, though, before larger events scuttled Rubi's get-rich-live-rich scheme. Starting in June 1940 when the Nazis finally did enter Paris, the status and even the location of the Dominican embassy shifted with disconcerting regularity. The Dominican Republic was still technically neutral in the European war, and it maintained diplomatic relations with the Nazis' puppet government in Vichy, a liaison that was difficult to maintain as the Germans continually forced the Dominicans to relocate their base of operations: Twice before midsummer the embassy moved, first to Tours and then to Bordeaux, where Rubi was ordered to present himself. "A lady friend accompanied me," he remembered in his memoirs, failing to mention that it was his partner in greed, lust, and social climbing, La Môme Moineau. "Officially, the Dominican legation was put up in a castle near St. Emilion. I presented myself there. It was filled with refugees—some crying old ladies, children with dirty noses, caged birds, kittens in baskets, and old men who had saved France in Les Esparges or Verdun." This wasn't exactly the duty he'd signed up for, and he immediately took advantage of the vacuum of authority—communication with Ciudad Trujillo had slowed to almost nil—and changed his and his companion's situation: "I stayed in a pension for a few days and then returned to Biarritz."

Eventually, a Dominican embassy was established in Vichy. Even though it enjoyed a prime location—it was situated in the Hôtel des Ambassadeurs directly across from the Grand Casino—the new embassy wasn't to Rubi's liking. "In Paris," he explained, "life had recommenced. I was neutral. I returned to Paris and then went to Vichy. Paris–Vichy, Vichy–Paris: This was my itinerary during the fall of 1940."

And so it was that when the French diplomat Count André Chanu de Limur invited him to a cocktail party in Paris that autumn he was available to attend. Truth be told, he might have made the effort to be there no matter where he'd been when he got the invitation: The guest of honor was just the sort of woman he would want to meet: the highest-paid movie star in France, "the most beautiful woman in the world," as she was billed, twenty-three-year-old Danielle Darrieux.

=====

At fourteen, there was a knowing depth to her eyes, and their audacity drew you to her soft, gamin face. By seventeen, she could play ten years older than she was and had learned how to steal scenes with such mature tricks as slowly unfurling her eyelids when asked a question. She was a bona fide natural, able to channel emotions—joy, sorrow, worry, hope—in such a way that the audience felt them instinctively through her. But she was at her best as a comedienne, with a delicious ability to squinch her features into a smile so that her eyes seemed two merry commas on either side of the aquiline exclamation mark of her nose.

She was a war baby, born in Bordeaux on May 1, 1917, to Dr. Jean Darrieux, a French ophthalmologist and war hero, and his wife, an Algerian concert singer. (Polish and American roots were hinted at in publicity biographies.) After the Armistice, her family relocated to

Paris. By the age of four she was playing piano; later, she would take up the cello seriously. But her path toward the conservatory was hindered by two fateful events: In 1924, her father died, leaving her mother to raise three children with whatever income she could earn as a vocal instructor; and in 1930, Danielle was recommended for a screen test. "My mother was distrustful," she recalled later. "At that time, the cinema was reputed to be a completely depraved world." But she nevertheless relented and allowed the girl to go.

Danielle auditioned for director Wilhelm Thiele, one of those Viennese maestros so stereotypical of the silent film era: autocratic, high-minded, and lecherous (a few years later, he would pick Dorothy Lamour out of a chorus line). The film he was casting was based on Irene Nemirovsky's novella "Der Ball" about a teenager whose social-climbing parents plan a grand ball but don't include her; jealous, she tosses all the invitations into the river. To deal with the vagaries of the new technology of sound film, which still lacked the capability for dubbing dialogue, Thiele employed the then-common practice of shooting two versions at once—a German and a French, with distinct casts made up of actors from each country. Danielle got the part of the headstrong daughter in the French version.

The impression she made was strong enough to guarantee her a full five-year contract. In the next three years she made nine films, mostly comedies in which she appeared as a sparkling ingénue. (She made one crime film, *Mauvaise Graine* ["Bad Seed"], which was cowritten and codirected by Billy Wilder.) And she appeared on the stage in several productions throughout Europe: in Paris, Brussels, Prague, Sofia, Munich, and, fatefully, Berlin, where, in 1934, she signed a contract to make six films.

The first film covered by that agreement was *L'Or dans la Rue* ("Gold in the Street"), the French-language version of a German thriller coauthored by a German named Hermann Kosterlitz and a Frenchman named Henri Decoin. It was a fateful meeting of star and writers. Kosterlitz was a Jew who had engaged in a few unwise run-ins with German authorities and would soon be leaving for America, where, as

Henry Koster, he would hit paydirt as the man who made Deanna Durbin a star and put Abbott and Costello in the movies; he would keep a savvy eye on Danielle as her star rose. Decoin was a former Olympic swimmer, World War I pilot, and knockabout journalist who had been working as a director and screenwriter for almost a decade; he would become, in 1935, Danielle's first husband.

The age difference may have raised eyebrows—he was thirty-nine, she just eighteen—but it made sense when Danielle's fatherless adolescence was taken into account. As she remembered tellingly, "I was always absolutely confident in him, and I obeyed him in all things." More striking was the way in which they wed their careers, turning them into one of those classic director-actress couples who do their best work together. In a span of seven years starting in 1935 with *Le Domino Vert* ("The Green Domino"), Decoin directed his wife in six features, establishing himself as a capable hand in a variety of genres and cementing a directorial career that would last into the 1960s.

But Danielle became an international star largely on the work that she made between Decoin's films; while he worked exclusively with her during this period, she made more than twice as many pictures without him. He gave her the confidence to take on meaty dramatic roles, and she did so brilliantly. The key step in her ascent was the romantic lead in *Mayerling,* Anatole Litvak's 1936 costume epic about the love affair between a married Hapsburg prince and a girl from a minor noble family. It was an international critical and commercial success (it won the New York Film Critics Circle prize for Best Foreign Language Film), and, opposite the lordly Charles Boyer, who had already begun making films in America, Darrieux made a brilliant impression: fetching, bright, and quick, as she had been in lighter fare, but capable of the melodramatic emotions the script called for.

Universal Pictures, prodded by Henry Koster, requested her presence in Hollywood. They offered a multipicture deal and brought her, Decoin, and their pet Scottie, Flora, over on the *Normandie* in September 1937 (Cole Porter, who never did find a way to use Danielle's mellifluous name in a rhyming couplet, was on board for that crossing, as was Sonja Henie). In California, the couple were introduced by Boyer to the small French colony of Los Angeles, and Danielle was tutored in English (she was quick) and the technical aspects of American film-making and PR. The studio mounted the traditional grooming-for-stardom campaign; she appeared on the covers of American movie magazines and in all the right newspaper columns; she was news. But her debut film was delayed because of problems in the script; she sat around, bored, collecting money but grousing.

The film, *The Rage of Paris*, turned out to be a lightweight screwball comedy that presented Danielle to a mass American audience as a gold digger on the make for a millionaire husband. Directed by Koster and playing opposite Douglas Fairbanks Jr., she made another dazzling impression: Her long, elegant face, wavy hair, bright eyes, and wide smile photographed exquisitely; her English was more than passable and charmingly accented; her timing and rhythm were acute; she did some sleight-of-hand tricks (she had practiced for years) and ad-libbed verbal jokes and comic physical bits; she was slim and frisky and sexy and fetching.

But the film—a harmless thing but hardly equal to the hype—did only so-so business, and Danielle and Decoin made it clear that they didn't appreciate the protracted process or the result. Contract or no, they went home. A tumultuous welcome from the press and fans in Paris greeted their return, and they resumed their series of joint projects. In the fall of 1940, they were shooting a film called *Premier Rendezvous*, or, as it was known in its American release, *Her First Affair*.

And at roughly that time Count de Limur decided to throw a cocktail party in her honor.

═══

It got so later in his life that Rubi was suspected of any and every subterfuge, and so rumors would swirl that he crashed the party to latch on to Danielle or that he turned his world upside down so as to live near her in Neuilly-sur-Seine.

But the truth was that he'd lived in the same place since he was married to Flor, and his being invited to the party probably had more to do with his diplomatic standing than any occult plan he was hatching. That said, his reputation was genuinely dodgy. When the host asked Danielle if she would accept a lift home from Rubi, she demurred. When it was pointed out that they were virtually next-door neighbors, she changed her mind ("If it was a film no one would believe it," she remembered). When another partygoer, the Mexican diplomat and high-liver Pedro Corcuera, noticed them leaving together and joked, "Careful, Danielle: This man is dangerous!" there was only nervous laughter all around—many a truth spoken in jest, and all that.

As it happened, he behaved like a gentleman. And then a few days later, at L'Aiglon, a posh Paris nightspot, he happened to see Danielle and Decoin hashing out the dissolution of their increasingly rocky marriage over dinner; the combination of their age difference and his insistent control both on and off the set had proved impossible. Soon after this accidental encounter, Rubi was invited to an evening at Maxim's and was on the verge of declining when his host mentioned that Danielle would be there; of course, he went. This time, he asked her out for an evening together and she accepted.

It was the first of several dates. "This might have been an agreeable flirtation, a light episode of the sweet life, in the eyes of others," he reflected in that perfumed persiflage he adopted when writing about amatory episodes. "But one day she said to me, 'I'll tell you, I think that this is very serious for me.' 'For me too, Danielle.' " In February 1941, she filed for divorce from Decoin, freeing her for whatever she and Rubi wished.

From Rubi's vantage point, Danielle was in most ways an improvement over Flor or La Môme Moineau or any of the fun-time gals that had filled his evenings of late.* She was gorgeous, she was spry, she had her own money, and, intoxicatingly, she was famous. "I was well-known in the night life," Rubi said. "But Danielle was a real celebrity." He felt a

---

* Flor was, of course, across the ocean during the war, and so, indeed, was La Môme Moineau, who left in Rubi's charge for safekeeping a valuable Delahaye motorcar while she sat out the hostilities in Puerto Rico with her husband.

big man alongside her; they made an impression when they went places.

Too much of an impression sometimes. In December 1941, after the attack on Pearl Harbor, the Dominican Republic, along with many Caribbean nations wanting no part of the strife afflicting Europe and Asia, threw in with the United States and declared war on the Axis; as an official belligerent, Rubi would no longer be permitted to bounce freely back and forth between Vichy and Paris. Trouble was, he was in Paris when Trujillo, through his puppet president of the moment, declared war—and in terms that personally insulted Hitler. Rubi needed to return to his post in Vichy, but the German authorities in Paris instead decided to hold him as a hostage, collateral, in effect, guaranteeing the safety of their ambassador in Ciudad Trujillo. He protested the decision, arguing that it was the Dominican ambassador in Berlin who ought to be held, not he, and that, besides, he was only in Paris because of—get this—"an accident of love." His arguments prevailed, and he was allowed to stay in Paris on the condition that he not try to leave without permission or face arrest.

A few nights after this reprieve, Rubi and Danielle were out at L'Aiglon, drinking and laughing in the presence of several Gestapo officers. From their glares Rubi could tell that they didn't approve of a cocoa-complected fellow escorting a fair European, but he ignored them and kept at his partying. Eventually, in the spirit of the evening, he began breaking glasses after drinking from them, in the Russian fashion, and this proved to be the last straw for one of the Germans, who threw a glass at Rubi, striking him. Instinctively, Rubi set on the fellow and hit him, a proper ruckus ensued, the police were called, and then a senior SS officer stepped forward and broke the thing up before it got truly bloody. He took Rubi's arm and walked him to the door, stating firmly through clenched teeth, "You shouldn't have done that. I understand, but you don't know who you're dealing with. Get going quick. Quick!"

It was a dumb thing to do, but, according to Danielle, within character. As she recalled, his diplomatic good cheer was a facade for a real loathing of the Nazis. "Rubirosa detested the Germans," she said. "He screamed it loud and wide and he didn't hesitate to lash out at them when he'd had a few drinks."

This time there would be no sympathy extended to these glamorous lovers whose stars had been crossed by war. Rubi was arrested at his home and taken to the Hessian spa town of Bad Nauheim, north of Frankfurt and hundreds of miles from the French border. The resort where the young Franklin Roosevelt, among other summering Americans, had taken the waters with his family had been filled since Pearl Harbor by hundreds of enemy diplomats and journalists—principally from the United States—and had developed a decadent wartime culture that would, seemingly, have suited Rubi nicely. "There were friends, women, girls, everything you would need to kill time," he recalled. "They organized card games and social events. You could dance. We indulged in drunken parties with white wine." It's hard to imagine he didn't find his enforced visit at least *somewhat* diverting.

Eventually, though, his pining for Danielle outweighed these fleeting pleasures. "Bad Nauheim is a spa city where people with heart ailments recuperated, but the therapeutic effects didn't work on me," he moaned. And then, a month or so into his sojourn, the most astonishing telegram arrived, lifting him out of his pet: "I'll arrive tomorrow morning on the 7:30 train. Tenderly, Danielle."

If a minor Dominican diplomat hefted no clout among the German authorities, a gorgeous French movie star did. Almost as soon as Rubi was taken from her, Danielle began looking into the possibility of joining him. Her stardom, her short tenure in the German cinema before the war, and the fact that she had a new film, *Premier Rendez-vous*, debuting in Germany meant that she had entrée not only to the Nazi state but to its ruling class. She went to Germany and . . . did something. According to the French Resistance, who took bitter note of the facts as they saw them, she performed for German troops; according to Rubi, she went on a publicity tour along with a number of French artists; according to her, she was still under contract in Germany and was required to present herself at the studio or suffer reprisals against her career. At any rate, she was certainly there, about that there would be no debate, and she certainly made the acquaintance of Joseph Goebbels, whom she charmed into the remarkable concession of a visit to Bad Nauheim and—again, it depended which story was true—the privilege to marry her interned lover.

She arrived too early: Bad Nauheim detainees weren't allowed to leave their quarters before 8 A.M., and her train got in just before that hour. Rubi reserved a hotel room and paid a bellboy to meet her train, holding up a sign that read "RUBI" and escorting her to their trysting place. He asked about the circumstances that brought her to him, and she told a story about charming Mrs. Goebbels with tales of her imprisoned lover and about how she was granted permission to leave Berlin for Bad Nauheim by the fearsome propaganda minister himself.

"Do you have written permission?" Rubi asked her, knowing the esteem in which paperwork was held by the German bureaucracy.

"No," she told him, "just verbal."

He got a little queasy and took her to the authorities, who laughed in their faces at the claim that Goebbels would authorize such a whimsical visit. Danielle begged them to call Berlin, which they did . . . and the mood quickly changed. Goebbels *had* approved. The official who was minutes before mocking the couple was now groveling. "He signaled his compliance by making me a gift of a month's worth of his ration tickets for butter," Rubi remembered, "and in Bad Nauheim in 1942, tickets for butter were like bars of gold. From that moment, I helped myself to all liberties. I went everywhere in the city with Danielle on my arm. Those 10 days of happiness gave me new hope."

And they also made every other internee mad as hell: Why couldn't *their* wives and lovers visit? The authorities had to choose between banishing Danielle or opening the floodgates to trainloads of tootsies—no choice, in other words. Regretfully, respectfully, with an anxious tone of "would you mind?", they asked her to return to France—quickly, like the next day. She complied and they parted, tearfully.

It would be another few months before negotiations between Berlin and Ciudad Trujillo were completed and the representatives of both governments were sent to Lisbon in neutral Portugal and freed to return home. "I passed the first two or three days without the sensation of walking," Rubi remembered. "It was like I was floating, dumbfounded, enchanted."

He must truly have been in love, though, because he left the seat of this enchantment, this paradisiacal war-free zone, this Casablanca with better plumbing, for Vichy and Danielle.

=====

He must have loved her: It would be the only explanation. She had money and means, but not so much to make him independent, and she was gorgeous, but he was already having his way with her. Maybe she needed the sanctity of marriage to protect her career rather than endure scandal as a woman living openly with a foreign man. But the simplest theory covered the most contingencies: They really were in love.

They wanted to get married straight away, but the paperwork for wartime marriage between a French citizen and a foreigner took so much time to process that they couldn't stand the wait and made for the Riviera, where the agony of the delay could be mitigated by the scenery and the cushy lifestyle. At Cannes, where, of course, Danielle was recognized, they drew crowds everywhere they went, so they would leave their hotel early in the morning for Eden Roc, where they would swim and dine and laze until the evening, when they raced back to their hotel to see if word had come from the authorities. (That they were able to get about a war-staggered country and chose to be married in the collaborationist capital would count against them in the eyes of many French loyalists later on.) Finally, on September 18, they got the green light and headed back to Vichy to wed.

It was all done, Rubi recalled, "very quickly, without publicity"—which wasn't entirely true. The tabloid *Paris-Soir* was there and the next day spoke glowingly of the groom as "a brilliant chargé d'affaires . . . a fine young brown man sent to us by his country."

They were gorgeous together. He seemed taller beside her than he had beside Flor de Oro, and he had grown into his looks, sculpted, rugged, and confident where a decade before he had sported baby fat and a foolish, self-satisfied little smile. He was dressed in a formal wedding suit: cutaway morning coat with a dashing pocket square; striped pants; white tie, light vest, and high-collared shirt. She wore a heart-shaped hat that dwarfed her head to a somewhat unfortunate effect; her suit was dark and demure (though hemmed short); and the crown of her head barely reached his mouth even though she teetered on significant heels. But despite her drab outfit (there *was* a war on, after all), she shone, and in the photos in which she flashed that million-dollar smile she was absolutely the picture of a twenty-five-year-old in the full bloom of love. It was the best they would ever look at any of their combined eight weddings.

The witnesses included the Brazilian ambassador, Luis Martins de Souza Dantas, and Mrs. Douglas MacArthur II, the wife of the famed general's nephew, who was himself second secretary of the U.S. embassy in Vichy. After the civil ceremony, a breakfast was held in the Hôtel des Ambassadeurs. Such was the fame of the bride that the *New York Times* carried a small item on the wedding, mistakenly reporting that the groom, of whose first wedding ten years earlier it had also taken brief note, was from San Salvador.

It was an innocent mistake, and perhaps it was down to the fact that the Dominican Republic no longer had an embassy in Vichy, leaving Rubi with no work to do and no means of communicating with Ciudad Trujillo. Danielle was being courted by various filmmakers, but she refused to work until the French regained control of their film industry from the Nazis, so the newlyweds found themselves rootless. They honeymooned in Portugal, where Danielle, recognizable throughout Europe, was greeted with "La Marseillaise" at bullfights, restaurants, and cafés. Back in Vichy, though, things were more tense. "I decided to put some distance between us and the German army," Rubi said. They considered fleeing for the Caribbean, and started off for Perpignan in the Pyrenees to contact a Resistance cell that might be able to get them to a boat in Spain. But Danielle got cold feet about meeting the Free French, and so they returned to Vichy, where Rubi continued to stew. Finally, he threw up his hands at the whole situation: "I couldn't telegram the Dominican Republic. I couldn't receive instructions from my government. And so I left."

And just where would a Dominican diplomat cut off from his country and married to a French actress who might be wanted by either or both the Germans and the Resistance go?

Skiing, of course.

They went to a chalet in Megève in the Haute-Savoie, a chic resort tucked into the corner where France, Italy, and Switzerland meet at the toes of Mont Blanc. The explanation was *echt* Rubi: "A number of my friends were there, supplies were easy to come by, Switzerland wasn't far off, and the occupiers were principally Italian. It was said that the atmosphere was completely unique."

Charmant.

With the permission of Vichy authorities, who asked only that he report daily to the local gendarmerie, they spent most of 1943 in the small town, skiing and otherwise disporting themselves, yes, but engaging, at least by Rubi's claim, in anti-German activities as well. (Again, all of this gadding about in the midst of war—and the Nazis' evident countenancing of it—led Allied intelligence officers to believe that Rubi was a Nazi agent; his name even showed up on a list of suspected Axis spies during the war.) However, when a Gestapo officer was assassinated by the local branch of the *maquis,* the French Resistance fighters, Rubi, who was by his own admission acquainted with the insurgents, was marked for reprisal by the Germans. As Danielle remembered, "One night we had to flee with just what we had on our backs." (Her forged papers declared her name to be "Denise Robira.")

They wound up on a small farm that she owned near Septeuil, about thirty miles east of Paris. From one ironic setting to another: Instead of high life in the Alps, Rubi found himself living the sort of existence he would have thought of earlier as the most awful doom. "I became a peasant," he remembered. "I bought a cow to get butter, pigs to make hams, sheep to make grilled chops. I learned how to herd cattle. Danielle saw to her chickens. Friends came to see us from time to time, bringing cognac and leaving weapons."

But truly there was no safe haven in a divided France in which various factions were seething over the many treacheries that had colored the war. Rubi was denounced in one newspaper as an enemy of Germany "in a perfectly repugnant article by a brave anonymous author who declared that I was a lackey of the judeo-marxist plutocrats and ought to be behind bars."

And it was actually worse for Danielle. The trouble began that winter, when a newspaper called *Bir-Hakeim* (after a ferocious battle the Free French had won under de Gaulle in the Libyan desert) wrote that she had been tried *in absentia* by the Resistance, who'd found her guilty of betraying her country with her activities in Germany and had sentenced her to die. It was so sensational a story that a version of it found its way into both the *New York Times* and the syndicated gossip column of Hedda Hopper. A movie star, a Latin diplomat, Nazis, a secret trial, assassins, a great scoop—and almost entirely untrue. *Bir-Hakeim* was, in fact, an organ of *Nazi* disinformation, established to sow infighting among the Resistance and its sympathizers and to direct attacks on enemies of the Germans by painting them as enemies of the Free French: Just a month before Danielle was tarred with a false death sentence, a newspaper editor in Toulouse who'd been similarly framed was shot dead in the street. She had every reason to fear for her life.

Where did she go for help? What did she do? She wrote a telegram to Hedda Hopper:

I have read your Hollywood column of December 8th and really don't understand where you picked this information STOP The reason of my trip to Germany was because I wanted marry [*sic*] my fiancé who was taken there as hostage and stay with him in same condition STOP I never entertained but Americans and Free French soldiers and I said no to the occupied movie pictures in 1942 and believe me it was rather dangerous with the Germans here STOP Trial is a big word there are no charges against me STOP I hope you will have the kindness to write the truth about me STOP would appreciate a cable from you addressed 7 Boulevard Julien Potin Neuilly Sur Seine STOP Happy New Year

And, strangely, this earnest little appeal had some effect, at least in the United States, where accounts of the true nature of the alleged death sentence made their way into print. Hedda was particularly sympathetic in setting the record straight.

Not, of course, that anyone in the Resistance was reading Hedda Hopper.

=====

After D-Day, life on the farm resembled less a restful country interlude than a dangerous game of cat and mouse. Somebody—Nazis? the Resistance?—was asking for them around the village, and they fled their home on bicycles, hiding in a friend's barn for a few days. Soon after, an Allied plane was shot down by Germans and they attended a ceremony where the dead airmen were memorialized by the locals; again they were noticed and subsequently hunted. They ducked in and out of their home, seeking shelter with friends on nearby farms. One afternoon in August when they felt it was safe, they went into the village to visit the café.

"A group of young men were talking loudly," Rubi remembered. "One of them suddenly froze. He pointed at Danielle and said 'Danielle Darrieux!' in an American accent." Handshakes all around and, Rubi being Rubi, a party ensued: "We invited him and his friends to dinner, where they reveled in fresh foods and we in American goodies." In the coming weeks, as the liberation of Paris was awaited as an inevitability, a group of American journalists happened upon the French actress and the Latin diplomat in their rustic retreat. On August 20, a reporter named James McGlincy dropped in, shared a bottle of wine, and reported to the world that the vagaries of war were such that the glamorous Danielle was wearing blue slacks with a big patch on the seat. Four days later, Paris—and with it all the couture houses a desperate movie star could want—was liberated by the Allies.

Finally they could live together as husband and wife.

Or at least try.

SIX

AN AMBUSH AND
AN HEIRESS

There may never have been a greater ecstasy in a place that
was better suited to host it.

Paris at its liberation: Nazis on the run, Yanks and Brits
pouring into town, hidden wine cellars unsealed, music and
color and smiles and food and champagne and everywhere
men and women finding in one another the perfect release for
the stifling and suffering of the previous years. Paris traditionally
closed for national vacations in August. That summer it was more
wide open than ever.

There were still signs of wartime scarcity—a curfew on electricity, for instance, and daily announcements about which bak-
eries would be operating that day. But those sorts of things felt
like ancient history when so much was new or newly revived:
Cafés were allowed to open every day of the week; English, American, and Russian movies showed up in newly reopened theaters;
telephone service outside the city was reinstated; the lottery resumed, as did horse racing. Novelties intended to entertain the
Allied troops made the world seem larger than it ever had been:

exhibitions of baseball and football, soccer matches between British and French soldiers, Fred Astaire—the actual Fred Astaire!—was on hand to perform for the enlisted men. (The lucky Yanks and Brits could stay for a week in a room with a bath at the Grand Hotel for 150 francs—about three U.S. dollars.)

The newspapers couldn't report it all, *literally.* Paper was so scarce that most published as a single folded sheet—four pages total—and were dedicated to serious matters such as the progress of the war and the arrests and purgings of Nazis and collaborators from all parts of liberated France.

So some stories were missed altogether.

Such as the mysterious events of the early hours of Saturday, September 23, which were never reported in Paris but made headlines elsewhere.

Somebody had thrown a party for some international big shots who were in town—William Randolph Hearst Jr. among them—and Rubi and Danielle were, naturally, on hand. Late at night, they bummed a ride home from Spiro Vassilopoulos, a press attaché of the Greek embassy, who was accompanied by his wife, Edmée, and a young man from Switzerland. Vassilopoulos, and his wife sat up front and Rubi, Danielle, and the Swiss took the backseat, with Rubi in the middle.

They were headed northwest along Boulevard Malesherbes with the windows closed against the early autumn air when Vassilopoulos heard the trill of a whistle and, thinking it was a policeman, slowed down.

Then Danielle heard something.

"That's a shot . . ."

The car stopped.

"A veritable hailstorm exploded behind us," Rubi remembered. "Edmée let out a shriek. A bullet had hit her. At the same time I felt as if I had been whipped on the back. But it didn't hurt much. Then I had the feeling that a hot object had lodged itself deeply within me. I didn't say anything because the poor woman was shouting. She was bleeding everywhere. In a minute, her seat was covered with blood.

Vassilopoulos took his wife in his arms and shouted, 'My love, don't die!' "

In contrast to the drama in the front seat, Rubi played the stoic in the back. "I opened my collar. I breathed with difficulty. I felt sweat cover my body. I murmured, 'There's no point in yelling here. I'm also wounded.' "

Danielle hadn't even noticed that her husband had been hit, and the news launched her into a panic of her own: "What's wrong? Where are you hurt?"

But he couldn't answer. "It was a struggle to breathe," he recalled. "I had the impression that something was escaping from me—my life, without a doubt. And at that very moment I felt within myself an extraordinary resolve." He muttered a single word: "Marmottan."

The tiny Hospital Marmottan was just blocks from his old family home on Avenue Mac-Mahon; he'd passed it a million times as a boy. It was no trick, even in his distress, even with Edmée screaming bloody murder, to direct Vassilopoulos, who had gathered himself sufficiently to take the wheel again, to the front door.

"We made a striking entrance," Rubi recalled. "Edmée didn't stop screaming." He felt just the opposite urge. "I felt like sitting down, because my legs wouldn't support me." He found a room where a few American servicemen were drying out after a night of binging. And for the first time he began to feel truly anxious. He blurted out to Danielle, "If they leave me here, I'll die."

Marmottan was, as he knew, a charity hospital, staffed with young doctors—interns and residents. He wanted his own physician, and asked Danielle to call him. She got on the phone and painted the most urgent scene she could—"Rubi has at least four bullets in him!"— but the doctor advised that they let the attending physicians see to him.

"For a moment," Rubi said, "I thought he hadn't come because he thought I was a hopeless case. But he had made a clever assessment of the situation. If we had waited for him, I would have died before he got there. But I nevertheless died a bit when I learned he wasn't coming."

He was uncomfortable sitting up so he slouched onto the floor for relief. He was so nonchalant, in fact, that he hadn't been noticed at all by the staff.

"Edmée was already in the operating room," he said. "The way she was yelling, they saw to her immediately. On the floor, I smoked a cigarette, convinced it was my last. Nobody paid me any attention."

Finally, a passing nurse noticed that he was in discomfort.

"What are you doing there?"

"I have a bullet in my back."

"And you didn't say anything? I'm going to get Dr. Adam."

They whisked him off for an X ray, and Dr. Adam whistled with amazement when he saw what it revealed. Rubi was rushed into a two-and-a-half hour operation to remove a slug from his right kidney. He made it through the night, but from there it would be a touch-and-go business.

═══════

If the shooting of a minor Caribbean diplomat couldn't be squeezed into the meager pages of the Parisian newspapers of the era, even if the bullets narrowly missed a major film star, mention of the incident did find its way into the *New York Times*. And in Ciudad Trujillo, it was front-page news, not in the least because it was the first time in years that anybody knew for sure that Rubi was even alive. Since he had quit Vichy in late 1942, he'd been entirely incommunicado. But the Dominican newspaper *La Nación* (edited at the time by Rubi's brother-in-law Gilberto Sánchez Lustrino) carried a full report of the shooting, including this telegram sent from Rubi's convalescent bed to his erstwhile father-in-law:

I've been liberated from German internment by Allied forces. Find me in Paris awaiting your orders. Found in a Greek car, I was gravely wounded Sept. 23 by shots aimed at that car. I believe I'm out of danger after surgery. —Rubirosa

(The newspaper declared, upon this evidence, that Rubi's "first thoughts" upon the liberation of Paris "were of his country, his relatives and his protector, Rafael Leonidas Trujillo.")

The following day, another telegram from Paris found its way into the paper.

> I have the good fortune to inform my family and friends in America that I'll soon be fine. Danielle has carried herself bravely. She has been at my side night and day from the moment I was injured.

Again, this was a pretty brave face to put on things. The operation may have been a success, but recovery was hardly a given. Edmée, it turned out, had merely, for all that screaming, suffered a flesh wound to the ass. Rubi might yet die. For several days, in vivid pain, he hovered in danger of infection in a convalescent hospital near his home in Neuilly.

"I began to weaken," he recalled. "The pain increased. I grew delirious. As if I had a cold, I coughed, and with each coughing fit I felt 20 bayonets in my body. I died of thirst, but they gave me nothing to drink; they only allowed me to lick a spoon of water that Danielle, who never left my side, offered me, trembling and in tears. I didn't stop running my hands over my body. I fought. I felt young. I didn't want to die so quickly and so stupidly for nothing."

As he lay there, he remembered a visit he had made to a fortune-teller in Berlin in 1936. "She told me that I would divorce within two years and that within eight years I would suffer a grave injury by firearms: 'Everyone will believe that you'll die, but you'll be saved.' "

She was right on both accounts. Fit and hale at thirty-five years of age, he made it through those crucial first five days without infection and would fully recover.

So who did it?

After the trouble over Danielle's wartime visit to Germany, there were suspicions that it was Resistance gunmen avenging themselves against a perceived collaborator. Another supposition lay the blame at the feet of Nazis or Nazi sympathizers still lurking in the city and seeking to stir up trouble. As Rubi was one of the injured parties, it seemed almost inevitable that rumors would circulate—jokes, really—that the assailant was a jealous husband.

According to Rubi, the Swiss lad in the car, perhaps because he came from a neutral nation, was able to follow up the incident and get to the bottom of it. The shooters, said the Swiss, were members of a group known as the *Francs-Tireurs et Partisans,* a splinter group of the Communist *Front National,* which formed to fight the Nazi occupiers in 1942. They were patrolling Paris trying to beat any lingering Germans out of hiding when the car sped past them in the night.

"They weren't devils," Rubi reflected. "They were young men who had begun fighting around the time the war ended and sought to make a mark."

When asked why they attacked the car, they said, "We asked for papers and you didn't stop, so we thought you were Germans and we fired. . . . We realized that we'd done something stupid and we beat it."

Typically philosophical, Rubi responded to this account with a shrug: "There's nothing to say to that."

But typically as well the brush with death inspired him in a way that recalled his reaction to Trujillo's anger after that fateful dance in Santiago a dozen years earlier: "There emerged in me a greater appetite for life and lively people than ever."

Danielle, in other words, had reason to keep her eyes open.

They passed part of his convalescence on the Riviera, where Rubi found himself under attack by an unjustly jealous husband at a party thrown by Aly Khan, another sportsman and playboy with a burgeoning global reputation. Right there in the luxe setting of a fine restaurant, the fellow challenged Rubi to a duel, slapping him on the cheek and swearing he would avenge the honor Rubi had allegedly stained. "Why should I fight you?" Rubi asked. "I haven't done anything wrong." (In fact, the fellow's wife, a fiftyish Argentine matron, had pursued Rubi doggedly to no avail.) Into the breach stepped Danielle, arguing that the man was mistaken and defusing the situation. Rubi watched placidly, enjoying the spectacle of his tiny tigress fighting for him.

When he was fit enough to resume work, Rubi was proposed for a position at the newly reestablished Dominican embassy in France. But the new French government was making a point of refusing to recognize diplomats who had been accredited by the Nazi-sponsored government in Vichy, and so an alternative commission fell his way: Rome, where he was named to the all-purpose post of chargé d'affaires in January 1945.

Danielle, having been cleared of charges of collaboration by a committee established to weigh guilt and innocence, was still waiting for the French film business to resume and her career to recommence. So she joined Rubi on his trip to Rome to present his credentials.

The arrival of a major French movie star in Italy was big news, and it would be reported not only locally but internationally by wire service correspondents and even freelancers looking around the Italian capital for colorful stories. One in particular made an impression.

"A journalist showed up the day after we settled into our hotel," Rubi remember. "We lunched together. She struck me as vivacious and jovial, with that certain something that Americans can have." She was, he recalled, "a typical enough journalist except for the fact that she was the richest woman in the world."

Her name was Doris Duke.

―――――

There was a certain audacity in wooing the daughter of a bloodthirsty despot. There was a thunderbolt fortune in winning the heart of a gorgeous and well-to-do film star. But sitting at lunch with your wife and turning the charm on the single wealthiest woman on earth—a recent divorcée, to boot—was brash even by Rubi's brazen standards. Doris wasn't nearly in Danielle's league as a beauty, although she possessed a kind of long-limbed, squared-jawed sexiness. But her hundreds of millions of dollars could have the same effect on the libido as a night of drinking and dancing and a bartender's shout of last call: All physical imperfections were magically transformed into comely assets—and she had neither a vengeful daddy nor a controlling husband to circumvent.

And more even than greed or the overweening nature of his inner *tíguere* was this: In Doris Duke Rubi finally confronted somebody as large as himself in spirit and self-image and appetite for life and sense of unlimited boundaries. They were kindred in a way that he hadn't been with either of his wives or any of his lovers. They deserved each other.

Of course, he was already married. But Danielle's career took care of that inconvenience in the short run. By spring she was in Paris working on her first film in nearly four years, leaving Rubi in Rome to see to his diplomatic and other tasks. Whatever, if anything, happened between Rubi and Doris in Rome after Danielle left—some said that the American heiress was satisfied with declaring frankly that he should look her up when he was done with Danielle, others that they had already made their plans and she had made a down payment of as much as a half-million dollars against future considerations—the groundwork was laid for a rollicking ride.

Danielle went back to work, making two films in France while Rubi dallied at diplomacy in Rome. After being together for more than five years, they were drifting apart. "Little by little," Rubi related in a poetic moue, "something besides 1000 kilometers came between us, something like absence, separation, different lives, social circles the other didn't know, the habits one picks up over time, day by day, living without your double, your echo."

He dutifully commuted to see her when he could—perhaps because Doris was too big and unlikely a catch for him to feel satisfied that she was well and truly hooked. But Danielle wasn't fooled: She saw things and heard things and had plans of her own. She signed to make a film in Morocco, *Bethsabée,* a flimsy modern updating of the story of David and Bathsheba. Rubi offered to visit the set, but she warned him off, saying there would be nothing for him to do and that he'd grow bored. He came anyway.

Big mistake.

"Danielle was right," he admitted. "My presence was useless. We had a long talk. Not one of those scenes where love and passion are translated into violent words and angry shouts. A long, slow, quiet, sad talk. I came to realize that she had noticed all my little madnesses, my deviations from strict conjugal orthodoxy. Nothing had escaped her."

Among other things, Danielle revealed that she, too, had found someone else—an actor named Pierre Amourdedieu who went by the screen name Pierre-Louis. They had performed together before the war when he had a bit part in one of the films she made with her first husband, and he had a small feature role in *Bethsabée*.

As she recalled, "Sometimes you need distance to really see somebody, to know what you really have." And apparently she wasn't crazy for what she had. According to Rubi, she said, "I waited until I was sure of myself to tell you all this. To be sure that I could live without you, sure that I wouldn't feel myself drawn back to your side. Now I can tell you goodbye."

He said he took it well: "I listened silently, without reaction, without argument. I still loved her, but I didn't defend myself or make excuses."

When she returned to Paris in February 1947, Danielle made public their mutual decision to part and agreed with his assessment of his behavior: "I made known to him my intention. He accepted like a gentleman."

But after the divorce became final on May 21, things changed in her mind. First Pierre-Louis backed out of the intended marriage. "Too much mother-in-law before the wedding," she groused. "His mother said I am a woman with a past, and Pierre obeyed her orders forbidding the marriage."

Then the press started to ask her questions about their five years together, and the happy veneer she had tried to put on the divorce cracked. "That man has ruined me," she told one reporter. To another, she revealed, "One woman is not enough for him. A man like him needs a harem."

(Years later, Rubi himself put a bittersweet varnish on the matter: "It was a very big love, and we had said from the beginning that the moment it stops being such a big love we will separate. We will not ruin this thing. So we separated.")

After a while, Danielle stopped talking about it altogether, refusing to answer questions about him in interviews and acting as if his name meant nothing to her. But she knew that people were aware of their whirlwind life together, and when she chose she could use the fact to her advantage. A decade after their split-up, she was appearing in a benefit performance in which the comic actor Fernandel used her as the target for a trick shooting act. The crowd seemed concerned for her safety, but she assured them that she'd be fine: "Nothing frightens me. Remember, I was married to Rubirosa."

And how did he, the man at the center of this tumult, succor his wounded heart?

"I returned to Paris," he sighed, allowing that "with the sadness of a break-up mixed the joy of recovered liberty." Of course, he had help through this arduous recovery: "Doris was there, happy, elegant, enchanting." (And rich.)

The waters of Lethe had nothing on this treatment for melancholy.

===

Throughout the nineteenth century and after each of the catastrophic wars that roiled it in the twentieth, Europe hosted a lot of Doris Dukes: American girls with money who visited the Old World in search of culture, refinement, and social standing and found themselves swarmed by gigolos, bounders, cads, and studs-for-hire. Some of these fellows were real catches, of a breed: scions of old families, some titled, whose ancestral fortunes had disappeared in wars and revolutions; for the price of a dowry and an allowance, they bestowed the gilding of their lineage on arriviste American girls whom they took as wives. Others more resembled the nightmares of rich daddies hard at work back in the States: outright fortune-hunters (as the male species of the gold digger is known) who offered good times and fast times and painless removal of token portions of their trust funds. Warnings against this predatory type were spelled out in boldface, but the combination of willful girls and dashing men produced inevitable sparks. A man with the right clothes, right connections, and right line of palaver might make a career out of a string of dalliances if not marriages.

Doris Duke knew the type. Indeed, back home she had been married to one, Jimmy Cromwell, one of the subspecies of bounder who sought to marry money even though he came from it. Cromwell (and he was descended from *the* Oliver Cromwell) was the coddled son of Eva Roberts Cromwell Stotesbury, a gold digger par excellence who married twice for money and whose social climbing, elbow rubbing, and vulgar excesses raised eyebrows in bastions of old American wealth in Washington, D.C., and on Philadelphia's Main Line.

Fit and dashing and chiseled, Eva's son Jimmy was also tinged with the becoming patina of a wicked history: A noted roué, he had been married to the daughter of automobile mogul Horace Elgin Dodge and had blown his own family's money in a utopian land scheme near Miami that bore the noxious sobriquet Floranada. In the summer of 1929, just months before the stock market crash that would create scores of Jimmy Cromwells with busted fortunes, he was on the make in Bar Harbor, Maine, and met Doris, not yet seventeen but plenty old enough for Cromwell's purposes. In particular, he was aware that as the sole inheritor of her father's interests in tobacco and hydroelectric power, she was, in plain fact, the richest girl in the world, with some $300 million to her name.*

Doris's father, James Buchanan "Buck" Duke, was born in 1856 to a family that was nearly wiped out by the Civil War but found salvation in the weakness of others and a certain ruthless cunning. Union soldiers had rampaged through the family seat of Durham, North Carolina, and when Buck's father, Washington Duke, returned home there was nothing left him save his children and a little bit of tobacco. That crop would become the seed, literally, of the family's new lease on the

* More than $3.15 billion in 2005 terms.

world. The tobacco business boomed after the war—Northern soldiers had acquired a taste for fine Southern leaves—and W. Duke, Sons and Company, propelled by the aggressive salesmanship and competitive savvy of young Buck, became one of its major concerns. With two wildly successful gambits—the use of cigarette rolling machines to create prepackaged smokes and the establishment of a monopolistic tobacco trust—the Dukes came to control the trade. By 1900, the Duke family controlled virtually all of the cigarette and snuff markets and more than half of the plug and smoking tobacco markets in America and Europe.

Buck Duke was living in New York by then, and with his money, his business savvy, and his raw Southern ways he was considered at once a nouveau riche vulgarian and a man worth knowing—and, of course, marrying. Lillian Nanette Fletcher McCredy was the lucky minx who snagged him; an aspiring singer from Chicago who had already wed and cuckolded one wealthy New Yorker, she got Buck to sign on the dotted line in November 1904, and proceeded to treat her vows to him with the same disdain she'd treated the ones she'd made to Mr. McCredy. By 1906, they'd parted.

Lucky for Buck, too, as he had spent a pile while married to her, chiefly on an ambitious estate in Somerville, New Jersey. Populated with exotic wildlife, dominated by a massive mansion choked with antique treasures from around the world, the three-plus-square-mile property included greenhouses, a racetrack, a clock tower, heated stables, vast flower beds, and a five-acre lake stocked with wildfowl and fish. In addition to serving as his personal kingdom, the estate also allowed Buck Duke—who'd acquired the nickname MegaBuck—to reincorporate his companies in New Jersey, which had more favorable tax policies than either North Carolina or New York. His fortune would multiply liberally in this bucolic redoubt.

Soon after his divorce, Buck found a more suitable mate. Nannie Lane Holt Inman twice belonged to prominent old Southern families, once by birth to the Holt line, which failed to keep its fortune after the war, and once by marriage to William Henry Inman, whose family fortune in cotton had fared better. She first wed in 1890, when she was twenty-one, and had two children—only one of whom survived infancy—before her husband's death in 1902 of complications of alcoholism. By the time she met Buck Duke at a North Carolina resort, she had taken to calling herself Nanaline, a Frenchified name that sounded a nice note in the moneyed circles in which she ran. They married in July 1907, and set about to work on two projects: a grand mansion on Fifth Avenue and Fifty-second Street and a family of their own. The former, under the auspices of the lordly architect Horace Trumbauer, would take nearly eight years to complete and stuff with the booty of Europe. The latter, too, took time: Baby Doris, "the richest mite of humanity in all the world," per one press report, arrived on November 22, 1912.

The advantages Doris had were staggering, even by the standards of royal children or the offspring of arriviste American robber barons: bodyguards, nurses, governesses, nannies, tutors; piano and dance lessons; a thirty-two-room New York brownstone as a principal residence, its ballrooms, drawing rooms, and bedroom suites stolid masses of marble, gold, antiquities, Louis XVI furniture and precious rugs; a chauffeur-driven limousine (there was, of course, a fleet of cars: the limo was hers alone); a private train car named *Doris;* a Newport, Rhode Island, cottage, Rough Point; and yet another estate, a fifty-three-room Southern mansion near Charlotte.

Buck doted on Doris shamelessly, going to extraordinary lengths to isolate her from germs and to buy her anything she ever hinted at wanting, however fine, rare, or dear. Even into her teens he called her "the baby," and she reciprocated his tenderness, composing little love notes that he would keep in his pockets to moon over when he needed a boost. But if she was unusually close to her big, loud bear of a papa, Doris was somewhat remote from Nanaline. The girl was rangy and gawkish—an ugly duckling among the delicate swans of her set—and her gracelessness unsettled her fashionable mother. Doris was a good student during her years at Manhattan's prestigious Brearly School—smart, sharp, funny—but she didn't make friends easily. And as Nanaline controlled her wardrobe and her associations, she seemed never fully to emerge as herself.

She grew shrewd and mistrustful. She watched with a cool eye as overindulged relatives on both sides of the family squandered their fortunes and, indeed, their lives. She read with studied indifference the bags full of mail she received daily—half beseeching loans, half threatening her for having the temerity to be born wealthy. She learned, oddly, to count pennies, expecting to be cheated because she had so much money and haggling with waiters and cabbies and shopkeepers over small sums.

If there seemed too much Nanaline in the girl, perhaps it was because Buck Duke so rarely ceased in his aggressive accumulation of wealth and standing to put more of a stamp on her. In the 1920s, the phenomenon of hydroelectric power—"white coal"—took hold of his imagination and he began buying up rights to streams with waterfalls and rapids, slowly building a huge interest in the power grid that covered most of the southeastern United States and stretched up into Canada; Duke Power would become one of the country's largest utilities. At the same time, Buck got involved with a small college in his hometown of Durham and endowed it with such huge sums that its name was eventually changed in tribute to the man who, in effect, built it—from Trinity College to Duke University.

In September 1925, with these twin efforts consuming him, his floozy first wife reappeared to wage an ugly public challenge to the legal standing of their divorce. All of it—the bad press, the pressing against the clock to build his empire and legacy—seemed to drain him. He collapsed, anemic, probably stricken with leukemia. From the first episode of weakness he lasted barely two weeks. In October, he died, leaving virtually everything to his twelve-year-old daughter.

If Doris had been sheltered, she was now positively quarantined. Her few school friends no longer saw her; she vanished into a world of international socialites and grown-ups. Her relations with her mother grew so tense that she actually sued Nanaline for sole possession of the various Duke houses, the provenance of which wasn't made entirely clear in Buck's will; Nanaline, fearful of losing everything, ceded ownership of the New York and New Jersey estates to Doris, while retaining the right to live in them, and kept the Rhode Island house as her principal residence. (The Charlotte property, like the private railroad car, was sold off.) At seventeen, Doris was presented at Buckingham Palace; that same year, she debuted in a massive all-night party in Newport featuring circus animals and three orchestras. At twenty-one, she inherited the first third of her father's bequest and secured freedom from her scolding, superior mother. The stays were off, and she was determined to live in the world she knew was out there.

That was the girl whom Jimmy Cromwell courted across two continents for the better part of six years, finally landing the prize in February 1935, when he married her in a brief civil ceremony at the Dukes' New York mansion, Doris defiant in the face of her mother's stern glare. Nanaline had, correctly, sized Cromwell up as a fortune hunter, but the groom was determined to do more than spend his wife's money. Yes, they traveled the world in grand style for a ten-month honeymoon that included not only a visit with Mahatma Gandhi in Wardha, India, but an idyll on Waikiki Beach, where Doris began construction of yet another palatial home. Yes, Cromwell kept up his amateur sporting life: boxing, golf, polo, sailing. But he kept earnestly at work, too, exploring serious business ventures and even a political career, finagling appointment as the U.S. minister to Canada in 1940.

The marriage hadn't ever been truly intimate—Cromwell, sixteen years his wife's senior, referred to her as his "Frigidairess"—and both spouses had roamed frequently. Doris had spent long periods of time in Hawaii overseeing the construction of her house, and when she was there she engaged in a widely known affair with Duke Kahanamoku, the Olympic swimmer and granddaddy of modern surfing. She was also seen around Europe and New York and Hawaii with Alec Cunningham-Reid, the British World War I aviation hero and rising Tory political star whom she'd met while touring the Continent as a debutante.

Doris and Cromwell were almost brought together as a family—he had hoped that a baby would knit them even as he realized that it very well might be another man's. But their only child, a daughter named Arden, survived just one day. After that, Ottawa would prove the last straw; with the world as her playground, there was no way Doris was going to act the quiet diplomatic wife in a frozen provincial capital. Not long after presenting herself as the new Madam Minister, she pressed Cromwell for a divorce.

But Cromwell was relying on his marriage not only for financial support but because he believed that his connection to the Duke fortune would boost him in his quest to become a U.S. senator. He fought Doris's efforts to free herself with all his political, financial, and emotional capacity; as his family's wealth had dwindled, he was trying to hold on, he must have felt, to two legacies. But she outflanked him in all areas and, after purchasing a small home in Reno, Nevada, to establish legal residency there, she was granted a divorce in December 1941. Cromwell would over the coming years so vehemently contest her right to Nevada residency that Doris cannily held on to the Reno property just in case.

Even more than freedom from Nanaline, the divorce launched Doris into the maw of the world—and this time a world that was newly at war. Although she had entertained but one thought when Pearl Harbor was bombed—"Did they destroy my swimming pool?"—she was determined to make a real contribution to the Allied effort. She joined the United Seaman Service, a kind of USO for merchant sailors. And then, seeking even more action, she went to Egypt. She lost herself in a series of affairs with, among others, playwright Charles MacArthur, gossip columnist Tex McCrary, actor Brian Aherne, and General George S. Patton. She made contact with the Office of Strategic Services, the fabled OSS, precursor to the modern CIA, and, befriended by OSS founder William Donovan (the same man who employed Rubi's poker buddy Fernando Gerassi in Spain), she was granted privileges that allowed her to fly between Italy and Cairo. (She had no official duties, and it was widely assumed that she used these trips to follow a British officer with whom she was having an affair.) By 1945, she had lost her standing in the spy community but gained employment of another sort as a correspondent for the International News Service, for which she reported about conditions for civilians in liberated Italy.

And it was as an INS reporter that she rang up Danielle Darrieux and met her husband, the recently appointed Dominican chargé d'affaires to Rome—who'd been waiting for her, in one way or another, his whole life.

SEVEN

YUL BRYNNER IN A

BLACK TURTLENECK

You needed a good closet.

You had to be proficient in at least one sport, the more dangerous and expensive the better.

Languages were an asset—for blandishments if nothing else—and smarts: not bookishness so much as worldliness.

It wasn't necessary to be drop-dead handsome but you had to be charming, and you got extra points for a reputation for danger and good times.

You had to dance well, it went without saying.

A little money didn't hurt, if only to get you into the right restaurants and nightclubs and casinos and hotels. (A lot of money didn't, of course, hurt either.)

Connections were essential, whether acquired through school or sports or socializing or business, if you were the sort who went in for business.

And time. Time was, as the saying went, of the essence: time to travel and time to play and time to lounge and time to get fit and time to get fitted and time to dally and time to take your time while others, less certain of themselves and what they wanted, scurried.

You had always to be on your guard; the least sign of ordinary sloth or slovenliness or boredom or fatigue or complacence could be a crushing turnoff, and you'd be through.

It helped to have an equanimous sense of humor about yourself and what you were up to, both of which could look pretty ridiculous if the light was aimed just so.

And taste, the *je ne sais quoi* that separated the vulgarian from the connoisseur: God help the fellow who went into this racket and lacked fine taste.

No, no, laugh though people might, whisper and snipe and grumble and disparage, when it was totted up and taken as a whole, if the thing was to be done as it ought, there was nothing especially easy about the life of a playboy.

═══

Years later, when he was internationally famous for his women and his sporting life and his diplomatic postings and his gaudy adventures and his seeming ubiquity in the scandalmongering media, chic nightclubs, and enviable boudoirs, a journalist asked Rubi when he found time for work.

"Work?" he answered. "It's impossible for me to work. I just don't have the time."

It was no joke. Gumption and pluck and guts and fortune he had in surfeit, but his chief employment, the thing that ate his time, was creating out of whole cloth the image of himself. He would become the most singular sort of juggler: twirling the hoop of Trujillo with one ankle, tossing the batons of his many women in his hands, spinning an active sporting life on top of his head, always well liked, always noticed upon arrival, always impeccable in dress, speech, mien, and manners, a marvel, a star.

And yet, for all his uniquenesses, he was of a breed.

Before the world spoke of playboys it spoke of Philanders, Romeos,

Don Juans, Lotharios, Casanovas—men of monomaniacal sensuality and prodigious sexual achievement, all celebrated in letters, all but one fictional.

Philander was a son of Apollo, suckled by goats and noted for his love of beautiful boys; his name, from the Greek *philandros*—or "fond of men"—was hijacked by English poets as the generic name for a predatory lover of women: a rake, a wolf, a tomcat, a lecher, a libertine.

Romeo was, of course, Shakespeare's model of the impassioned young heart, mercurial, yes (recall how quickly his affection flitted from Rosaline to Juliet), but when focused focused in whole: a swain, a suppliant, a suitor, a truelove, a slave.

Don Juan, most famous of them all, came to the world through the pen of the Spanish playwright Tirso de Molina, whose *El Burlador de Sevilla* inspired two centuries of plays, operas, novels, and poems about the unrepentant seducer who goes so far as to flout Satan in his quest for physical pleasure: a profligate, a debauchee, a gallant, a lady-killer, a stud.

Lothario was the antihero of Nicholas Rowe's *The Fair Penitent,* a cruel user of women who ended up cruelly used himself, murdered in repayment of his desires: a roué, a letch, a goat, a satyr, a whorehound.

Casanova really existed: Giacomo Girolamo Casanova, born in 1725 in Venice, a law student, monk, bureaucrat, violinist, translator, healer, gambler, pamphleteer, linguist, librarian, and, of course, lover, whose bedroom adventures scandalized and titillated all of Europe upon the posthumous publication of his massive autobiography: a swinger, a reprobate, a dallier, a skirt chaser, a wanton, a dude.

It wasn't until a half century after the appearance of Casanova's memoirs that the term "playboy" became part of this notorious word tree. As early as the eighteenth century it was an obscure term from the theater meaning "child actor": a boy who performed in plays. By the late nineteenth century, it had also accrued the meanings of "musician" and "gambler" and perhaps with all of those implications taken together it gained currency in Ireland as another name for the devil or those who would emulate him: hence J. M. Synge's 1907 comedy *The*

Playboy of the Western World, one of the earliest instances of the word being applied, if ironically, to a ladies' man. In the 1852 first edition of *Roget's Thesaurus,* "playboy" doesn't appear; by the 1920s, it was a standard term in most thesauri and dictionaries of slang.

There had always been playboys, of course, but the specific use of "playboy" that would inspire Hugh Hefner's naming of a magazine focused on his ideal of the modern male lifestyle came to its full meaning in the Jazz Age, when the word acquired all of the undertones that Hefner heard in it: a sensually inclined male, generally of financial means, who roves from woman to woman, party to party, thrill to thrill. It implied all the license and inconstancy that its predecessor synonyms held, but it had a jolly lightness that they lacked: "play," as in fun; "boy," as in innocent—the happy face of a dark and seamy business.

But the 1920s were also, recall, a golden age for Latin men, when their music, manners, dark looks, and sultry ways were celebrated in the media—particularly the cinema—as the ne plus ultra of male sexual allure. The Latin Lover, as this subspecies of libidinous male came to be known, first entered the consciousness of northern Europeans through fictions from Shakespeare to Byron and was cemented as a type by the real-life experiences of young ladies who took the Grand Tour to Italy and southern France and found themselves the subject of unfamiliar but not necessarily unwelcome attentions. Beyond the predilections for female companionship and easy living stereotypical of the playboy and his brethren, the Latin Lover had some unique qualities of his own. The cultures of the Mediterranean (and of lands colonized by Mediterranean powers in the Caribbean and Central and South America) were, perhaps, more overtly sexist than those of northern countries; Latin men paraded peacockishly as if unconcerned that their virility would be doubted, and they kept their women determinedly under cover at home.

But if women in southern Europe had fewer outward privileges, they were, paradoxically, more venerated. A subtle matriarchy held sway in the home; Spanish men bore their mothers' surnames in their own legal names. The veneration of women was so integral to the culture that speech and writing themselves were impossible to conceive without it: the very languages—the Romance languages—lent their name to the art of love. The first recognizably modern love poems—and, arguably, the very notion of idealized romantic love—came from the troubadours of Languedoc, who wrote in Provençal, which, like Spanish, French, Italian, and Portuguese, was more prolix and florid, more sensual on the tongue, than the rough, glottal idioms of the north. The very forms in which a fellow from the Mediterranean pitched woo had a dreamy sound to northern women who would have laughed heartily at the same sentiments expressed in their own languages.

There was a note of condescension in the association in the northern mind of the southern and the sexual: Latins, the stereotype held, were more passionate and impetuous, as befit people born closer to those exotic climes where civilization hadn't yet gotten a firm foothold. There was a fear of miscegenation in this way of thinking, but the languid sensuality of Mediterranean life exerted an undeniable pull on northerners—the music, the wine, the food, the sultry weather, the sense that what happened there stayed there. The pasty, terse, beer-drinking Protestant boys back in London and New York didn't, in comparison, stand a chance.

So in the 1910s the tango craze and in the '20s the cult of Rudolph Valentino, the sloe-eyed seducer with the grace of a dancer who melted women the world over first with his films, then with the stories of his offscreen amours, and then with his pathetic death from blood poisoning at the age of thirty-one. For a period thereafter the Latin fad waned: The scourges of global economic depression and ghastly world war seemed to focus the attentions of women on the boys at home—the title of a famous and rather ludicrous article published in *Esquire* in 1936 declared without irony that "Latins Are Lousy Lovers."

But with the ending of the war and the resumption of travel for pleasure and, indeed, of pleasure for its own sake, the love of things Latin—music, especially—was reignited. The international high life, the milieu of the playboy, resumed. And the likes of Doris Duke, rich and worldly and unafraid of gossip and fond of dark-skinned men, emerged back into the world like the bottles of vintage wine Parisians cellared away from the Nazis.

═════

History, in short, was on Rubi's side.

But Rubi was not alone.

Throughout postwar Europe and, in this newfangled era of commercial air travel, in such removes as Palm Beach, Hollywood, and Havana, casinos and nightclubs and polo pitches and resorts filled with well-dressed men on the make.

Some were born to privilege, like Aly Khan, Rubi's friend and sometime rival, heir to the throne of his father, the Aga Khan, hereditary leader of fifteen million African and Asian adherents to the Ismaili sect of Islam. Technically per the precepts of his faith a god on earth—no lie—and a millionaire many, many times over, Aly fulfilled his dynastic duty by fathering two sons and attending various religious rites. But he barely otherwise comported himself like a holy man, running with and after the most beautiful women on earth (a true democrat, he paid little notice to their purses) and, incidentally, becoming an important breeder of thoroughbred horses. Like Howard Hughes, another noted aficionado of the ladies, Prince Aly had the means to lavish his attentions on whomsoever he chose. And after the war, and despite his wife and sons, he chose Rita Hayworth (despite, for that matter, the child she'd had with her former husband, Orson Welles); their marriage kept him more or less occupied so that he and Rubi could bond in rascalhood over their shared tastes rather than compete for this or that hand.

Some of Rubi's rivals were gangsters, raw thugs with deep ties to the most vicious sorts of power but who themselves possessed manners and wardrobes of unlikely refinement, ruthless murderers and thieves like Johnny Roselli, Pat DiCicco, Bugsy Siegel, and Johnny Stompanato who chased and sometimes caught actresses and models and heiresses and the like, sometimes satisfying themselves with the thrill of the hunt, sometimes with sex, sometimes with money. Through their hands passed the likes of Gloria Vanderbilt, Marilyn Monroe, Lana Turner, Thelma Todd, Virginia Hill: a constellation of glittering desires dreamt and realized.

Actors and singers and other such celebrities counted in the ranks of playboys, of course, but so did their chums. The infamous Freddy McEvoy so resembled his fellow Aussie Errol Flynn that he helped quash a statutory rape case against the actor simply by standing up in court and revealing the accuser to be unable to say who exactly did what to her; McEvoy, a sportsman, adventurer, and pimp, bagged a couple of oil heiresses before drowning when his yacht, in which he was likely smuggling arms or drugs, broke up off the coast of western Africa.

On the strength of such big personalities and the relative calm of the postwar period, international playboyism became a kind of craze. In the late 1940s and early '50s, dozens of fascinating new faces would swell the ranks. There was Francisco Pignatari, a Brazilian mining millionaire who dallied with a former queen of Iran and a few hot actresses and married a princess—and all that despite being widely known as Baby. There was Don Jaime de Mora y Aragon, descended, he liked to note, from fifty-six kings, the brother of Queen Fabiola of Belgium, a sometime nightclub singer and official greeter at the posh Marbella Club on the Costa del Sol, with a playboy act so polished and precise that it seemed almost a send-up of the species. There was Nicky Hilton, the hotel heir, who was Elizabeth Taylor's first husband and gave his occupation as "loafer" when he was arrested for drunkenness—which was his curse—in Beverly Hills and died of heart failure at forty-two. There was Jorge Guinle from Brazil, who also inherited a hotel fortune and squandered it—if you can call it squandering—chasing after the likes of Jayne Mansfield and Janet Leigh and Hedy Lamarr and Veronica Lake and Anita Ekberg. There was Howard Hughes who, well, *everything.*

And there was—deep breath—Alfonso Antonio Vicente Eduardo Blas Angel Francisco Borija Cabeza de Vaca y Leighton, Grandee of Spain, Count of Mejorada, Count of Pernia, Marquis de Moratalla, Marquis de Portago, and Duke of Alagon, who went, for obvious reasons, simply by "Fon." He was, depending on how you counted, third in line for the Spanish throne, impossibly handsome and charming, and, wouldn't you know it, a brilliant sportsman: Olympic-class swimmer and bobsledder and fencer, high-level steeplechase jockey, valued member of the Ferrari Formula One team—and, by all accounts, a swell fellow all around.

Yet even amid this pantheon of high livers and lover boys, Rubi stood out. For one thing, he was, like most Dominicans, Creole in heritage— partly African, in short; he was so naturally dark that he had to watch out for the sun lest he take on too negroid an aspect for the circles in which he ran, and he straightened his hair with the same sort of stuff with which black American hepcats konked theirs. Most people who knew him as a grown man thought of him as a Mediterranean Latin as opposed to Caribbean black. For another, he was from an obscure back-water that few, if any, of his chums and conquests could find on a map; indeed, like a Columbus-in-reverse, he was conquering the Old World from the New almost as if by accident of fate. And, perhaps most im-portant, he had no money of his own and no prospects of making any. Women were drawn to Rubi for Rubi, not for the perks. And men—par-ticularly those of his special ilk—found him fine company.

One night, probably in the 1950s, Rubi, Aly Khan, Baby Pignatari, and Juan Capuro, another South American mining heir with an eye for the ladies, found themselves stag at a Paris nightclub, drinking to-gether. The maitre d' was delighted with the assembly. "Tonight," he crowed, "in my place are gathered the four most famous playboys in the world!" Everybody had a good laugh, but Rubi had the last. "Yes, that's true," he responded, "but there is a big difference between me and these other gentlemen: They all pay their women, and all my women pay me!"

———

And, so, what was it that elevated Rubi from dictator's son-in-law to movie star's husband to the sort of man who might capture the hand of the world's wealthiest heiress?

Well, there was his native charm.

People who knew him, even if only casually, even if they were pre-disposed to be suspicious or resentful of him, came away liking him. He picked up checks; he had courtly manners; he kept the party gay and lively; he was attentive to women but made men feel at ease; he was smoothly quick to rise from his chair when introduced, to open doors, to light a lady's cigarette ("I have the fastest cigarette lighter in the house," he once boasted): the quintessential chivalrous gent of manners.

The encomia, if bland, were universal. "He's a very nice guy," swore gossip columnist Earl Wilson, who stayed with Rubi in Paris. "I'm fond of him," said John Perona, owner of New York's El Morocco. "Rubi's got a nice personality and is completely masculine," attested a New York clubgoer. "He has a lot of men friends, which, I suppose, is unusual. Aly Khan, for instance, has few male friends. But everyone I know thinks Rubi is a good guy." "He is one of the nicest guys I know," declared that famed chum of famed playboys Peter Lawford. "A really charming man—witty, fun to be with, and a he-man."

There were a few tricks to his trade. A society photographer judged him with a professional eye thus: "He can meet you for a minute and a month later remember you very well." An author who played polo with him put it this way: "He had a trick that never failed. When he spoke with someone, whether man or woman, it seemed as if the rest of the world had lost all interest for him. He could hang on the words of a woman or man who spoke only banalities as if the very future of the world—and his future, especially—depended on those words."

But there was something deeper to his charm, something irresistible in particular when he turned it on women. It didn't reveal itself in photos, and not every woman was susceptible to it, but it was palpable and, when it worked, unforgettable.

Hollywood dirt doyenne Hedda Hopper declared, "A friend says he has the most perfect manners she has ever encountered. He wraps his charm around your shoulders like a Russian sable coat."

Gossip columnist Sheila Graham was chary when invited to bring her eleven-year-old daughter to a lunch with Rubi in London, and her wariness was transmitted to the girl, who wiped her hand off on her dress after Rubi kissed it in a formal greeting; by the end of lunch, he had won the child over with his enthusiastic, spontaneous manner, full of compliments but never cloying. "All done effortlessly," Graham marveled. "He was probably a charming baby. I am sure that women rushed to coo over him in the cradle."

Elsa Maxwell, yet another gossip, but also a society gadabout and hostess who claimed a key role in at least one of Rubi's famous liaisons, put it thus: "You expect Rubi to be a very dangerous young man who personifies the wolf. Instead, you meet someone who is so unbelievably charming and thoughtful that you are put off-guard before you know it."

But charm would only take a man so far. Rubi was becoming an international legend not because he could fascinate a young girl but because he could intoxicate sophisticated women.

What was *that* secret?

═══════

In the mid-1950s, at the height of Rubi's glory and success, the Cuban guitarist and composer Eduardo Saborit wrote a hit song that bluntly asked the musical question "¿Qué Es El Tuyo, Rubirosa?"—"What Have You Got, Rubirosa?":

> *Rubirosa tiene una cosa,*
> *Que yo no sé qué será,*
> *Qué será, qué será,*
> *Lo que tiene Rubirosa . . .*

> Rubirosa has something
> I don't know what it could be,
> What it could be, what it could be,
> That Rubirosa has . . .

What indeed?

Recall the testimony of Flor de Oro concerning her honeymoon: "When it was over my insides hurt a lot." Another paramour, the Parisian floozie known as Manouche, who ran with gangsters and operated her own nightspot, put it this way: "It was long and pointed and it hurt . . . I suppose it hit my uterus." One of his wives wrote in her diary that he was "priapic, indefatigable, grotesquely proportioned" (was that praise?). Another lover, famous worldwide for her men, put it more frankly: "He could have been a carnival attraction."

There is no way around saying it out loud: The man was well-hung, hung, indeed, legendarily, his superhuman endowment a calling card that recommended him to circles into which he might otherwise never have gained admittance. Women heard about it, wondered about it, whispered about it, had to see it, hold it, have it—and who was he to deny them?

The stories were legion.

A fellow polo player once called on Rubi at home and was admitted to see him as he soaked in a tub. "All I can tell you," he recalled, "is that when I saw it, I knew that if I ever tried to follow it, I'd be like a drunk in a corridor." (Another acquaintance, also from the polo pitch, admitted to stealing one of Rubi's jockstraps and nailing it above the door of the barn where he kept his breeding stallions as a good luck charm.)

The old saying held that no man was a hero to his valet; Rubi was. The Russian fellow who dressed and looked after him for years testified thus:

> One afternoon when I thought Mr. Rubirosa was out of the house,
> I went into his bedroom to put away some shirts. He was there and
> he wasn't alone. I had interrupted him at a very crucial moment. In
> his fury, he jumped out of bed and rushed toward me cursing like a
> stevedore. What a sight! I was stunned!

And then he cupped his hands and moved them up and down as if weighing melons. *"E le ouve!"* he declared, resorting to the Italian for "eggs" to describe the indescribable. *"Le ouve!* They were so enormous that they bothered him and he usually wore a jockstrap."

Jerome Zerbe, a society photographer who snapped dozens of celebrities at New York's famed El Morocco nightclub, was said to have gotten into his cups at the casino at Deauville and, on a dare, followed Rubi into the men's room. He skittered out gleefully, the story went, with the intelligence, "It looks like Yul Brynner in a black turtleneck!"

Tabloid magazines brushed as close to the subject as they could, calling him the "ding dong daddy" after a phrase made famous in country and soul songs.

Truman Capote described it in *Answered Prayers*—without ever seeing it, of course—as "that quadroon cock, a purported eleven-inch café-au-lait sinker thick as a man's wrist."

A British journalist who interviewed Rubi in his suite at the Savoy reported that after she repaired to the powder room to freshen up she reemerged to find "a grinning Mr. Rubirosa in his boxer shorts, through which stood a donkey-style member. He threw me on his unmade bed and a wrestling match ensued as this grotesque thing swung about." (She cooled him off, she said, and was impressed by how easily he took rejection: "He simply shrugged, looked in the mirror, patted his hair and returned to a business-like discussion of the interview.")

Jimmy Cromwell, the sportsman first husband of Doris Duke, had seen or at least heard tell of it: He referred to Rubi as "Rubberhosa."

And Doris, well, Doris never forgot or got over it. "It was the most magnificent penis that I had ever seen," her godson Pony Duke recollected her saying. "There has never been anything like it since." In Pony's account of Doris's description, it was "six inches in circumference . . . much like the last foot of a Louisville Slugger baseball bat with the consistency of a not completely inflated volleyball."

His tailors were said to have had a job on their hands to hide the thing in the folds of his famously impeccable wardrobe. And his custom-made underwear, complete with monogram, proved a bonanza to his Russian valet, who cut up used pairs and sold the swatches around Paris as souvenirs. When Rubi found out about it, he acted the outraged patron and fired the fellow. But he quietly reinstated him a few days later; the moneymaking scheme, in point of fact, had been his own.

At the helm of this notorious weapon, Rubi was moreover reputed to be something of a machine, able to forestall ejaculation almost indefinitely (in this, Aly Khan, who practiced a yogic form of control over his orgasms, was once again a peer). Rubi was said to be in a constant state of semistiffness even during the actual act of coitus, nicknamed *Toujours Prêt*—"Always Ready"—by Parisian gossipmongers. He was even believed to be unable to ejaculate, a full erection, they speculated, would cause him to pass out from loss of blood. (The baroque theory helped explain, to some minds, his lack of children despite the ample opportunities he'd had to conceive them.) He was rumored to have numbed himself with whiskey, marijuana, morphine, Japanese mushroom tea, meditation. But he couldn't have resorted to any of those performance enhancers as often as he used his penis for pleasure. Rather, he applied his mind to the domination of his body. "It's a muscle like any other," he explained to his chum, fashion designer Oleg Cassini. "It can be strengthened." And in this physical application, he was—as in other pursuits he undertook—simply a gifted athlete. If some of his lovers remembered him as rough and unfeeling, there were many others who remembered him as spectacular—and in a pre-Kinsey era when nobody spoke about sex, the fact that he was associated with it at all made him a sensation.

It finally had a life of its own, this legendary member, long after the man who was attached to it was gone: More than three decades after Rubi was buried, an otherwise sober writer for *Vanity Fair* magazine found himself asking women with firsthand memory of it to compare it to his size-11 shoe. And cheeky waiters at Continental restaurants would celebrate it perennially, if not always knowingly, referring in knavish fashion to the largest peppermill in the house as—what else?—the "Rubirosa."

So it was on the strength of a prodigious banality that he rose, and rose audaciously. His gifts couldn't be discussed in newspapers or polite society, but he didn't depend on the press or proper people for his success. His career was based on a secret, on a fluke of genetics, on a whisper, on a myth. And it elevated him steadily.

When he married Flor de Oro Trujillo he was nobody: an upstart.

When he married Danielle Darrieux he was a mystery man, not easily placed—*vide* the *New York Times* declaring him Salvadoran—but *somebody*, or at least that was the sense you got.

But when Doris Duke zeroed in on him, he became front-page news and his name became synonymous with adventure and high life and intrigue and flamboyance and—as much as anyone in that delicate time could speak of it out loud—sex. He became famous just as the era of audacious-celebrity-for-its-own-sake was blooming. And the genius of it was that the reason for his celebrity, even if it were known, couldn't actually be spoken of—not firsthand, not out loud.

Anyone anywhere could understand why the world's most desirable women would date wealthy men like Aly Khan or a Baby Pignatari or a Fon de Portago.

But Rubi?

"*Qué será, qué será, lo que tiene Rubirosa,*" indeed.

EIGHT

BIG BOY

On September 24, 1947, in an account of a society wedding published in the *Washington Times-Herald,* an unnamed friend of Doris Duke's declared of Rubi that "the FBI is said to have a bulging dossier on him."

The sentence was highlighted twice by one particular reader who clipped the article and added a note at the bottom in a cursive hand before sending it to a subordinate:

> *What do we have on*
> *Rubirosa?*
> —H.

The following day, pursuant to this request from the desk of J. Edgar Hoover, the FBI, which had taken no formal notice of Rubi to date, opened a file on him with that annotated article as its first entry. Eventually it would swell to nearly eleven hundred pages.

Since skipping out of New York on the eve of the murder of Sergio Bencosme twelve years earlier, Rubi had assiduously avoided setting foot in the United States. And as the FBI had apparently demonstrated little interest in that shooting, there was no specific reason for it to monitor his activities or dig around in his past. But Hoover, of course, was a famous collector of gossip, and by the fall of 1947 Rubi was an up-and-coming superstar of gossip. If he had heard *anything* about Rubi's particular physical genius, Hoover would certainly have hoarded dirt and secrets with real relish.

But he had a more pressing need for information about Rubi, and several branches of the United States government shared his urgency: On September 1 in a quick, informal ceremony at the Dominican legation in Paris, Rubi and Doris had wed.

The courtship had been both brisk and peripatetic. They were seen together in Paris and Rome and the French Riviera throughout 1946, at restaurants and nightclubs and golf courses and resorts. "We had a lot of tastes in common," Rubi recalled. "We loved Paris, the subtle poetry of the Left Bank, music. We often went to Cap d'Antibes, where we sported in the sun and the shining sea." Doris, who was possessed of a considerable libido, found herself as if drunk on the magnetic power of his massive organ. And he was held in a death grip by thoughts of getting hold of a game girl with one of the largest fortunes in the world.

Indeed, such were their respective stocks at the time—she an aloof and rangy girl of attractive energy but no great beauty, he a studly mystery man in his physical prime rebounding from a passionate marriage to a renownedly gorgeous actress—that the calculus of the relationship seemed transparent: She was in it for the sex, he for the money, and he had far more to gain from the relationship than she.

It was easy to see Rubi's devotion to Doris in the least flattering light. In the south of France, the couple visited a resort where British actor Stewart Granger and American producer Mike Todd were vacationing. Granger saw something almost pathetic in Rubi's attentions to the heiress. "Poor Ruby [*sic*] was in there really pitching," he wrote later. "She used to keep him waiting around at all hours to take her to lunch or dinner, and both Mike and I were amazed that any man would stand for it." The movie men decided to make sport of Doris's interest in them and asked her to dinner while Rubi looked on. "Poor man," recalled Granger. "With us it was all fun. With him it was business." Finally, they let her alone and made amends to Rubi: "We apologized for our behavior and swore we wouldn't interfere with his romance any more."

While Rubi worked on Doris, Doris worked at a job. In March 1947, when Rubi was in Paris seeing to the dissolution of his marriage with Danielle, Doris was there as well in her new position as a correspondent for *Harper's Bazaar*. The two were seen constantly together, and the air buzzed with talk of marriage, but Doris wasn't the sort to confide in people, and Rubi wouldn't dare open his mouth for fear of queering the deal.

But the State Department—perhaps alerted by Doris's contacts in the OSS—wanted to make it clear that they didn't approve of the heiress's choice of beau. When earlier she had been running around Rome with a shady lot, the U.S. government saw fit to demand she turn over her passport and return home; she submitted the document but stayed in Italy where, for a time, lacking the proper credentials, she had been unable to travel, to secure ration books, or even to visit the Correspondents Club. It took some judicious string-pulling for her to get her papers back, but she eventually did, and, emboldened, she pointedly ignored warnings that Washington didn't care for Rubi. (Whether race played into the equation wasn't clear; the authorities probably didn't care about Rubi's bloodline so much as his connections to the Dominican government.)

Yet if Doris was headstrong—or simply lust-sick—she was also shrewd, particularly when it came to her money. She may have refused to back away from her man when threatened by Washington, but she would fight ruthlessly to protect her prodigious fortune. When plans for the wedding were being finalized, Rubi cagily insisted on holding the ceremony on Dominican soil and under the aegis of a Dominican authority—consul general Salvador Paradas, one of the men who had steered him toward the Aldao jewels. This would, of course, mean that Dominican law, which followed the Napoleonic code granting authority over communal property to the husband, would pertain. Rubi would have his fingers on hundreds of millions—and Trujillo, at that judicious remove from which he preferred to do his dirtiest work, would have indirect control through Rubi over Duke Power and the electrical grid of the southern United States.

Officials of the State Department and OSS were apoplectic, but they had no sway over Doris. Rather, it was, ironically enough, in the world of haute couture where she found her best counsel. She wandered into the offices of *Harper's Bazaar* and, announcing she was planning to marry, spurred editor Carmel Snow to set into motion a plan to protect the Duke millions. Lawyers were called; contingencies were considered; a prenuptial agreement was drawn up.

All that remained was to tell the groom.

They waited until the wedding ceremony.

Rubi arrived at the embassy that morning in what might very well have been the same suit in which he married Danielle: striped pants, dark cutaway coat, pale vest, white shirt, shiny tie. He had selected as his witnesses two friends from the world of motor racing, which had come to consume him in the months of his courtship with a woman who could fund such an interest: Jean-Pierre Wimille, the ace driver of the Alfa Romeo team, and Pierre Leygonie, like Rubi one of the gentleman amateurs who had begun buzzing around auto sports after the war.

Ana Rubirosa Sánchez, the groom's sister, had moved to Paris to school her son, so she was there, but there were few other guests, mainly Doris's acquaintances from *Harper's Bazaar.* The bride herself arrived in a green taffeta Dior New Look dress and chic dark hat, an artificial rose pinned to the right of her décolletage. She fought through a throng of reporters on the street—*this* wedding, compared to the couple's previous nuptials, would be a truly hot story—and then disappeared into the embassy.

Inside, a bare-bones reception awaited the guests, who amused themselves at the bar while . . . something went on behind closed doors. Few had taken note of the two men with briefcases who met Doris on her arrival, but they were as important to the proceedings as the bride and groom themselves: They were lawyers from the Franco-American law firm Coudert on hand to present Rubi with the bad news.

The groom had begun celebrating a little early, perhaps, the finishing line so close he could feel the tape across his chest. He'd been sipping whiskey highballs and chatting amiably. His mood changed when he got wind of the lawyers and their purpose. "He looked like one of those fierce Miura bulls about to charge a red cape," said an eyewitness. "I've never seen anyone madder."

The prenup was painfully clear: Rubi would renounce all claims to Doris's fortune and her holdings in the various companies and trusts her father founded in exchange for cash and gifts. He kept drinking as the impossibility of his situation became patent. Other than walk away with nothing, what could he do? He signed, no doubt harboring the thought in the recesses of his mind that there would be time later to get his hands on the mother lode.

After all the delay, the brief ceremony proceeded as something of an anticlimax. Rubi tried to play the gallant, laughing and drinking and lighting up a cigarette which he held in his hand through the vows. (A waggish observer, having heard about the sucker-punch prenup, said of the groom, "He refused the blindfold but accepted the cigarette"; a New York headline read "Doris Duke Weds Smoking Latin.") She promised to love, honor, and obey in English; he took his oath in Spanish. They exchanged rings: Hers to him was a traditional gold number that some observers thought resembled a handcuff; his to her was a delicate gold band laced with rubies (he gave her several lavish presents through their courtship and marriage, often ruby-encrusted, and she held on to them her whole life). The proceedings were muted and swift. And then Rubi, drunk or anxious or angry or overcome . . . fainted. "Big boy passed out in my arms," Doris laughed.

But he got back at her exactly where it hurt. They had been intending to honeymoon in Hawaii but went instead to the Riviera, where Rubi revenged himself on Doris for her secret wedding day maneuvers by withholding his favors: no sex. Even with all the gifts she eventually coughed up—the cash, cars, suits, polo ponies, a plantation in the Dominican Republic, a B-25 bomber fitted out as a private airplane—he made sure that she remembered that he had assets of his own.

Back in Paris after that brief, chaste honeymoon, they moved into yet another manifestation of Doris's munificence, a massive *hôtel parti-*

culier on Rue de Bellechasse in the Seventh Arrondissement, midway between the buzzy cafés of the Boulevard Saint Germain and the courtly hush of the Invalides. Bought at a cost of $100,000 from Princess Chavchavadze, née Elizabeth Ridgeway, the American-born wife of a Georgian prince and concert pianist, the three-hundred-year-old house presented a blunt aspect to the street but was singularly sumptuous within. Passing through a courtyard—where Rubi eventually installed a pair of stationary bicycles and a mechanical bull for sharpening his taurine skills—visitors entered a massive three-story home furnished by the celebrated interior decorator Henri Samuel at a cost of a half-million dollars with antiques, artworks, marble, rosewood, silk, gilding, and the like. The top floor was rebuilt so that Rubi could have a gymnasium and boxing ring installed, as well as storage for polo trophies and tack.

Doris was used to such grandeur—she had four other homes at least as big and plush—but for Rubi this new life was heady, even if he'd long reckoned himself entitled to it. He filled his days with more pleasure than seemed possible.

His nights went on forever: dinner out; clubbing at Tatou or the Vieux Colombier or Jimmy's or some other of the chic new spots—at once swank and bohemian—that dotted the Left Bank; back home with a co-terie of musicians, dancers, hangers-on, women, demanding hot food from servants who'd been jolted from their beds; not thinking about going to bed himself till morning roused.

But that wasn't a daily routine. More important even than his evening *parrandas* were his daytime rituals—so important, in fact, that he would limit his exhausting nighttime bacchanals to two or three a week. Nearly forty, he came to value his sleep because he so valued his mornings, which were given over to polo, his latest passion. Under the tutelage of French champion Pierre Dobadie, who put him through his paces on the pitch at the Bagatelle in the Bois de Boulogne, the game became the single most constant passion of his life.

He had been drawn to riding since his father scooped him up in the Cibao night and rode him briskly through a paddock; now, addicted to polo, he envinced the slight bowlegs of the inveterate horseman. (A fellow polo player, the Spanish writer José-Luis de Vilallonga, met Rubi and his new wife at around this time and observed dryly, "I always wondered if it was the love of horses that made Rubirosa marry Doris Duke or if the equine spectacle of her femininity made him so fond of equestrian sports.")

But dressage, steeplechase, hunting, and other horsing sports didn't quite evoke the same sense of competitiveness or danger that this Dominican general's son relished. In his memoir, which barely took a deep look at anything, Rubi paused for a few earnest pages to tell the history of polo and pay homage to the way Argentine fans celebrated the great teams and players their country boasted.

It was an auspicious time to take up the sport. In England and the United States, polo had fallen off following a pair of golden ages that roughly bracketed World War I, but Continental polo, particularly French polo, thrived after World War II. Major tournaments were held in Paris and Deauville each season, attracting teams from throughout the world. Indeed, the latter was an unofficial world championship—the Coupe d'Or—that drew an international field and the high livers and hangers-on who made polo not only a sport but a social spectacle.

Rubi loved that part of it, recalled a fellow player: "He always brought the prettiest girls to the party after a game, and not just one, but two or three. He danced with them all and made sure they were all happy. We would party until 7 or 8 in the morning."

The gilded aspect of polo, and, especially, polo as it was played in such places as Deauville—with its trappings of casinos and seaside chateaus and luxury cars and bored rich women—would have made it attractive enough to him; even if he'd never played, Rubi might well have been a habitué of the grandstands and boxes. But he found he had the game in his blood. As he explained it, "The physical force that a match required, the risks you ran, the peaceful reenactment of savage rituals, it all suited my temperament perfectly." Polo was a terrifically perilous, expensive, and hallowed pursuit—those traits appealing to him in something like that order. Mounted on horses bred for quickness and agility, surging forward at thirty-five miles per hour, swinging at a four-ounce ball with a four-foot-long bamboo shaft with a slender tapered headpiece, ranging over a pitch the size of ten football fields, coordinating attack and defense with a team of only three other players, it combined the precision of golf with the nonstop activity of soccer and the determination-in-the-face-of-physical-peril of boxing. It was the nearest thing to war he ever experienced, and, considering the equipment, the time, and the multiple mounts it required, was nearly as expensive.

"To play polo well," he told Vilallonga, "you should be young and poor. Young because to be truly contemptuous of danger, you must be an idiot. Poor because if you really want to give everything you have nothing to lose." Laughing as he said it, he reckoned himself well suited on both scores.

As a player, Rubi was aggressive and moderately talented—very good for a gentleman but not quite up to professional standards. The sport was governed by a handicap system of ranking players: ten goals denoted a world-class superstar, while numbers below zero were used to indicate the players who paid for teams and insisted on riding with them but truly didn't belong on the pitch. Over the years, Rubi was anywhere from a two-goal player to a five (as in golf, players often lied about their handicaps for reasons of vanity and to sandbag rivals into bets). In Paris, where rankings were more lenient, he could be handicapped very high. "He was a three," remembered his frequent polo partner Taki Theodoracopulos, "but he could play a four or five. But he was a good three. He really played his position. You could rely on him. He might have got up to five for a moment, but he was a good three."

In friendly matches in Paris, Rubi would often be his team's best player, always recognizable in the red helmet he wore—a little touch of Rubi color. For serious tournaments, he organized and sponsored a team called Cibao–La Pampa—named for his birthplace and for the Argentine home of the sport—and was often the weakest player on his own side. He kept up with the Argentine pros he hired, but he didn't truly rank with them. Instead, he made his place by pampering them with gifts and money and rode with them to victories throughout the 1950s and '60s, most notably the 1951 Coupe d'Or at Deauville. The team took championships in Italy, the Caribbean, and France, especially Paris, where it owned the Coupe de France for a dominant run of three years starting in 1953. Later in his career, Rubi limited his tournament play and most often competed in amateur matches in Paris. Even then, "at the head of a team of fat bankers," in the words of Vilallonga, "he acquitted himself without shame." And as late as 1961, at the age of fifty-two, he bragged to the *New York Times* about his handicap, by then, he claimed, two goals.

Still, if he wasn't a world-class player, he was one of the only international celebrities associated with polo in the public eye. And he proselytized for it. He introduced Ramfis Trujillo to the game, and Ramfis brought it to the Dominican Republic, where it would be played ever after, a curious rebuke to the general poverty of the nation but utterly in keeping with the imperial self-image and bread-and-circuses mystique that the Trujillo family so scrupulously cultivated.

Rubi also introduced the Polish novelist Jerzy Kosinski to the sport, which the author would play and write about for years. In the early '60s, Kosinski was wintering in Florida and happened to attend a match at the Royal Palm Beach Polo Club, after which he met some of the players. Rubi immediately assumed that Kosinski played as well.

> "Of course, as a Pole, you must love horses." I said I wasn't sure I did. "How can you say you are not sure whether you love horses? How can a man not love horses?" "I guess it all depends on the man's past," I replied. "No," said Rubirosa, "It all depends on his horse. . . . In polo you forget about everything else—but not the horse!"

Polo became such an obsession that it bled into all aspects of his life. At least that's how he explained the strange turn he next took. As a reward for marrying into one of the world's great fortunes, Rubi recollected, Trujillo offered him his choice of diplomatic posts. Italy held no particular allure for him, and because of his service in Vichy he was still unable to hold the chief spot in Paris. "Argentina is the Mecca of polo," Rubi wrote. "I asked him to give me Buenos Aires . . . the heart of the world of polo."

It was an especially apt place, all things considered. If there was outside of the Dominican Republic a single country in the Western Hemisphere with a cult of personality dominating its political and cultural life, it was the Argentina of Juan Perón. Like Trujillo a former soldier who had come into power on the strength of a coup that promised stability, Perón was an object of Trujillo's envy and even fear. He was genuinely popular, in no small part because of the mass appeal of his wife, the former Eva Duarte, adored as Evita, champion of the *descamisados*—"the shirtless ones," the poor of Buenos Aires; with such an asset, Perón didn't need to impose the same cloud of fear over his people that Trujillo found essential to his rule. As well, Perón commanded the largest army in South America and was sufficiently distant from the United States to operate without a superpower breathing down his neck.

The two men shared a mutual esteem that would last throughout their tenures as leaders of their respective nations. But each as well sought to secure wider influence in the region, and in this their ambitions clashed. In 1946, a group of more than one thousand Dominican exiles led by the writer and politician Juan Bosch amassed a force in Cuba with the aim of invading the Dominican Republic; they were armed, in large part, with weapons they had purchased for a mere $80,000 from Perón. Trujillo accepted the Argentine leader's claim that he had helped the aborted rebellion only inadvertently, but he determined at the same time to keep a closer eye on his fellow *caudillo*. Rubi would serve as that eye; on October 25, 1947, he was named ambassador to Argentina; two weeks later, he was accepted by the host country. He would move there before Christmas.

And he would do it alone. While he endured a forty-eight-hour plane journey from Paris to Buenos Aires, via Lisbon, Dakar, Recife, Rio de Janeiro, and Montevideo, Doris went to the United States to wrangle with the State Department and her legal and financial advisers. All of them were determined to drive a wedge between her and her boy toy husband from the land of Trujillo; they had gone so far as to refuse to grant her the visas she would need to accompany him to Argentina. She was sat down and told about the most sordid aspects of Rubi's past: the Bencosme murder, the Aldao/Kohane affair, his ties to the ghastly regime in Ciudad Trujillo. Threats flew willy-nilly: "She has let her country down," whispered an unnamed friend in a gossipy newspaper account, "and faces a life-and-death fight with Washington, which is thoroughly displeased with her and may refuse to allow her to go to Buenos Aires. It may even use its influence with the Argentine to have Rubi refused accreditation." None of it mattered. Doris probably understood that the threats from officialdom were composed more of bluster than muscle. She wanted to be with Rubi, and she *would* be with him; she flew down in mid-December, meeting a plane that bore the servants from Paris and her furniture and china (a couple of their cars would follow by boat); once again, despite herself, she was an ambassador's wife.

And once again she didn't care for the way things went. Much of the time he was in Argentina, Rubi was off playing polo or scouting horseflesh or watching wild polo matches among gauchos, the raw Argentine cowboys who—young and poor, like he liked 'em—were the best players in the world. In Buenos Aires, he did his dancer's best to juggle the demands of Trujillo with the strange pressures of life around the Peróns, Evita, in particular, with whom it was widely suspected that he had more than just a traditional statesmanlike relationship. He certainly knew how to finesse the divalike first lady: One evening, Doris and Rubi attended a reception for one of Evita's charitable enterprises prior to attending a formal dinner; as a litany of speeches glorifying Evita's good works droned on, Rubi put the honoree's nose out of joint by continually glancing at his wristwatch. Evita upbraided him in a stage whisper for what she called his poor manners; everyone heard. The next day, Rubi presented her with a check for her charity in the neighborhood of $1,500 (reckon nearly ten times that in 2005 dollars). That gesture was enough, apparently, to mend the broken fence, but it did nothing to enhance Rubi's reputation among his fellow diplomats. Evita continually brought up Rubi's largesse as an admonitory example to other ambassadors who had failed to match his generosity; word of the gift even found its way into the *New York Times*. One of the fellows who was browbeaten with the tale finally found the silver lining in all the scoldings: "We'll be able to boast to our grandchildren," he told his fellow diplomats, "that we assisted at an unprecedented event—the only time in recorded history that a pimp ever gave money to a harlot."

The atmosphere in Argentina brought out an aspect of Rubi that he rarely, if ever, revealed in Europe. Vilallonga, who accompanied him on his horse-buying journeys into the countryside, looked on as he engaged in a wild folk spectacle called *pato,* a primitive variation on polo in which players, mounted on horses with neither saddle nor stirrups, chased a live duck with their hands. The game wasn't, like polo, imported from Asia, but rather of genuinely local origin—and strictly against the law. Watching Rubi pursue furiously a squawking mass of blood and feathers, Vilallonga saw into his friend's core: "This man, so polite and charming in daily life, was transformed into a savage covered in blood, willing to risk his life so as not to submit to defeat."

With all this chasing of ducks and polo ponies and presidents' wives, Rubi managed to awaken the ire of both Doris and Trujillo. The latter was outraged at the dearth of inside dope that Rubi was providing from Buenos Aires and recalled him to Ciudad Trujillo—the sort of summons from which people more important than Rubi never returned. Cleverly, Rubi brought Doris along with him on the trip: Starstruck, Trujillo not only failed to upbraid his prodigal ambassador but he feted the couple in Ciudad Trujillo and at his private ranch. Rubi escaped with his scalp—but lost his post in Buenos Aires, which probably suited him just fine.

From there, however, Doris and Rubi parted: He went directly to Paris, she to New York. By March, they were back together on Rue de Bellechasse and, increasingly, miserable with one another: the bickering George and Martha of the Left Bank.

There were his women, a nonstop train of floozies, grandes dames, and whores—anyone he could get his hands on, really. With all the money in the world at his disposal, he gave himself over to his animal instincts more, perhaps, than ever. With waitresses, showgirls, old flames, there was a stream of quickies and one-nighters abetted by the subtle machinations of Victor, the Russian valet and sometime sparring partner whom he'd hired when he acquired the house. With capital and an in-house enabler, Rubi lost all sense of self-control; he had landed the most enviable prey in the entire sport of fortune-hunting, and he was acting, perhaps with the encouragement of his wife's confessions of obsession with him, as if he could do nothing to lose his grip on his catch. He was shameless, as if daring her to expel him from her graces.

One evening, Doris was feeling ill and sent for the doctor, who prescribed a regime of sulfa; Rubi was sent for it, but driving around looking for an all-night pharmacy, he was distracted by the sight of Tabou, one of his favorite nightspots, and stopped in for a drink; he didn't get home until dawn. Another time, when they were on vacation on the Riviera, Doris sent Rubi for cigarettes; in the hotel lobby he ran into Manouche, the gangster's moll and club owner who, like Doris, so vividly recalled his sexual singularity; he didn't return with the smokes for three days. It was as if he was playing *pato* with his marriage, risking his neck to prove his independence and catch a few kicky thrills.

As if this wasn't enough, the house on the Rue de Bellechasse became a kind of hotel and crash pad for their respective retinues of friends. Gilberto Sánchez Rubirosa, Rubi's nephew by his sister Ana and her newspaper editor husband, stayed for months, witnessing a string of marital squabbles; Cesar Rubirosa, now working in Switzerland as a diplomat for Trujillo, stayed there whenever he was in Paris. Rubi, of course, had his string of hangers-on and partiers who followed him home for reverie and eats after his bouts of nightclubbing. And Doris, drawn increasingly to the world of jazz, had her own coterie, musicians and pianists whom she courted and supported and even took piano lessons from.

One of Doris's musical acquaintances particularly irked Rubi. "She was a jazz musician who gave piano lessons and to whom Doris was deeply attached," he groused. "A strange American woman, bossy, who always had something to say and who felt that my presence stood between Doris and her own whims." As in when he was with Flor de Oro, his wife's friendship with a woman who might have some insight into his marriage caused him to bridle. In Rubi's view, the woman's meddling too closely echoed the way Flor de Oro's cousin had torpedoed his first marriage, and it magnified what might otherwise have been harmless marital disputes into real trouble.

"The tone of our little quarrels grew angrier," he revealed. Sometimes Doris would simply leave the house and move into a suite she kept at the Hotel George V across the river near the Champs-Élysées. And then she'd make her way back home, lonely or horny or hopeful or contrite or a combination of them all.

One afternoon in the early summer of 1948, in the company of the nosy piano teacher and her friend, a French attorney, a lunchtime disagreement turned into a full-blown shouting match. As Rubi recalled, he and Doris childishly escalated to a fateful climax: "Doris spoke of divorce . . . 'Fine,' I said brusquely. 'Perfect. Fortunately this gentleman is here. For once he'll be of use. Let's divorce.' Doris, who never once failed to contest a point, answered, an octave higher. Three minutes later, the pens were drawn, the documents signed. The same afternoon, Doris left the house and returned to the U.S."

The paperwork wasn't filed, but Doris made sure Rubi couldn't smooth-talk her out of their rash decision. She decamped for Hawaii, where she spent the better part of a month before returning, via New York, amid gossip reports that they were finished. (Rubi was once again on a tear in Paris—it was even rumored that Flor was in town, though she later denied it—and word of his escapades fueled speculation.)

In July, Doris sailed back to France on the *Mauritania* to see if it would be possible to mend things. Rubi met her boat and they had a warm reunion, but the troubles that impelled her to leave hadn't disappeared in her absence. Indeed, for someone like Doris who believed in signs and omens and the paranormal, things were worse. In September, the B-25 she'd bought him and which had been christened *La Ganza* ("the wild goose") and outfitted with a kitchen, full bathroom, and several sleeping areas, crashed in a marsh in Teterboro, New Jersey; Doris wasn't aboard and no one in the crew was hurt, but the idea that she might have died terrified her. Soon after, she was, according to whispers, hospitalized for a nervous breakdown after an attempt at taking her life.

The situation was quickly devolving from an amusing bit of Feydeau to an ugly slice of Hitchcock, and the people who had all along advised Doris against the marriage finally prevailed. In October, she took those divorce papers that she and Rubi had so heatedly signed and moved to the house in Reno that she'd never sold. Three days later, not quite fourteen months after their whirlwind wedding, she gave Rubi the house on the Rue de Bellechasse and a promise of $25,000 a year in alimony until he should remarry, and they were divorced.

———

But it hardly ended there.

As Rubi said, "We had divorced realizing we didn't really want to be apart."

Within a few weeks of the decree, the phone rang in his Paris bedroom. It was Doris.

"What are you doing, Rubi? Are you bored?"

"No."

"Are you in a bad mood?"

"No, I'm doing fine."

"Are you angry?"

"Why would I be?"

"Well, then come see me."

"If you wish. . . ."

And so he went—to Hawaii via New York, his first visit to American soil since he'd snuck out after giving his cousin Chichi the order to kill Angel Morales. And after a few days, he was back in Paris. And then she rang him again. And this time *she* visited *him*. They went to Mexico together, the Riviera, Italy, Doris's various homes. The back-and-forth lasted far longer than their one year of marriage.

During all that time, Rubi remembered with painterly melancholy, "I did nothing but break up with Doris, reunite with her, break up again, reunite, all in a tumult of planes that dragged me from Europe to the United States and back. When I was in Palm Beach, nothing seemed more beautiful to me than the fading light on the Île St. Louis. When I encountered the gray light of autumn in a Paris that was still recovering from the war, I wanted nothing more than the sun of California."

Tragique, no?

From Doris's vantage, if it no longer could be called true love—she was spending time in Hawaii with her old flame Duke Kahanumoku and was said to be seeing other men—then it was certainly passion, maybe even obsession. And, too, there was a genuine fondness: Rubi gave her gifts (the only one of all the men in her life, she later said, who ever did so) and was always reliably good company. There was enough sentimental attachment for her to race to Egypt to be at his side in 1950 when he injured his neck playing polo in matches organized by his new chum and poker buddy, King Farouk; the estranged couple were photographed together at the pyramids after his recovery, he astride a camel, she atop a donkey.

For him, though, it would be one more of the clean breaks he was always able to make in his life. He spoke fondly of Doris and, indeed, of the marriage, at least in the abstract: "She was gay, elegant, charming—and rich. I had everything a man could desire: a car, a home—and an allowance." But he admitted that he was too easily distracted: "In the end, other women began to attract me again."

Of course, he hadn't waited until the end to act on those attractions. And he could get involved as deeply as she, even during this phony second marriage. For several months, he carried on an affair with Christina Onassis, wife of the shipping magnate, who was actually in his bed one afternoon when Doris showed up unannounced at Rue de Bellechasse. Victor the valet, startled, sounded the alarm and helped avert catastrophe: "Mr. Rubirosa flung on a dressing gown and took the stairs at a giant leap. He held the señora down in the hall while Madame Onassis put on some clothes so that I could hustle her through the garden."

Would Doris have forgiven the faux pas of catching her ex-husband and on-again-off-again lover with the wife of a man almost as rich as she? She may well have, according to one of the frequent guests in that eccentric household. "She was by far the nicest of any of Porfirio's wives," reflected his brother, Cesar, years later. "She had a sense of humor, which is more than can be said for Danielle and her successors, and she was fabulously generous with him."

Cesar had good reason to wax nostalgic about the time he spent at Rue de Bellechasse. Soon after Rubi and Doris split up, he found himself in a massive pickle of his own owing to his lack of funds. Although he was periodically employed by Trujillo at the Dominican legation in Berne, he was sentenced to six months' imprisonment in Athens and fined $200,000 after being convicted in a smuggling scheme.

Apparently the golden aura of his little brother's fabulous life—which he had sampled vicariously when he was occasionally mistaken for *that* Mr. Rubirosa—had inspired Cesar to attempt his own simulation of it. He was married with a couple of kids, yet Greek authorities had caught him trying to leave their country with $160,000 in cash in the company of one Yvonne Neury, a French national who was pregnant with his child. Cesar at first pled diplomatic immunity, but, as he wasn't accredited by the Greek government, he was refused. Then he tried to sneak out of the country but was caught—once again with contraband: a cache of luxury watches that he had purchased, so rumor had it, with money fronted him by his brother. When he was finally convicted in December 1948, he declared that he hadn't the means to pay the fine, so the authorities created a schedule whereby he could live it off, as it were, slashing a percentage off the debt for every month he spent living in a kind of house arrest in Corinth. There, on a salary of about $50 a month earned as a teacher of French and English, he supported yet a third woman—a Greek—whom he eventually married. (Neury, who bore him a son, served a three-month sentence and had a $70,000 fine levied on her.) Only the steady devaluation of Greek currency against those of other countries kept him from living out his days in his quixotic Hellenic prison to the slow, drip-dropping rhythm of drachmas.

No wonder he sighed when he remembered his brother's third marriage. "I'll never understand why," he muttered, "after getting his hands on somebody with hundreds of millions of dollars, he didn't hang on to her."

Put it to that damnable Rubi restlessness. Or a fear of stability. Or—and why not?—the comforting knowledge that if billionairesses didn't grow on trees, millionairesses did.

A mansion, cars, clothes, polo, and a big brassy name: Who would want a wife to queer all that?

NINE

SPEED, MUTINY, AND OTHER MEN'S WIVES

n the wake of a world war, at the dawn of an age of civilian jet travel, in an era of accelerating technology and increased leisure time, auto racing became a truly global sport. Once the province of an ardent but finite cadre—car wonks, R-and-D men at European auto companies, daredevils with money to burn, and burly-armed drivers who could control big, heavy cars—it was spreading in popularity, popping up everywhere, and organizing itself into a series of races that would constitute a true world championship.

In 1947, one of the more colorful spots in the motor race circuit was Buenos Aires, where two newly inaugurated races, the General Juan Perón Grand Prix and the Eva Duarte Perón Grand Prix, were contested on a circuit in Palermo Park, where the national polo championship was decided in front of tens of thousands of fans each autumn. In 1948, when Rubi was installed in Argentina as an ambassador, the two races were dominated by Italian cars and Italian and Argentine drivers.

But the best driver in the world at that moment was French—

none other than Rubi's best man at his wedding to Doris Duke, Jean-Pierre Wimille. There were approximately eighty-five Grand Prix races held worldwide between the end of the war and the dawn of 1949, and Wimille won ten of them, including the major races in Switzerland, Italy, Germany, and France. There wasn't yet a Formula One tour or an official world championship, but if there had been he would have won it handily three straight years.

He was a bouncy, charming fellow, something of a rogue but not of Rubi's stripe: By most accounts, his marriage to the French Olympic skier Christiane de la Fressange was a happy one. There was no brighter star in the French sporting firmament, and it wasn't surprising that Rubi, who was becoming interested in a sport that still attracted as many gentlemen amateurs as it did young hungry gearheads, was drawn to him. It may, in fact, have been Rubi who convinced Wimille to enter the Argentine races in the winter of 1949—even though, having been removed from his post by Trujillo the previous autumn, he wasn't there to watch them.

As a result, he missed out on a catastrophe. On January 28, Wimille was steering his Simca-Gordini through a practice lap at Palermo Park when he either swerved to avoid spectators who had accidentally wandered onto the track or was blinded by sunlight as he turned a corner. His car crashed at nearly full speed into a makeshift wall of straw bales and launched into a sideways spin that ended when he smashed into a tree. His head and chest crushed, he was still conscious when he was pried from the vehicle and loaded, muttering, into an ambulance, but he died before he reached the hospital. His body was flown home to France, where he was posthumously awarded the Légion d'Honneur. A monument was raised to his memory, a multipurpose sporting center bearing his name near the Port Dauphine of the Bois de Boulogne; Rubi would have had occasion to remember his friend almost every day as he rode in the park or drove back and forth to the polo pitch.

The memory of Wimille's painful death didn't deter Rubi from pursuing his nascent interest in motor sports. Like so many things, he simply put

The Benefactor and his brood: Rafael Leonidas Trujillo and his wife, Doña María, flank little Colonel Ramfis on a 1940 visit to New York. *Copyright © Hulton Archive/Getty.*

Flor de Oro Trujillo—sometime after her marriage to Rubi and possibly between a few of her nine husbands. *Copyright © Bettman/CORBIS.*

War bride: At their 1942 nuptials, Rubi and bride number two, Danielle Darrieux, billed in films as "the most beautiful woman in the world," make merry. *Copyright © Bettman/CORBIS.*

After the ambush: Rubi and Danielle, lucky to be alive after the mysterious shooting in the streets of newly liberated Paris, in 1944. *Copyright © Photofest.*

Doris Duke, bride number three, probably the richest woman in the world, in Dior on the occasion of her 1947 wedding to Rubi.
Copyright © New York Times Co./Getty.

All the trouble, none of the flair: Cesar Rubirosa, the woebegone brother, and his mistress, Yvonne Neury, on trial in Greece. *Copyright © Bettman/CORBIS.*

The fastest thing on wheels: Rubi, race official Alec Ulmann, and a Ferrari before a marathon race in Sebring, Florida. *Copyright © Bettman/CORBIS.*

Rubi weds another heiress, Barbara Hutton (his fourth, her fifth). Among the witnesses, the fixer Leland Rosenberg (far left), the debonair Ramfis Trujillo (moustache), and the bride's heir, Lance von Reventlow (fidgeting).
Copyright © Keystone/Getty.

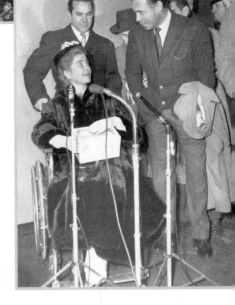

The bride wore Everest & Jennings: Barbara and Rubi off to their Florida honeymoon. Their bliss—and their bond—lasted barely two months.
Copyright © Photofest.

Hungarian for "meow": Zsa Zsa Gabor, wounded by Rubi, laughs at the Hutton wedding photos. *Copyright © Photofest.*

After a public quarrel in Paris, Rubi and Zsa Zsa make nice in a stable.
Copyright © Bettman/CORBIS.

Man at work. *From the top: copyright © Thurston Hopkins/Getty; copyright © Express Newspapers/Getty; copyright © Hulton Archive/Getty.*

Look what I found: Introducing wife number five, Odile Rodin, to the press, autumn 1956.
Copyright © FPG/Getty.

Kingfish out of water: Ramfis Trujillo at the military college, Fort Leavenworth, Kansas, 1956.
Copyright © Grey Villet/Getty.

||| The Goat in his glory: Rafael Trujillo in 1959. *Copyright © Hank Walker/Getty.*

||| July 5, 1965, the Bois du Boulogne. *Copyright © Keystone/Getty.*

||| Odile's farewell (Rubi's nephew Gilberto holds an umbrella behind her).
||| *Copyright © Agence France Presse/Getty.*

it behind him as he leaned forward into a world of anticipated thrills and pleasures. In late 1948, Trujillo reinstated him as an envoy in Rome—a precious anecdote had him showing up to present his credentials to the head of state with a trace of lipstick gracing his cheek—and during his stay in Italy he swapped the luxury cars he'd acquired from Doris for a pair of Ferrari road cars powerful enough to give him a taste of the professional thing.

During the next fifteen years, Rubi would own at least a half-dozen Ferraris, both road cars and Grand Tourismo models. These latter were no mere production line sports cars but rather wicked little rockets, stripped of all nonessential luxury components (the upholstery was canvas, not leather, for instance), amped up with oversized carburetors, supplied with high-performance clutches and brakes. Access to these vehicles was carefully monitored by Enzo Ferrari, pasha of the auto dynasty, who wanted to assure that they would be owned and raced only by people who wouldn't tarnish the name by losing in them—or by killing themselves in them (the blood-red paint job on those cars was no joke). Rubi, who knew Ferrari and his rival auto magnate Giovanni Agnelli from evenings trotting about Rome, was deemed to be qualified.

That a Dominican should fashion himself a race car driver was a curiosity that distracted nobody. It wasn't Rubi the diplomat, Rubi the charmer, or Rubi the lady-killer who was being put behind the wheel of Sig. Ferrari's precious cars—though all of that certainly imparted an air of glamour to the sport. Rather, it was Rubi the daring polo player, who thought nothing of leaning off a careering horse and sticking his upper body in harm's way in pursuit of a little ball. Grand Prix racing of the postwar era was—witness the fate of Wimille—a staggeringly dangerous enterprise. The tires were less than half as wide as those of passenger cars; the brakes wore quickly and even caught fire in the heat of action; the courses were improvised, often rocky or wet or uneven, and rarely equipped with barricades to separate the cars from spectators or roadside dangers; there were no harnesses or restraints to protect the drivers, who rode with their chests and heads above the chassis, protected only by goggles, tiny windscreens, and helmets that didn't extend down to the tops of their ears. You needed money to get involved in this hazardous activity, yes, but you also needed hair-trigger reflexes and unblinking courage.

Of his inner resources there was no doubt: Rubi's daily heroics on the polo pitch proved his guts, even more when you considered he was engaged in them into his forties. But living on the leftovers of his wedding gifts and an annual alimony check that barely kept him in bespoke suits, he had to watch his fiscal resources scrupulously. As he acquired various racing and touring Ferraris in the coming years, he executed a number of fancy steps to eschew the steep duties on imported sports cars. He was close enough to Ferrari to prevail on the factory for help in evading taxes, identifying his new cars as his old ones—swapping the serial numbers on the paperwork—and making it seem to the revenuers as if he only had the one, aging racer. Likewise, he would occasionally pass ownership through a friendly straw man—usually Italian, again to circumvent import duties—who claimed ownership and, for races, sponsorship, of cars that actually belonged to Rubi: In some cases, he drove in competition cars that he was said on paper to have sold and which were subsequently said to have been sold to a *third* party.

He ran his first race in Le Mans in June 1950, in a 2-liter Ferrari 166 MM with Pierre Leygonie, his other witness from the Duke wedding, as his partner in the twenty-four-hour marathon. By the eighth hour, they had made 44 laps of the 13.5-mile course—not exactly tearing it up—and then they had to withdraw because the clutch failed. Three years later, showing up in another 166 MM, a Series II Spyder Vignale, he and Leygonie weren't permitted to enter at all due to an irregularity in his registration. In 1954, his new driving partner, the Italian Count Innocente Baggio, who, charmingly, raced in shirt and tie, crashed their 375 MM Berlinetta Pinin Farina Ferrari in the fifth lap. Rubi never tried Le Mans again.

In Reims in July 1953, he and Leygonie showed up in that same royal blue-and-white Spyder Vignale that officials at Le Mans wouldn't allow into the race a month earlier; in addition to the spiffy two-tone styling, the car bore the legend "Porfirio Rubirosa" in stylish script on the passenger side of the chassis. The car didn't finish the race: another malfunction.

The following winter, Rubi wandered into El Morocco in New York; the nightclub had been one of Doris's favorite spots and Rubi had become sufficiently chummy with owner John Perona that he was always welcome even without his billion-dollar bride. That particular night, Perona, a motor sport buff, was in colloquy with Alec Ulmann, the doyen of a Le Mans–style endurance race held each March at a disused bomber base in the central Florida town of Sebring. Ulmann and his fellow directors had launched their twelve-hour race just two years earlier and were still courting the major European race teams, whose entry would signal to the sport and the press that the event was legitimate. Ulmann had in his hands a letter from the Lancia Company, characteristically the least publicity-minded of the Italian manufacturers, proposing a four-car entry. There was much delight, but there was a hitch: Lancia could only supply seven drivers; Ulmann and company had to recruit an eighth of their own. Perona went to the club's famous Round Table (or Wolf Table)—where playboys, married men, and other cats about town met up when stag of an evening—and asked Rubi over to meet Ulmann. It was quickly agreed that Rubi would copilot one of the factory cars.

The field included entries from Ferrari, Maserati, Porsche, Jaguar, Aston Martin, Triumph, MG, and Austin-Healey; among the drivers were the Spanish playboy Fon de Portago; the German daredevil Harry Schell; the American racers Phil Hill, Carroll Shelby, and Briggs Cunningham; the great British drivers Peter Collins and Stirling Moss; and the magnificent Juan Manuel Fangio, the Argentine who had given Jean-Pierre Wimille the toughest battles of his career and had supplanted the late Frenchman as the best in the world.

The Lancia team, which included Fangio, gathered in Palm Beach and were escorted by John Perona to the finest rooms at Harder Hall, the premiere hotel in the area. They were so supremely confident of their fame and skill that they actually insisted that Ulmann provide police escorts for them when they went anywhere—to keep away the autograph hounds and the like. Ulmann, who knew how little American fans knew or cared about the event, disbelievingly obliged.

On race day, the Lancia team leapt out to a commanding lead and then started toying with their opponents. Rather than work as a four-car unit and ensure that they won the top spot, they began challenging each other to see who could achieve the best time for a lap. But the thing about endurance races was that they challenged the durability of the cars as much as they tested the drivers. One of the Lancias—the Fangio car—suffered a broken axle after 51 laps and dropped out. Another suffered brake trouble about 30 laps after that. That left two Lancias: one of which was well in the lead, and Rubi's car, which puttered along gamely but well behind. Then, disaster: The lead Lancia was disqualified on a technicality. Rubi's was the only car left on the imperious Lancia team.

Rubi had gained steadily on the cars ahead of him as night had fallen and given the car a real chance of winning, but he was removed in the final laps for his more professional partner, the Italian Gino Valenzano, who pushed valiantly but was finally overcome by Stirling Moss and American Bill Lloyd, who completed 168 laps to the Lancia's 163. (Moss, years later, rated Rubi's driving as "only fairly good.") It was the only time that Rubi would ever be sponsored by a manufacturer—all of his other races were as private entries—and it would be his best-ever result.

From Sebring, Rubi went on to Mexico for the fifth annual Pan-American race—a multiday two-thousand-mile rally through some truly rough country; he didn't finish. The following year, he put in a strong race at Santa Barbara and at the Governor's Trophy race at Nassau in the Bahamas, where his copilot was Fon de Portago. In 1958, he entered the second Grand Prix of Cuba, an event best remembered for the absence of Fangio, who was kidnapped by Fidel Castro's guerrillas two days before the race in a bold bid for attention from the world's press.

But over the years Sebring proved Rubi's favorite track, if only because the race came in March, at the height of the nearby Palm Beach social and polo seasons. He returned in 1955, '56, and '58, each time at the wheel of his own Ferrari. In that second year, he was interviewed by sportscaster Barrett Clark for a recording that was released on an LP phonograph record. The announcer introduced their brief chat with a précis of the generally held impression of Rubi's driving:

> Better known as a man about the world than as a driver, Rubirosa has achieved small success. His driving is nervous and unsteady. He seems more drawn to sand banks and oil drums than to the finish line. But he is on occasion very fast, which indicates that with more experience, he might well become a threat to factory teams.

But there were no derogatory notes in their conversation. In a voice that bounced and sang in notes that could sound Spanish, Italian, and even French, Rubi shared some banalities about his car and the track.

CLARK: Could you tell us a little something about the car that you're driving today?

RUBI: Well, I'm driving a two-liter Ferrari, and I think the car is in good shape. We had a little accident the day before yesterday— my copilot hit the gasoline drums. But we repair it, and everything is all right.

CLARK: What do you think of the course?

RUBI: I think the course is in very good condition. It's harder than last year because they put some gasoline drums in the curve over there, and it makes it harder, more difficult.

CLARK: Who are you driving with today?

RUBI: With Jim Pauley, an American boy—evenly, three hours each. I start and he follow with the next three hours and then three me and he finish.

CLARK: Are you worried about tire wear?

RUBI: Well, uh, no, maybe we can finish the whole thing with one set of tires.

Later, Rubi was among the voices commenting on the new American car, the Corvette, that was making its Sebring debut that year: "Well, I think it's a fast car but maybe they are a little heavy for the small curves, you know, but, uh, they are fast enough." (Fon de Portago, who also sat for an interview, was much blunter on the subject of the Corvette: "I don't think they have any chance.")

In the race that followed the interview, Rubi finished tenth overall and top among the cars in his engine class; the following year at Sebring, in the last competitive race he ever ran, he finished eleventh overall and second in his class.

Even if he wasn't behind the wheel, he loved to attend races—he was captured by newsreel photographers in the grandstands and pits at several big events over the years—and he counted among his friends some of the best drivers in the world: Portago, Harry Schell, Count Wolfgang von Trips. Indeed, he was so associated with the racing world that he was filmed by newsreels as a spectator when he showed up for the big events and he even popped up as a character in *Twenty-four Hours at Le Mans,* a 1958 novel by Jean Albert Gregoire. But as he neared fifty, he limited his behind-the-wheel kicks to hair-raising high-speed rides home through the Bois de Boulogne after nights out on the town. "He had a Mini Cooper," remembered his buddy Taki Theodoracopulos, "and he knew how to drift it. In those days you could make the car go sideways—you would accelerate and lose the back and then catch it. He used to do that in the park at five o'clock in the morning."

═══════

If you weren't sponsored by a manufacturer—and but for that single race at Sebring, Rubi wasn't—race driving was an enormously expensive sport: the cars, the maintenance, the travel, the entry fees. As when he played polo or picked up a check at a chic Parisian boîte, an uncomfortable question hung over him and permitted all sorts of dark innuendoes: Where did he get his money?

There was the Duke money, of course, both the signing bonus he got on his wedding day and the alimony, which amounted to nearly $200,000 a year in 2005 terms. And there was his diplomatic salary of perhaps a tenth of that: not a lot of dough, but a considerable sum, especially considering how little he actually had to do to earn it. (Ramfis

Trujillo Jr., grandson of the Benefactor, declared decades later, "My grandfather would send him a blank check whenever Rubi needed it," although that could have been the grousing of an heir who felt that a chunk of his inheritance had been poached.) Profligate with money that came so easily, he had the habit of succumbing to dubious deals with shady partners, such as his $200,000 investment in some botched enterprise in Argentina proposed to him by Juan Duarte, Eva Perón's brother. But there were a few credible investments in his portfolio: the plantation in the Cibao he received from Doris as part of his wedding goodie bag and a fishing fleet that operated off of the west coast of Africa, near the Congolese port of Pointe-Noire.

Rubi was never particularly good with money—he didn't trust banks, probably with good reason given what he knew about business practices in the Dominican Republic—and he always had piles of cash on hand; his luggage often included a suitcase crammed with bills. But the idea of trawling off the coast of the Congo to sell fish to the natives—who were even poorer than the most rustic Dominican peasants—was laughable; people *left* places like West Africa to find food and fortune. There was suspicion that the operation was some kind of smuggling scheme: When Rubi's friend Freddy McEvoy died in a shipwreck off the coast of Morocco, it had been widely assumed that he and his crew were up to no good, probably running guns. But Trujillo kept Rubi on a leash sufficiently short to make any truly risky freelancing unlikely. No, it was far easier to believe that Rubi had simply bungled into a rum business deal with no conceivable upside.

Well, at least *one* upside. In late 1951, Rubi's phone rang, and someone named Alexandre Korganoff was on the line. Korganoff was a strange, ascetic little fellow—Rubi described him as "a man of perhaps 30 years who had an adolescent appearance . . . tall, svelte, fair, with very clear eyes and chapped lips"—with an expert's knowledge of naval history, deep-sea diving, and techniques of treasure salvage. He had been busily working with maps and historical documents to pinpoint the likely locations of several fabled wrecks in the Silver Bank, a reef some 125 miles north of Hispaniola, and he had learned that Rubi was well equipped with ships and connections to the Dominican government and might be interested in doing a little treasure hunting. A few vessels from Rubi's fishing fleet were in La Rochelle for repairs, and, as he put it, "I was, as they say, free and available." The unlikely partners agreed to go find a fortune together.

The ship they were looking for was *Nuestra Señora de la Concepción,* a galleon of forty guns that had left Havana in September 1641 with a huge cargo of Mexican silver, plus some gold and precious stones. Nine days out of port, the lumbering fleet of six in which the ship was sailing was smacked with a hurricane; the damaged vessel tried to limp toward Puerto Rico, but it hit an uncharted reef north of Hispaniola and broke apart. In 1687, one of the survivors assisted a North American colonist named William Phips in recovering more than thirty tons of silver and a little gold, a mere lagniappe.

The wreck wasn't deep—perhaps one hundred feet—but the waters around it were treacherously pocked with reefs that could founder a ship or rip it to shreds. As a result, nobody had successfully reconnoitered the site in the centuries since. Korganoff was convinced there was plenty of treasure that Phips hadn't found and that he knew where it was and how to bring it up. Rubi was persuaded, and he had one of his ships, the *Ile de Re,* fitted out for the expedition, which was to employ a cache of six hundred kilos of dynamite, an old-style diving cage, and a newfangled drilling device that could pierce a ship's hull underwater. As a crew, Rubi had hired ten men from La Rochelle who were experienced in diving in the rugged conditions of the North Atlantic.

In February 1952, the ship sailed for the Dominican Republic; Rubi flew ahead, preferring his accustomed luxurious mode of first-class travel to weeks at sea with Korganoff and the French sailors and divers. They would rendezvous at Puerta Plata, not far from Columbus's first footfall on Hispaniola. In the intervening time, Rubi would be in Ciudad Trujillo petitioning the Benefactor for the right to salvage the treasure. By Dominican law, dibs on anything brought up from the Silver Bank went to Trujillo's brother José, known as Petán ("the bomb" or "the fart"), a onetime chicken thief, cattle rustler, and hooligan who had, under the aegis of his older brother, become a rich man with a monopoly on plantains and control of the propagandistic national radio station. Rubi won a concession from Trujillo—likely in exchange for a bigger taste of the action than Petán would have shared with him—and got the green light, Petán cursing him and wishing his expedition the worst as he made for Puerta Plata.

Petán apparently had some real pull with powers greater than his brother: Virtually every step Rubi and his cohorts took was disastrous. As the *Ile de Re* left Puerta Plata for the diving site, it nearly collided with a sloop and got tangled with its anchor line; the chief diver at first refused to go down to extricate the vessel and had to be threatened with loss of his portion of the proceeds. It was a telling flash of attitude: The French crew proved truculent and even mutinous as the expedition wore on. The captain was homesick for his sweetheart; the rest of the crew drank heavily of the red wine they'd brought along, heedless of the heat and sun, while Rubi wisely stuck to the beer he kept in a cooler on his launch, *El Pirata;* the Caribbean sharks so frightened the divers that Rubi had to stand guard with a rifle to scare off the predators while the men were in the water; the diving cage was too bulky and clumsy to use in the coral reefs; the divers and sailors swore at Rubi and Korganoff and gambled and laid about with hangovers and wicked sunburns. Worst of all, the *Concepción* was nowhere to be found: The French maps Korganoff had consulted turned out to be so old that they were nearly useless, thanks to several centuries' growth of coral since the site had last been explored. Now and again, thinking they were in the right place, they would blast a reef with a bit of dynamite, but the treasure continued to elude them.

After a period of fruitless, agitated searching, Rubi was faced with a crisis: "I quickly realized that for the expedition to have any chance of success, which every day seemed more doubtful, it was imperative to rid ourselves of this awful crew immediately." He directed the *Ile de Re* to shore, where the crew angrily demanded advances on their salaries. But Rubi didn't have any money to pay them: He had reckoned their shares would come out of the back end, when the treasure was recovered; there was no cash on hand.

What did he do? Why, he rode *El Pirata* up the coast a few miles to a little beach town and encamped in a tavern beneath the palms to drink beer and brood. "I needed to be alone to think and get some clarity on this mess," he explained.

Two days later, an alarmed Korganoff found him. As Rubi recalled, he had a riot on his hands. " 'Come quickly,' he said. 'It's mutiny. They're going to kill themselves. They're crazy on booze.' " When he arrived in Puerta Plata, Rubi saw that the crew had somehow found the means to get loaded on rum and were threatening to blow up the harbor: The lead diver, Rubi remembered, "displaying a courage he hadn't previously shown, amused himself by throwing detonators among the explosives." Rubi cut all connection to the anarchic scene, explaining to the harbormaster that the crew had been infiltrated by Communists and had mutinied, scuttling the expedition. The C-word elicited the expected response: Trujillo's militiamen seized, incarcerated, and "interrogated" the sailors, then sent them back home via Martinique.

Rubi hired a second crew—Dominicans—but found that the French sailors had sufficiently damaged the *Ile de Re* that it would have to be put in dry dock and repaired in Ciudad Trujillo. It never got there. Hobbled—and well insured—it sank en route, with all hands saved. Rubi went back to Paris. And the diving cage, left on the dock in Puerta Plata after the fracas, fell into the hands of a local pig farmer who used it as a feeding pen for his hogs.

End of fiasco? Not exactly. Korganoff, having come this far, went back to the presumed wreck site and continued his search. After a couple weeks, he found it: the *Concepción*, visible from the surface under a calm sea. Rubi returned and hired a small ship and a new crew, and they went out one more time. But when they reached the spot, the wreck was no longer visible because the sea was no longer calm; indeed, all signs indicated that a brutal storm was kicking up. They turned tail for the harbor, but they were hit with motor trouble. As a wicked squall approached, they dropped the anchor, but it didn't hold. They fought the weather to get away from the reef and into the open sea, then battened down for the duration of the tempest. When it passed, they tricked the engine alive and rode through the night to land. As Rubi recalled, "The sailors thanked the heavens. 'The depths didn't want us to get their treasure. We will never again, for anything in the world, return to the Silver Bank.' "*

And Rubi returned to more familiar means of uncovering fortunes.

=======

He gadded for a while: polo in Paris, Deauville, Palm Beach, Ciudad Trujillo, and Argentina (he ran into his old chum Aly Khan there, also buying horses, and they partied with Gene Tierney and a Hollywood crew filming a gaucho western); the motor racing circuit; the high life of the French Riviera; a very little work in Rome and then, in jobs of low enough rank that they didn't violate the ban against diplomats who'd served in Vichy, in Paris. He ran into King Farouk in a casino and became a chum of the prodigal monarch whose zeal for life made him so much less ominous and nerve-racking than Trujillo; Rubi took several whirlwind trips with the king and visited Egypt as his guest.

Wherever he went, he played, as always, the big man. One night in Monte Carlo he was introduced to an American businessman and made a great show of his pleasure at meeting the fellow. The next night, in a nearby restaurant, the two bumped into one another again. "He came over to the table," the Yank told a journalist, "and shook hands all around. Somehow I'd got the notion that he was a freeloader. I thought, well, I'll have this suave bum on my hands the rest of the evening. But all he did was nod to everybody in my party and then go on to a table of his own. Later, imagine my surprise—and shame—when I called for the check and found he'd picked it up for my party."

And his legend as a lover grew exponentially. From the moment in 1947 he hit the papers as Doris Duke's new husband, he entered a rarefied company of pseudocelebrities known chiefly for their sexual escapades—if only to a select demimonde of international gossips. To some degree, it was the fame of the women he was linked to that fanned his legend: actresses such as Gene Tierney, Dolores Del Rio, and

* In 1978, explorers discovered the wreck of the *Concepción* and salvaged a small fortune in gold, jewels, and antiquities. Other expeditions continued to turn up silver on the site until the end of the century.

Veronica Lake; the great Portuguese *fado* singer Amelia Rodrigues; no-name showgirls in London and Paris; the wives and girlfriends of his polo and race-car driving peers; women from noble circles such as the Contessa Nicola-Gambi of Italy, Countess Marita of Spain, and Queen Alexandra of Yugoslavia. ("Rubi," an old friend joked, "has become a baron by a process of bedroom osmosis.") An exhausting retinue—and one with the most unexpected benefits in the form of widespread renown: At a party at a ski resort, for instance, a friend watched in astonishment as a woman to whom Rubi had only just been introduced declared with no trace of irony, "I will leave my husband for you."

Rather than recoil at news of Rubi's exploits, Trujillo and his government saw his fame as a valuable public relations coup for the Dominican Republic. "Few people had ever heard of the place until he came along," confided Rhadamés Trujillo to a reporter. Another relative of the Benefactor's concurred: "He was the best public relations money could buy for the regime." Concluded an official in Ciudad Trujillo, "The only way Rubi can fall from favor in the Dominican Republic is if he loses his sex appeal. I don't think that's going to happen for a long time. In our country, we have a saying that Rubi is so virile his sex glands will go on functioning even after the rest of his body is dead!" And Trujillo himself managed to put the matter concisely and undebatably: "He's good at his job," the Benefactor liked to say, "because women like him and he's a wonderful liar." Few resumes could compare.

But for all his glorious successes, Rubi behaved as if he were compelled to sex beyond any aesthetic or romantic sense or even profit motive, recalling nothing so much as Vilallonga's description of him covered in blood and chasing after a wounded duck in Argentina. There were whores, either in discreet brothels or picked up on the street, and hardly exclusively of the high-class breed; there were casual one-off encounters that couldn't even be counted as one-night stands since they didn't last nearly *that* long ("Come on, let's do it and just forget about it in the morning" was, a friend recalled, one of Rubi's staple come-ons for a quickie in a handy bathroom or closet). And when he had been drinking—and his valet claimed that he could drink so much that he would piss himself before he got home—he wasn't necessarily a choosy lover. He spoke of the *petit cochon,* the "little pig," inside his head and blamed it for some truly satyric behavior: Manouche, his lover of the 1930s, revealed that Rubi sometimes took his sport in her restaurant after the customers went home with a hag who worked there; a British diplomat recalled the astonishment that struck him and his colleagues at a formal event when it became clear to onlookers that Rubi had completed a discreet tryst with the wife of a Swedish official, a woman so unappealing that she was known in embassy circles as "the diplomatic bag." He was known for his sexual prowess, and he careered forward acting on it as if to endorse his own publicity. He was licensed, in effect, to indulge his lowest urge or most capricious whim, an exemplary *tíguere* whose successes and graceful comportment forgave the most galling tactlessness or shabbiness.

This sort of carrying-on inevitably provoked consequences, even in the jaded world in which Rubi lived, and in 1953 he had occasion to learn just what those consequences might be. In two high-profile society divorces, Rubi was named as a corespondent by wealthy men seeking to separate themselves from the young, beautiful, and not entirely faithful women they had wed. This was the sort of notoriety that came with a payment-upon-receipt notice, and Rubi would be made to pay.

In 1946, tobacco heir R. J. Reynolds Jr. married Warner Brothers contract player Marianne O'Brien after extricating himself from a previous marriage with a $9 million handshake. The new couple's happiness didn't last but a few years, despite the birth of a son. To be precise, Marianne felt herself trapped in a gilded cage: "I was standing on the deck of one of the largest boats in the world," she told her son years later, "wearing a beautiful gown and some of the world's best jewelry. But I was a prisoner on that yacht because every night by five your father had passed out." Rubi happened to turn up a few times where the Reynolds yacht was docked and caught the scent of the former actress's boredom; he pursued her. "When Rubi kept calling me, asking me to dinner and the casino, by God I went," she declared. The romance was consummated in Paris, by which time Reynolds, realizing something was amiss, had hired detectives to track down his wayward wife. The proof they provided of her infidelity saved Reynolds from a second hefty chunk of alimony in less than ten years.

An even more sensational bust-up befell the marriage of champion golfer Robert Sweeney and his celebutante wife, Joanne Connelley. Sweeney had cut a wide swath through the world in the thirty-eight years before he met his bride: He won the 1937 British Amateur golf tournament and had squired Barbara Hutton, the Woolworth heiress, for several years before she dumped him for Cary Grant. In the late 1940s, he found himself, like much of New York, enchanted by the lovely blond Connelley when she was thrust into the spotlight by publicist Ted Howard, who met the girl when she was an eighteen-year-old department store clerk out of whom he reckoned he could fashion a superstar. Because Connelley's father and stepfather were both on the fringes of New York society, she was eligible to be a debutante, and Howard banged the drum so loudly for her that he got her on the cover of *Life* magazine. Sweeney sought her out and they married six months after they met.

Two daughters followed, and Connelley presently found herself bored by the dull languors of Palm Beach, where Sweeney's set sported in the winter ("She was like a well-decorated cake," one of the older women in the circle sniffed, "good to look at, but nothing of substance"). Inevitably, she fell prey to the attentions of a number of fast men, Rubi among them. The story goes that they met in London at the chic Les Ambassadeurs club and Joanne asked Rubi for a lift home, then to walk her to her door, then for a nightcap and then . . . "She returned in a negligee that truly was negligible," Rubi remembered. But he swore that he made a chaste getaway, rushing past a chambermaid who was arriving with fresh towels. Even if nothing did happen, one needn't have been a smutmonger to put a seamier spin on the evening, and Sweeney successfully divested himself of his wayward wife by mere recourse to the maid's story. The suit was brought in London and uncontested by the bride; the court decreed that Rubi, as corespondent, was responsible for the costs of the proceedings.*

* During the divorce, Joanne found comfort in the arms of Jaime Ortiz Patino, a Bolivian mining heir whom she married within weeks of the final split with Sweeney. That alliance lasted barely three years, as Joanne became hooked on prescription drugs and Patino sought to have her committed as an addict. That divorce, preceded by many months of nasty back-and-forth, came down in June 1957, and one month later Joanne was dead at age twenty-seven of a self-induced drug overdose that the coroner mercifully called a heart attack.

These scrapes made headlines, and Rubi genuinely hated all the adverse publicity. "I've become a fad," he complained, "like Mah-Jongg or miniature golf. Wives that I've never heard of swear that I call them long distance and make love to them. It's getting so that when they can't think of whom to blame for a divorce or break-up in a love affair, they name me." But what was worse than the ill repute was the crushing recompense it reaped for him: In December 1953, Trujillo dismissed him from his diplomatic position in Paris, declaring in a press release that "complaints received in connection with the personal conduct of Señor Porfirio Rubirosa have led to the cancellation of his appointment."

Crucially, Rubi was still in possession of his diplomatic passport when this grave edict was declared. He would need it, after all, if he was to hunt down a reason for Trujillo to allow him back into his good graces.

And, as it happened, he had just such a plan.

TEN

HOT PEPPER

n January 1952, Generalissimo Rafael Leonidas Trujillo visited the United States on a goodwill mission. He hadn't been his country's president since the mid-1930s, finding it more comfortable to operate the government and his myriad businesses from a remove (his youngest brother, Héctor, known as "Negro" for his dark complexion, was the current puppet of choice). In fact, Trujillo was merely traveling as special ambassador at large for the Dominican Republic. But despite his well-known cruelties, he was treated like a head of state. He was feted by official Washington in January, and he showed up in a stunning display of pomp at the United Nations in February, serving for that month as a delegate and bestowing upon the International Children's Emergency Fund a check for $50,000. On his voyage home, he was scheduled to sign a treaty at the State Department and stop off for a chat with President Eisenhower (for those meetings, he was briefly named secretary of state for foreign affairs).

It was a first-class show all the way. And it demanded first-class accommodation for the generalissimo, his wife, Doña María, their youngest son, Rhadamés, and an entourage of more than a dozen staff members, aides, and bodyguards. In Washington, the party stayed at the Mayflower Hotel. And in New York, they encamped at the Plaza Hotel.

For that portion of the trip, Rubi was in tow (he hadn't yet been named in the divorce suits and still enjoyed the Benefactor's good graces). And one afternoon during his visit, Rubi got into the elevator and found himself agog: "Her blonde hair was swept up," he recalled. "She was wearing a mink coat and leading two poodles. She was a staggering sight."

It was his first eyeful of Zsa Zsa Gabor.

As it happened, sometime in the previous year, when she was in London visiting her husband, actor George Sanders, on a movie set, Zsa Zsa had had *her* first eyeful of *him*. She was dining, as she recalled, with Count John Gerard de Bendern at Les Ambassadeurs, the same club in which Rubi had his unfortunate encounter with Joanne Connelley Sweeney. That night, Rubi was in his usual stellar company: the Princess Hohenlohe (née Patricia "Honeychile" Wilder) and Ayisa, the Maharani of Jaipur. Zsa Zsa couldn't help but notice.

"That's that Rubirosa guy," the count told her.

She checked him out. "Not my type at all," she decided.

In New York the following winter, however, things were different. This time, Sanders was off in Naples making a picture with Roberto Rossellini and Ingrid Bergman, and, as was his practice, he had insisted that Zsa Zsa stay away. This time, Zsa Zsa herself was in the throes of fame and stardom: She was in New York for the premiere of her breakout picture, *Moulin Rouge,* a coronation that Sanders seemed almost deliberately to go out of his way to miss. This time she decided that Rubi might very well indeed be her type.

Rubi didn't know anything about all that; he just knew that he liked what he saw. He broke the ice: "Madame, what are you doing in New York?" He invited her to join him and Trujillo for a drink. She demurred; she had to dress for her premiere.

As she told the story in two autobiographies and countless talk show interviews, the rest of the day was a dream out of a bodice ripper. She went to her suite for a nap; when she awoke, her room was filled with roses, dozens and dozens of blood red roses. Amid them, an engraved card reading "Don Porfirio Rubirosa, Minister Plenipotentiary, the Dominican Republic." Handwritten below that, "For a most beautiful lady, Rubi."

The phone rang: him: "May I come over for a drink?"

By this time, her hair was half done and she was working against the clock to get ready for the big show. Not a chance.

"Perhaps later?"

"His voice was low," she remembered in a purple fog, "of such timbre that even over the telephone it seemed to me he was whispering in my ear."

And then he whispered something that gave her an uncanny sense of shock and thrill: "This is a world of strange coincidences. Would you believe it: we have adjoining suites."

Earlier when she had got off the elevator, he had stayed on, as if headed for a higher floor; while she napped, along with ordering the flowers, he had apparently switched rooms. She could palpably sense him on the other side of the door.

No matter; she had things to do. And then—wouldn't you know it?—just as she was nearly ready, she found that she couldn't quite zip up her skintight couture dress. She was contorting herself in an effort to grab at the thing when the phone rang: Rubi again. This time she wanted to see him: "I hope you won't think I'm silly, but I can't zip up my dress, and there's no maid. If you will be good enough . . . ."

He was over in a flash, zipped her up, helped her on with her coat: a complete gentleman. But the air between them was as thick and electric as before a thunderstorm. She extricated herself from the pregnant pause and made off for her premiere.

When she got back, after a wild success, an invitation to join Rubi and a party that included Prince Bernadotte in the Plaza's Persian Room awaited her. Rather than sit alone and stew over Sanders's absence, she accepted. She watched as he conversed gaily in French and English. She listened as he described his homeland. She took note as he sent a bottle of champagne back as corked and as he walked with an intriguing spring to chat with somebody at the bar. She stole appreciative glances at his dark hair and deep eyes. And she felt his intensity, his purpose. "This is a primitive," she gushed. "This man does not toy with a woman. He is all purpose. He plays for keeps."

When the party broke up, she later recalled, he escorted her to her door and asked if she would welcome him in for a brandy. She froze and he stepped nearer, eyes locked, hands still to himself.

Then he stepped closer yet.

"So," she remembered, "it all began."

<hr/>

She was born in 1919. Or 1918. Or 1917. Or earlier. Whatever: As she put it, "I wasn't born. I was ordered from room service."

She was Miss Hungary of 1936. Or 1938. Or 1937. But the first one ever, at any rate. Except she wasn't: She had been snuck in among the official entrants, and, besides, somebody else won, despite the row and ruction her pushy mother put up in front of the judges.

Her name was Sari. Really, it was.

But history knew her as Zsa Zsa.

Like her older sister, Magda, and the baby of the family, Eva, Zsa Zsa Gabor was groomed for grandness from birth by her mother, Jolie, who determined that her daughters would live the life of riches and fame that early marriage and motherhood had denied her. Zsa Zsa emerged as the aptest of the bunch. After her Miss Hungary fiasco, the cunning and gorgeous girl was discovered by composer Franz Lehar and singer-composer Richard Tauber in a Viennese restaurant and given the soubrette role in their 1934 operetta *The Singing Dream.* She made a splash but wound up back in Budapest nonetheless, where Jolie's counsel was that she marry well as a means of doing well.

First came a Turkish diplomat, Burhan Belge, who whisked her off to live in Ankara in a veritable seraglio. The Turk was much older and something of a brute, but he was a realist, and when she started wandering from her vows, he let her go. She went all the way to America—the long way, east, through India and Asia by rail, boat, horse. Eva was already there, working as an actress, and in 1944, in a very near thing,

Magda and Jolie made it as well (papa Vilmos stayed behind to be forgotten but as a punch line or point of trivia).

In Hollywood, Zsa Zsa pursued the business for which Jolie had bred her: the hunting of wealthy, powerful men. She was stunning: curvy, with a cascade of red hair and a clear-skinned face in the shape, wouldn't you know it, of a diamond. At Ciro's, the luminous Sunset Strip nightclub, she scored: Still in her early twenties (guessing at her age would turn from parlor game to necessity after a world war and the fall of the Iron Curtain rendered the vital records forever inaccessible), she locked eyes with Conrad Hilton, the fifty-four-year-old multimillionaire hotel magnate from Texas.

The courtship was high melodrama. A devout Catholic, Hilton had divorced his first wife and lived in a cloud of guilt ever since, unable to take Communion; nonetheless he hoped that his aged, religious mother would approve of his new romance. Even that blessing, when it came, wasn't sufficient to push him past the mere engagement. Before he could settle on a wedding date, he went off to a monastery in New Mexico so as to more clearly hear what his heart—or his God—was trying to tell him. It told him, apparently, to break things off, which is what he did . . . but only for four days. He begged Zsa Zsa to have him back, and she did. They wed in the spring of 1942 in Santa Fe.

Married to a fortune, Zsa Zsa felt entitled to its fruits. But Hilton hadn't inherited his millions; he'd built them out of a combination of smarts, daring, and obsession. Zsa Zsa may have been utterly sincere in declaring that she *needed* closets full of stylish clothes in which to lunch, to go to dinner, to attend nightclubs and social events, and to, of course, go shopping, but he didn't see the need. He put her on an allowance: $250 a month. (This at a time when he was earning about $5 million a year.)

Somehow Zsa Zsa managed. But what she hadn't counted on any more than Hilton had her extravagance was his aloofness and absence. Hilton was constantly caught up in business plans, money matters, charitable activities, thoughts of religion. Zsa Zsa came to feel like an objet d'art brought from the Old World to the New at high expense and then shut away from the adoration that was her due. And when he finally decided that he needed to wrest himself legally from a marriage of five years to which he'd never truly committed himself, he sent a priest to tell her the news. They separated and made a few stabs at détente. But they had grown weary of each other, and it came out in ugly ways: Hilton once, she said, dragged her to a brothel, and she claimed as well to have slept with his son—*her stepson*—Nicky Hilton, who would underscore his taste for the big and the brassy soon after by marrying Elizabeth Taylor.

It was no wonder that this Grand Guignol drama wore her down; equally, it was little wonder that when she saw a doctor about her fatigue she found herself drifting into the classic Benzedrine-for-breakfast, barbiturates-at-bedtime cycle. It gave her the energy she felt she'd lost, but she grew unsteady and unpredictable. A brutal intervention followed; someone had her slapped away into a sanitarium. (Hilton was in on it, for sure, and Zsa Zsa always suspected Eva was involved, a charge that Eva vehemently denied: Gaborology would always remain an imprecise science.) The mental health professionals into whose clutches she fell subjected her to real snake pit treatment: straitjackets, insulin shots, physical and verbal abuse, total isolation from the outside world. A friendly night nurse took pity on her and asked her if there was anyone who might help. Zsa Zsa remembered some friends, and they sent a lawyer who got her released.

Despite the sordid drama, Zsa Zsa managed to get pregnant (after Hilton's death, she claimed that the conception had been an act of rape): A daughter, Francesca Hilton, the sole issue of the three Gabor sisters' combined *twenty* marriages, would be born after the divorce. And the settlement itself was hardly a bonanza: a Bentley, a New York hotel suite as a home, a lump payment of $35,000, plus another $250,000 (each would be about nine times as much in 2005 terms) to be paid out in ten years of monthly payments . . . or until she married again. (Talk about hedged bets!)

The din raised by her cacophonous divorce from Hilton had barely settled when Zsa Zsa found herself at a Manhattan cocktail party standing in front of yet a third older, jaded man of imperious standing and notable fame.

"I have been wanting to meet you for so long," she purred. "I have such a crush on you."

"How very understandable," George Sanders purred back.

Sanders was one of those brilliant actors whose demeanor away from stage or screen was virtually identical to the striking figure he cut when doing his job: in his case, debonair, cynical, worldly, wry, imperturbable, urbane. His voice was at once feline and serpentine, like velvet marinated in cherry brandy. His bearing was somehow both military and decadent. He could be so boldly aloof and condescending that those qualities, normally alienating, transformed to possess a kind of magnetism.

He had been born in prerevolutionary St. Petersburg to English parents and raised after the age of ten in a working-class household in Birmingham. He tried to make a go of business but was a bust; his bearing and palaver were sufficiently impressive, however, that friends recommended he try acting. He was a natural. He made a few forgettable films in England and in 1936 arrived in Hollywood, where he impressed, usually as a villain. By the end of the decade he became a leading man in the role of Simon Templar in RKO's series of thrillers based on Leslie Charteris's novels about "The Saint." Finally, in 1943, a real breakthrough: the Gauginesque lead in an adaptation of Somerset Maugham's *The Moon and Sixpence*, a role that combined worldweariness, decadence, artistic passion, and drollery as if it had been dreamt up with him in mind. By 1947, when he stared amusedly down his nose for the first time at the bombshell known as Sari Hilton, he was an international star. And the gorgeous divorcee in front of him was his perfect match in both physical appeal and glittering self-regard.

Sanders was married at the time, yet he had no compunction about leaving the party with Zsa Zsa and spending the night eating caviar and toast at her penthouse apartment. That night he rechristened her—Cokiline, for a Russian cookie beloved in his youth—and they were presently a couple, even though his divorce was still only a matter of intent. They traveled together to Bermuda and Cuba; she moved into his Los Angeles apartment building. In September 1948, gossip queen Louella Parsons hinted that they might marry, and so they did, in April

1949, in a quickie ceremony in Las Vegas. After their first kiss as husband and wife, he gave her one of those down-the-snout glances and declared, "My dear, now that we're married, I'm not sure if I will be able to make love to you any more."

He wasn't kidding. He had warned her that years of psychotherapy hadn't stopped him from being a real mess: "I don't know what sort of fellow I'm likely to be at any given moment. I might make you miserable." But Zsa Zsa was content to serve as his handmaiden, bringing him late-night sandwiches, cleaning his apartment, staying in evenings even as he made the Hollywood party circuit, sitting up with him to play chess—which was how they spent their wedding night.

Soon, however, the unlikely hausfrau felt the need for larger quarters in which to make ham sandwiches and listen to the phonograph, and Sanders encouraged her to go house hunting. She found an estate that she adored: 11001 Bellagio Place, in the hills above the Bel-Air Country Club, with gardens, a pool, and fourteen rooms: a real Hollywood movie star pile. Sanders agreed she should have it . . . and then refused to contribute a penny toward its purchase or upkeep. He would retain his apartment—he required a lair to retreat to, he claimed—and he would outfit a suite in the house as his home away from home.

The year after the wedding, Sanders was cast in one of those once-in-a-lifetime roles so aptly suited to his talent and demeanor that it couldn't have been played by anyone else: Addison DeWitt, the viperous, Machiavellian theater critic in *All About Eve,* a character he could have played to perfection if he had sat bolt upright out of a coma. In the glory that accrued to him from his magnificent performance, including an Academy Award as Best Supporting Actor, he not only ignored Zsa Zsa but he positively pushed her aside, refusing to let her participate in interviews or photo shoots even when they were conducted in the house that *she'd* bought with her settlement money from Hilton. At the same time, Zsa Zsa had reason to believe that he was philandering with his costars, who included Hedy Lamarr and Marilyn Monroe. Yet she always swore that she adored him, and so she endured his absences, moods, and slights.

It got worse. He seemed to relish belittling her. He chided her for not being wealthy, even though by marrying him she had kissed off the bulk of her alimony. "The only sensible thing for a man of taste and intelligence is to marry a rich woman," he declared, "and look how I've allowed you to thwart my purpose." When they were invited to a party at Ciro's, this complaint was amplified into a truly cruel insult; introduced to one of the hostesses, it became clear to Zsa Zsa that her husband had slept with her.

It was Doris Duke.

"That's the woman I should have married," Sanders sniffed. "There's no greater aphrodisiac than money." Zsa Zsa, blinded with rage, shot back at him with the only weapon she could summon. She knew that Duke had once been married to some man famous for his amours. "I'm going to have an affair with Rubirosa!" she screeched. As she said later, "Rubirosa was just a name to me, a face, not too clear, that I had seen in the newspapers." But she saw that Sanders had been appropriately chastened by the threat, and, she claimed, "I never gave Porfirio Rubirosa another thought."

―――――

If that incident at Ciro's revealed anything, it was that Zsa Zsa had a quick, sharp wit—something that Sanders's brother, the actor Tom Conway, must have noted. Because when *Bachelor's Haven,* a TV chat show on which Conway was a regular, found itself short a panelist at the last minute one day, he rang Zsa Zsa and asked her if she could sit in. George was overseas making a film; why not, she thought. The format suited her: Letters from lovelorn viewers were read aloud to the panel, who offered their advice.

With her first two utterances, Zsa Zsa became a hit.

"I'm breaking my engagement to a wealthy man," read the first letter. "He gave me a beautiful home, a mink coat, diamonds, an expensive car, and a stove. What should I do?" "You must be fair, darling," came that soon-to-be-familiar Hungarian mew. "Give him back the stove."

Huge laughs, capped by the expression on her face that made it seem as if she hadn't even been trying to be funny.

"My husband is a traveling salesman," wrote another advice-seeker, "but I know he strays even when he's at home. What should I do?"

Another ad-lib: "Shoot him in the legs." Bigger laughs.

The producers had her back and then signed her as a regular. And director Mervyn LeRoy sought her out for a role in *Lovely to Look At,* an all-star musical. She was so beautiful and such a natural that LeRoy—who'd made such classics as *Gold Diggers of 1933, Tugboat Annie,* and *Little Caesar*—didn't even bother with a screen test.

She was signed up as well by Russell Birdwell, the publicist who had orchestrated the classic PR campaign around the casting of Scarlett O'Hara in *Gone With the Wind* and who immediately got her on the cover of *Life.* She was cast in two more films: *We're Not Married,* an anthology of romantic vignettes, and *Moulin Rouge,* John Huston's big-budget biography of Toulouse-Lautrec, in which Zsa Zsa was cast in the crucial role of Jane Avril, the Parisian entertainer who was the painter's muse.

When he returned home to all this, Sanders wasn't happy. There was supposed to be only one star in the family, and he was it. Not only had Zsa Zsa seemingly shot past him, the world committed the sin of reminding him of it: When they were out on the town, more people recognized her than him. His iciness grew in direct proportion to his resentment. Zsa Zsa thought he would be pleased that she had managed to occupy herself—and earn a living—in his absence; instead he grew more vicious than ever.

The frictions between them hit a climax in November 1951, when they were scheduled to appear together on the radio show of the actress and high liver Tallulah Bankhead. At the rehearsal, Bankhead fawned on Sanders and completely dismissed Zsa Zsa; worse, the dialogue mocked their marriage in a way that Zsa Zsa didn't quite understand.

SANDERS: We've been married two years and I haven't spoken to Zsa
    Zsa since she said yes.
BANKHEAD: Doesn't Zsa Zsa speak to you?
SANDERS: Only in Hungarian.
BANKHEAD: Do you understand Hungarian?
SANDERS: Not this one.

One line really got Zsa Zsa's goat.

SANDERS: She's deliriously happy. After all, she can catch fleeting glimpses of me as I walk in the garden or dive into the pool and we do have a certain intimacy. We do share the top drawer of the dresser.

Bad enough to make light of their marriage: But the house was *hers*, bought and paid for, and for Sanders to joke about his domain over it was infuriating. Zsa Zsa refused to read the few lines she was given; in fact, she bared her claws on Bankhead, stomped out of the studio, and refused to be on the show at all. Sanders, to save face, moved his few possessions out of the house and told the papers that he was splitting from his wife: "I have been discarded like a squeezed lemon," he whined to the Hollywood press. "My wife took the lines personally and thought I was to blame for them. When we got home, she asked me to move out."

Again, she fought back. When asked if this behavior wasn't to be expected from Addison DeWitt, she retorted, "I'm his wife. I won't have him talk to me, even in a radio script, as he talks to other women." And she laughed at the thought that he would leave her. "The last three things he packed before he left home were my photographs," she told Louella Parsons. "He'll be back."

In response, he whinged some more: "Like all women, my wife resembles the queen bee who ultimately extinguishes her mate. Her pattern is perfectly clear. She's caught me. She's breaking me, and when she has utterly cowed me, she'll trample on me." But there were her charms, and those midnight snacks, to consider. He came back but by the spring, divorce talk was still in the air. "Living with the Gabors is like living in a perfumed whirlpool," Sanders sighed.

He had no idea.

During this back-and-forth with her husband, on the first morning that she woke up beside the minister plenipotentiary of the Dominican Republic at the Plaza Hotel, a cable made its way to Zsa Zsa: "Am in London I miss you terribly I love you I love you George." Stupefied by what seemed his uncanny intuition about her behavior, she returned home to Los Angeles, where Rubi peppered her with phone calls from all over the world. (He had code names by which he identified himself to her: Mr. Perkins was a favorite, for some reason, and he also used M. Bellechasse.)

She heard again from George; he was in Italy, where he'd become ill with food poisoning; she rushed to join him. Then she raced to Las Vegas, where her agents had managed to put together a curious little show around her at the Flamingo. (Rubi flew from Paris to join her there for a single night—the trip made her certain he loved her, she said.) Then she went back to Rome and Sanders.

In Italy, as she endured her husband's usual hot-and-cold temperament, a telegram arrived from Rue de Bellechasse: "No word from you. Miss you and love you much. Wire me. Rubi." Sanders read it first and made a grand, mocking show of delight: "Cokiline, what a conquest! The great Rubirosa! He's in love with you! Now that's really an achievement!" Belittlingly, right in her face, he himself composed a response— "Mon Cheri, I love you too and cannot wait to see you again, Zsa Zsa"—and sent it off, triumphant in his scorn.

And then, fatefully, she was offered a part in a gangster comedy starring the French music hall great Fernandel. It would be shot in Paris. She accepted.

For the next several months, she and Rubi were inseparable. Zsa Zsa made a show of propriety by staying at a hotel, but they were on the town together constantly and she found herself addictively drawn to him. A few years later, she and a ghost-writer depicted her as the heroine of a drama of forbidden love.

He had such power over me that I had no will of my own. I remembered myself not once but many times putting on a black skirt and a huge black wool sweater so that no one would recognize me and slipping out the side entrance of my elegant hotel and into a cab. I could not help myself. How many times in my black sweater and skirt I stood before that house just before dawn, and touched the bell . . . knowing how loudly it rang inside, that it was heard everywhere, that neighbors' windows lit up and faces stared out to see who stands at Rubirosa's gate.

She adored the house: the aromas of leather and tobacco, the juxtaposition of ancien regime décor and polo gear and trophies, the deliciously piquant spices of the Dominican food he served her and which reminded her of the Hungarian meals of her childhood. She respected his aesthetic. "He is the only man I've known whose taste extends to women's clothes," she said. "He has an unfailing eye for the right color, the correct line, the becoming curve. If he says, 'Zsa Zsa, take that hat off, it doesn't suit you'—I do!" She loved the way he bore himself when they were out on the town: the vivacity with which he could fill a nightclub, the trance into which he seemed to fall as he joined a band in drumming, the way he merrily insisted that the party continue on into the dawn, paying the musicians to follow him to another spot or even to his house for a ham-and-eggs feast.

And, not surprisingly, considering the regal men she had already married, she quietly loved the way he seemed so smitten with her that he was prone to angry fits of jealousy. One night they dropped off another couple after a bout of nightclubbing and Zsa Zsa kissed the gentleman good-night and got back into the car. "Rubi turned the key in the ignition," she remembered, "then suddenly, without warning, his eyes blazing like hot coals, slapped me hard." Another time, they entered a restaurant and she bade hello to a lady friend. Rubi grabbed her by the arm: "So now you like women too, eh?" And yet another time, as they drove through Paris and she stared out the window daydreaming, she was jolted by a smack: Rubi presumed she was spooning after some young man on the street. "But I was thinking about my taxes!" she protested. (Beastly behavior, but she perversely read into such acts proof of affection. "A man only beats a woman if he loves her," she explained.)

She was drunk on him. Her mother tried to get her to see how ill suited they were for one another: "Rubi is not for you. He drinks a lot. At the most you have a wine spritzer. He loves nightclubs. You don't smoke. You hate nightclubs. For a husband he is not good."

"Yes," Zsa Zsa admitted, "but for a lover, he is the most exciting. . . . Rubi is a disease of the blood. I cannot be without him."

And besides, Jolie was *wrong:* They were perfect for each other—maybe *too* perfect. If there was ever a female *tíguere*, it was Zsa Zsa, clawing her way to the top and landing on her feet no matter how outrageously she tempted fate. And if there was ever a male Gabor, it was Rubi, flamboyant and exotic and laughable in his bald ambition but deadly serious about what he wanted from life. Their ambition and zest and greed and passion and shamelessness and obviousness all meshed. Zsa Zsa remembered it with exquisite slashes of purple.

> We were like two children: pleasure-seeking, hedonistic, perhaps spoiled and selfish, but full of an unquenchable lust for life and an insatiably strong appetite for excitement. . . . Rubi and I both suffered from the same curse: Life held too many possibilities for us. It was as if there was too much potential surrounding us, too much love, too much excitement. We were too greedy for life and too greedy for each other.

And why not? They were gorgeous specimens: he with his temples graying and his physique still lean and his face now chiseled with the becoming gravity of his forty-five years; she impossibly lovely and curvaceous and impeccably styled in just the fashion of the day. (A tailor dropped by Rue de Bellechasse to fit them for matching outfits for some party and came away reeling from proximity to her body: "She stood wearing a flimsy brassiere and the *tiniest* panties embroidered with sequins. She was a shattering sight.")

Even Doris Duke wasn't as well matched with Rubi—not counting, of course, the inestimable difference-eraser of her fortune. Was there truly such a thing as soul mates? Rubi and Zsa Zsa may well have been a perfect instance of the species. ("They reminded me of two flames shooting toward each other—yet having no control over their flight," observed society columnist Elsa Maxwell.)

Despite Sanders, inseparable in the heat of their affair, they traveled together openly as his diplomatic duties, her acting jobs, the polo and race car seasons, and the ebbs and flows of society demanded: Deauville, Rome, Cannes, where they were seized upon by reporters there to cover the film festival and word of their affair finally made its way back to America. When autumn came, she went back to Los Angeles, a blizzard of telegrams and telephone calls from Rubi following her, beseeching her to leave her husband for him.

She tried to ignore his pleas—she swore she loved Sanders—but she couldn't get him out of her head: "Rubi was a sickness to me."

She hemmed and hawed, and in August he wrote her with an ultimatum: "I love you darling but after reading your cable I see that you are not willing to separate and come here. So be frank and decide once and for all."

She couldn't do it; she had to do it. She would meet him in New York; she wouldn't see him again. He would come to see her; she would forbid him to come.

Enough: He went to Deauville for the polo championship and tried to put her out of his mind.

Maybe he could lose himself in some distraction.

ELEVEN

COLD FISH

s his brother Cesar had despairingly noted, Rubi had failed to hold on to Doris and her hundreds of millions. But there was one woman out in the great big world with a fortune nearly as large and a marital history even more checkered: Barbara Hutton, or, more properly, at the time Rubi bumped into her at Deauville in the summer of 1953, Princess Barbara Hutton Mdivani Haugwitz-Reventlow Grant Troubetzkoy—something like that.

As that ungainly string of names indicated, Barbara was a serial bride, with four husbands already in her wake by the time she cut into her fortieth birthday cake. And although it was hard to say afterward whether she had used her men or vice versa, there was no doubt that she could afford to be profligate with them: When her grandmother died in 1924, Barbara, then eleven and a half, had inherited a cool $28 million.*

The money came from two streams. As her name indicated, she

* About $3 billion in contemporary terms.

was a Hutton. Her father, Franklyn, was the younger brother of Edward Francis Hutton, the Wall Street tycoon who founded the famed brokerage firm that bore his name, E. F. Hutton. But Franklyn Hutton was the black sheep of his family, a boozer and skirt chaser who was kept on at his brother's business out of nepotistic kindness. The real money came from Barbara's mother's family, and a fortune with even more resonant fame than the Duke billions.

Edna Hutton was born in 1883 Edna Woolworth, the middle of three children, all daughters, of Frank Winfield Woolworth: *that* Woolworth. Four years before Edna's birth, F. W. had opened his first five-and-ten-cent store in Utica, New York, and promptly saw it close within two months for lack of custom. In a demonstration of true American stick-to-it-ive-ness, he went ahead and opened another store later that year in Lancaster, Pennsylvania. This time he had a hit. By the time Edna was taking her first steps, there were 25 Woolworth stores in five states; by 1917, Woolworth's company was grossing $100 million a year (nearly $1.5 billion in 2005 terms) from 1,000 stores—a massive fortune built literally on the nickels and dimes of consumers all over North America and Western Europe.

Old F. W., a humble son of Rodman, New York, only partly shared MegaBuck Duke's vaunting ambition to remake the world and himself in it. True, when he moved his family and his corporate headquarters to Manhattan, he settled in increasingly grand houses; He owned a sizable chunk of property at the Fifth Avenue and East Eightieth Street portion of Millionaires' Row, where he lived in a four-story, thirty-six-room palace near smaller homes he had built for his daughters and servants. But he maintained only one other residence—sixty rooms in Glen Cove, New York—and, unlike Duke, didn't invent whole new fields of business. Rather, he merely built the world's tallest building and named it for himself: 792 feet of gabled neo-Gothic rectangles rising above lower Manhattan an oversized copper finial, a sandstone cathedral pointing a splinter into the sky: the Woolworth Building was the tallest building in the world for nearly two decades.

Barbara was born the year before the building was finished, in November 1912, an only child who arrived eleven years after her parents first met and four after they wed. Her birth may have been well planned, but more likely it was a stab at salvaging a rocky marriage. Edna hadn't the constitution to keep up with Franklyn's vices. He publicly escorted various women, yet still she stuck to him, eating away at herself until she finally took her own life in May 1917: strychnine. Four year-old Barbara found the body.

For some time, Barbara bounced among aunts and uncles until Franklyn married a flowsy but kindly former beauty parlor operator from Detroit. The newly reshaped family resettled in the wealthy San Francisco suburb of Burlingame. By the time Barbara was old enough to be sent back to New York for proper schooling, old F. W. and his wife were gone, and she had inherited, as her late mother's only child, a third of their estate, establishing the foundation of her fortune. Naturally, she entered society, introduced by her family, among them her aunt, the regal Marjorie Merriwether Post, wife of E. F. Hutton, and her cousin, the outrageous Jimmy Donohue, with whom she would be close for life. She attended parties thrown by socialite and columnist Cobina Wright; she met Doris Duke, starting a lifelong acquaintance—and contest for the title "poorest little rich girl." And she got interested in men, both in America and, when she first traveled abroad, in Europe.

Among the first to catch her eye was Prince Alexis Mdivani. At least he *said* he was a prince. Like his brothers, Princes David and Serge, Prince Alexis claimed to be the fruit of a noble Georgian bloodline (Mdivani, with a silent "m," was said to be a reference to a *divan*, or throne, and indicated, they said, their elevated heritage). In reality, they were just a White Russian family who seized on the confusion of the times in such matters to claim a lineage that didn't even exist; their father joked that he was the only man ever to have inherited a title from his children. The boys and their sister proved notably ambitious in their private lives: Despite having neither money nor careers (not even ambassadorships!), David had managed to marry Mae Murray, the wealthiest and most popular actress in Hollywood; Serge had equaled the feat by snatching up silent screen siren Pola Negri; sister Roussie had pilfered the muralist José Maria Sert from his wife (and still managed to keep her as a friend!); and Alexis had lined up a fortune in the guise of

Louise Astor Van Alen, a teenage heiress descended from several fine American families.

The Marrying Mdivanis, as they were called in the tabloid press of the 1920s, were brilliantly successful at their chosen craft despite their insolvency, their shady business practices, their phony history, and even their queerly exotic looks: David a dark, sinister Harpo Marx; Serge with a lantern jaw and large credulous eyes; and Alexis, with the tough, broad features of a movie hoodlum or a veteran cop. In latching on to their various spouses they got their hands on fame and real fortune—boats, houses, touring cars, polo ponies, oil fields—not to mention entrée into the sort of society in which they might meet other, richer prospects for conquest.

Alexis was already established in select European circles, an exemplar of the fallen noble (in this case, faux) on the make for an heiress wife. Hence Louise Van Alen. And hence Barbara Hutton, who, despite the plump, mousy, drab appearance she cut as a teenager, caught his eye on her visit to France. At the time, she was too young to be considered for marriage, and Alexis had already seen to his immediate future, anyhow. But he proved a patient sort.

Barbara debuted at a formal party for one thousand held at the Ritz-Carlton in New York and costing an estimated $60,000—a bigger fiesta by a considerable shot than had declared the formal arrival of Doris Duke into grown-up society. Then she was whisked off to London to be presented at court and then to Paris, where Alexis finally put the moves on her. Brazenly, with his wife about, Barbara let him; they were literally caught in flagrante at a house party near Barcelona in the summer of 1932. Alexis's missus got a divorce, and plans were made for a big Mdivani-Hutton wedding in Paris the following spring.

Doris Duke's two weddings were hushed, hurried, discreet affairs. Barbara's first marriage would be celebrated as if she truly were a princess (and why not: Franklyn's family had invested wisely enough to turn her money into $42 million by the time she legally inherited it soon after the wedding). The ceremony was held in Paris at the Russian Cathedral of Saint Alexander Nevsky; the massive display of wealth and antique ritual drew enormous crowds of reporters, photographers, and onlookers. And it nauseated a lot of people: at the height of the Great Depression, an American girl spending all that money and making all that noise—and marrying a foreigner to boot. Compared with relatively tasteful Doris, Barbara was seen as showy, supercilious, a wastrel. With the wedding she began a lifelong struggle to be treated kindly by the press, a battle in which she was very often her own worst enemy.

Indeed, though she was in a superficial sense prettier than Doris, the other of "the Gold Dust Twins" as the press called them, Barbara was far less suited for world in which her wealth made her susceptible to predators, temptations, and infinite—and often dangerous—choices. She was more fragile—physically and emotionally. She was restless like Doris, but with a more nervous air and an undercurrent of sadness. In some key ways, she was more refined than her friendly rival: She was less prone to outré enthusiasms; she had a finer eye for art, architecture, collectibles, and fashion; and she wrote poetry—publishing two slim volumes over the years, in fact. But she broke down more often and was more easily swayed by even moderately powerful forces—a more tragic if not quite so sympathetic figure on the whole.

Take the matter of her body. The story goes that Alexis took advantage of his wedding night to declare, "You're too fat." Crushed, she punished herself to lose weight, devising a coffee-only diet that whittled more than forty pounds off her body and initiating a lifetime of bulimia and crash diets that sapped her vitality.

Of course, Alexis was sapping much more than that. He had agreed to a prenuptial settlement that kept him from getting his mitts on all of her dough—$1 million in dowry and an annual allowance of $50,000. But he found ample ways to spend money on things that he insisted they *both* needed—cars and clothes and horses and property in France and Venice and antiques and travel and the like. For a year they toured the world, lapping up extravagant tchotchkes and bickering like brats. When they finally got to London, their one-year-old marriage was collapsing, and Barbara was grateful to turn to her right at a formal dinner party celebrating her twenty-second birthday to meet the gaze of Count Court Haugwitz-Reventlow, a Danish *genuine* nobleman—tall, erect, nearing forty, with a snooty air and the chiseled good looks of an Old World army officer in a Hollywood movie. Six months later, in a single twenty-four-hour period, she shed herself of Alexis and became a genuine countess by marrying Court.*

This act of caprice brought out the venom of the press more than ever: Barbara was positively barracked in headlines, gossip columns, and editorials, treated rudely by doormen and waiters, spoofed in movies, even cited as an example of the callous wealthy by a Canadian Parliament inquiry into the operation of Woolworth stores in that country. She considered herself "the most hated girl in America," and she had the press clippings and bruised feelings to prove it. She started a counteroffensive, a PR campaign of charitable contributions and good acts. But at the same time she spent outrageously and said and did utterly foolish, self-destructive things. In 1937, for instance, in a byzantine plot to curtail her tax obligations, she renounced her American citizenship in favor of the Danish nationality she acquired upon her wedding to Court; and she acted unconcerned when shopgirls from Woolworth's all over the country went on strike for better wages and working conditions. True, she had nothing to do with the operations of the company, but the pattern of her behavior was so tone-deaf and superior that no hospital wing she might build could erase its impact.

By the time of these missteps, Barbara and Court had begun living in a mansion near London's Regents Park and had seen the birth of a son, Lance. In the wake of the kidnapping of the Lindbergh baby, they worried fervently, and with good reason, about the safety of their son: The animosity directed at his mother more than once manifested itself in genuine danger. Barbara had had an awful time with pregnancy—Lance was a C-section—and that and the threats and her characteristic nervousness made Court's severity all the harder to bear. With a soul

---

* Alexis would have gone on to more spectacular things yet, no doubt: By the summer of the following year he was engaged to marry Baroness Maud von Thyssen, the estranged wife of a German steel tycoon. But he drove his Rolls-Royce into a spin-and-roll, killing him and severely injuring the baroness. The following year, Alexis's first wife, Louise, married his brother Serge . . . who was himself killed in a polo accident almost immediately after the wedding.

like an epee, he poked everyone in his world toward propriety, respect, and discipline, even his wife. (He once upbraided her for giving an order to a maid, insisting that "the Countess Reventlow doesn't speak to servants!") It was a rotten match, and it ended at a kind of apogee of horror, with Court, according to Barbara, dragging her to watch a sex show in Paris then taking her by violence and forcing her to watch him defecate. By 1938 they were living apart.

If anything, the divorce that followed was even uglier than that barbarous ultimate scene of their marriage; negotiations and litigation dragged on for years. Unlike Alexis Mdivani, Court had an heir, and he used his son as a weapon to pry concessions and riches out of Barbara. She in turn set the boy against his beastly father, turning him into a petulant, angry, brooding little firecracker batted cruelly back and forth between his parents—an awful business to which the 1941 divorce decree did nothing to put an end.

Barbara began to spend time in California, where she could see relatives and indulge a new fascination: Hollywood. There was a brief affair with Howard Hughes and a longer one with Robert Sweeney, the very fellow who would one day name Rubi in a divorce suit. And then, before her thirtieth birthday, there was a third marriage—to the one and only Cary Grant.

At the wedding, they were beautiful together, both at the height of their natural charm; she had grown into her looks with a kind of exquisite delicacy—up close, it could appear brittle—and had found a more natural (indeed, more *American*) way to dress, and he was simply himself: perfection. They partied and entertained and spent quiet time together, but once again there was something less than a harmony of personalities between them. Barbara was a doer and spender, always looking to expand the world as she fancied it; Grant was a workaholic and a tightwad, still feeling the sting of growing up as wretched Archibald Leech in Bristol, England. She was distracted by the continuing battles with Court over the custody and rearing of Lance and by FBI inquiries into her friendships with European nationals who may have been Nazi spies; he hated the strange, adverse publicity that came with proximity to her and the way that she threw money around.

Inevitably, she wandered. She acquired a flat in Los Angeles that she used for trysts, including one that her swain of the moment, designer Oleg Cassini, then married to Gene Tierney, recalled as being ethereal, spooky, and a little disturbing. (As he surmised from the experience, "She divided men into two groups—those she loved and those she took to bed. Her marriages were essentially sexless, and her affairs were bereft of love.") Inevitably, two separations and, after three years of marriage, divorce. And as always, nothing but kind words in public for her ex; as always, a declared resolve not to marry again.

For a brief while, it seemed possible that she might stick to her resolution. She poured her energy into acquiring and furnishing a house, a palace, truly, in Tangiers. But when in Paris she was squired by the notorious Freddy McEvoy, and that was likely only to lead to trouble. McEvoy, the Australian sportsman and playboy, was best known for being a chum of Errol Flynn's and for his adventures as an athlete (he captained England's bobsled team in the 1936 Olympics); Suicide Freddy he liked to be called. He had a brace of broken marriages to American heiresses behind him, a shadowy reputation as a sex machine and as a doer of rich folks' dirty deeds—both of which qualities recommended him, of course, to Barbara. Their affair was physical, but it was even more a kind of business arrangement: She seemed to have fronted him money, which he poured into suspicious operations such as selling black market American military goods and performing illegal currency exchanges; Barbara, of course, had no knowledge of these dealings and sought no profit from them, but it was with seed money from her that he was able to open an office on the Champs-Élysées to put a shiny face on his dirty work.

It wasn't surprising, then, that McEvoy didn't wed Barbara but rather brokered her introduction to the man who would serve as the fourth in her line of failed marriages: Prince Igor Nikolaievitch Troubetzkoy, heir to a worthless Lithuanian title, then employed as a journeyman bicycle racer and one of Freddy McEvoy's bagmen. Less than two years after signing divorce papers with Cary Grant (the only of her husbands who had insisted on neither a dowry nor parting gifts), she was once again a princess. This one endured until 1951, with most of the last year being given over to separations, fights, and his authorship of a tell-all book as a weapon of blackmail. She cut the check. *Dasvidanya,* Prince.

All of it had ground her down. She had never been robust but, now nearing forty, she was continually sick, with surgeries for mystery ailments and an increasing taste for the oblivion induced by booze and pills. She suffered from depression and a restless inability to stay in one place or heed the advice of her doctors. The mainstays of her life, such as they were, disappointed: Lance, a teenager in private school in Switzerland, was snarky and remote; cousin Jimmy Donohue had evolved into a world-class hedonist. Barbara, still writing poetry, still seeing herself as a misunderstood, abandoned soul, yearned for the solace of a true love. In the summer of 1953, she packed up Lance and went to Deauville hoping she might find it.

═══

It was a mad season.

Barbara ran into her former beau, Bob Sweeney, who was in the process of shedding himself of his unfaithful wife Joanne Connelley. And milling around the place as well was Rubi, the very man with whom Mrs. Sweeney had provoked her husband's outrage. Rubi had won the Coupe d'Or at Deauville with his Cibao–La Pampa team just two years prior and never missed the event—if not for the polo then for the social opportunities. Meeting Barbara certainly ranked high among them.

How did it happen? Take your pick. Elsa Maxwell claimed to have introduced them and then later claimed it wasn't she but somebody named S. Leland Rosenberg, a school chum of Lance's who was along for the holiday. Others say that it wasn't Rosenberg but his Parisian acquaintance Manuel de Moya, a Dominican pretty boy and diplomat in the Rubi mold that was becoming a stereotype of sorts among their countrymen.*

---

* Of all the Rubi imitators the Dominican Republic would produce, de Moya was the most successful. A former model, dancing instructor, and Broadway chorus boy with fluency in several languages, he knew enough girls and tough guys and political clout–wielders in Europe and the Americas to be named by Trujillo as ambassador to the United States in the '50s.

And Rubi offered an account that only partially cleared up the confusion: "I had known Barbara since she was married to my friend, Igor Troubetzkoy. . . . Later we often had lunch together when I was married to Doris. . . . Rosenberg was my special secretary during this time when I met Barbara, but he had no part in our union."

How Rosenberg came to be Rubi's special secretary—and, in fact, who Rosenberg was in the first place—would be one of the more persistent mysteries of the decidedly murky episode. He was born in Switzerland and came to America in 1946 on a passport that described him as a lawyer; while working at the United Nations, he married the daughter of the Chinese ambassador to Mexico, a union that failed to last out a year but served to introduce Rosenberg—who claimed vague war heroics and blood relation to several different industrial tycoons—to the son of Mexico's then-president. That friendship brought him to Hollywood, where he had a brief fling with the ubiquitous Gene Tierney and met Lance Reventlow, with whom he sailed to Europe on the same ship that was carrying Manuel de Moya.* At the time of this fateful nexus of characters in Deauville, he was perhaps working for the UN, perhaps engaged in some sort of business with de Moya and Trujillo, perhaps both—and, perhaps, special secretary to Rubi, a man who barely did enough desk work to warrant an *actual* secretary: boxes within boxes within boxes.

At any rate, contact between the two famous divorcés was made. Rubi renewed his acquaintance with the fragile Miss Hutton and turned on the charm: dancing, chats in between chuckers of polo, moonlight serenades outside her hotel window with the accompaniment of some musicians he'd hired at a nightclub. He considerately showed Lance about the resort city and its pleasures: the horses, the boats, the dances. The boy was only thirteen, but Rubi sincerely enjoyed young people; at around this time, he met the schoolboy Taki Theodoracopulos and be-

* De Moya was on board as part of the Dominican delegation to the coronation of Queen Elizabeth II, a body that was to be headed by the Benefactor's daughter, Angelita, until British authorities indicated that they would not recognize a fourteen-year-old as the head of a diplomatic mission.

friended him as well. "In those days, people didn't give a fuck about young people, their feelings or their sensibilities," Taki recollected. "But Rubi was very kind and interested."

That summer, Barbara was too frail and confused to respond to Rubi's gentle siege—and, to be fair, he was himself caught up in the hurricane of his affair with Zsa Zsa. So many possibilities! The season ended—Cibao–La Pampa failed to win the Coupe d'Or—and they parted.

In early December, Barbara left Paris for New York, where she kept an apartment at the Pierre. And then she left the Pierre for Doctors Hospital to be treated for what was characterized as bronchial pneumonia but was more likely a deep general malaise. Three weeks she was there and twice she was visited by Rubi.

He had homed in on Barbara and was preparing to swoop down as frankly as any bird of prey. For all the perennial talk about his ruthlessness and his selfishness and his eyes always being on the next prize, it was hard to see it for certain until now. Flor he had fortunately stumbled across; Danielle he had met as another face in the glittering Parisian throng; Doris, well, why not shoot for Doris and a lifetime of security, especially as his white-hot marriage was dimming. But Barbara was a wreck; he was way ahead of her; and he was clearly in it for himself and his future comfort alone. Ever the charmer, he put it over on her, and he tried to find a way to express it years later that made it seem something other than what it was: pure, wicked calculation: "Our friendship took a new course. We discovered a powerful attraction for each other. As soon as she regained her health, I discovered a new woman: with a delicate beauty, intelligent, cultivated, sensitive, around whom I took increasing pleasure."

That second visit, when she was truly on the rebound, must have been an especial pleasure. Afterward, Rubi made a beeline for Dunhill's, thirty blocks south, and ordered a closetful of $300 suits—a *large* closetful—to be billed to Barbara Hutton, to whom, he whispered to the store's owner, Norman J. Block, he would soon be wed.

And then he flew back to L.A. and Zsa Zsa.

By the fall of 1953, George Sanders had well and truly had it.

Bad enough to be married to an explosive temperament. "Life with Zsa Zsa is like life on the slopes of a volcano," he mused. "It can be very pleasant between eruptions." But when that volcano demonstrated the temerity to outscale him as a performer and *then* flaunt a torrid affair across two continents, he determined to return to his vinegary bachelor ways. He moved his belongings out of Bellagio Place on October 20 and two weeks later filed for divorce in Santa Monica Superior Court. "I have separated from my wife, Sari E. Sanders, also known as Zsa Zsa Gabor," read his petition, "and after this date I am not responsible for any debts she may contract." (As *if!*) He went on to complain that Zsa Zsa had been a constant source of "cruelty and inhuman treatment, causing great humiliation, mental anguish and embarrassment resulting in great mental suffering, health deterioration, nervousness and a rundown condition."

In New York, Zsa Zsa, discreetly accompanied by Rubi, initially didn't respond to reporters looking to get a rise out of her. That resolve lasted a day, and then she let loose. "I really don't understand it," she commenced. "For eight months I have begged him for a divorce. But nothing he does surprises me any more—he does whatever his psychiatrist tells him. He goes to the analyst every day. He's all mixed up. And only a little while ago the analyst told me George would have a nervous breakdown if I divorced him." In particular, and with reason, her gorge rose at the idea that Sanders was somehow amicably leaving her with the fruits of their joint financial lives: "When was he ever responsible? He's lived in my house in Bel-Air that I bought and paid for. He drives my car. That's why I've been away in NY and Europe—I have to earn a living to support my baby. . . . George just walked out of the house and left the child with a new maid." Upon vacating the house, she claimed, he had helped himself to several household items that weren't his—radios, chairs, candlesticks, a cheese set. "Why, he even took all the liquor in the place! I'm glad he left the air in the tires of my car! George never bought a ticket or paid a hotel bill. He used my car, my house. This man didn't buy one hat for me. . . . I didn't even get an engagement ring . . . I'm a nice lady, so I don't sue him, but he sues me." She ended with her sole note of understatement: "I don't think he's a gentleman."

She didn't know the half of it. Sanders apparently had no confidence that he could count on Zsa Zsa to let things die a quiet, natural death. He was advised that he needed explicit evidence of Zsa Zsa's infidelities, and he knew just how to get it.

———

Christmas Eve on Bellagio Place: Grandma Jolie, little Francesca, Magda, and Eva with their beaus of the moment, Zsa Zsa hovering over the stove and the bar, and, acting as the gentleman of the house, Rubi. There was more to celebrate than the holiday. The sisters would all three meet up again at the Last Frontier hotel in Las Vegas in just two days for the December 28 debut of a new stage show, a grand extrapolation of Zsa Zsa's solo act—a little singing, a little dancing, lots of droll, scripted one-liners about men: not bad for $15,000 a week.

A lavish meal, the opening of gifts, and then kisses all around and it was a night. After putting Francesca down to enjoy her visions of sugarplums, Zsa Zsa and Rubi went to bed.

Accounts diverge as to what exactly happened next in that bedroom. Either a gift-wrapped brick flew in, shattering the panels of a French door, or a window smashed under the weight of a ladder and the fellow it supported, or somebody simply sauntered in from the terrace. At any rate, it's agreed that the happy couple soon found themselves confronted by Sanders and a pair of private detectives, one of whom was busily flashing photos even as Rubi and Zsa Zsa bolted in their birthday suits for the bathroom.

A cutting "Merry Christmas" oozed out of Sanders.

"How could you do this?" Zsa Zsa shouted from behind a closed door. And then she emerged with a sangfroid that would have given pause to a Medici. "It was perfectly awful of you to come, darling, but since you did, please take your Christmas present. It will save me the trouble of delivering it."

She took him downstairs and offered him a glass of champagne and handed him his gift. In turn, he swept a hand toward his accomplices. "And this, Cokiline, is my Christmas present to you." And he walked out the door.

"He had entered like a thief," she recalled. "He was leaving like the master of the house."*

<hr>

By Christmas morning, a Friday, Rubi had emerged from the bathroom and was off to New York to see to the other woman he was so frantically juggling. Satisfied that Barbara was still on the string, he flew to Las Vegas, arriving there on Saturday as the Gabors were honing their act.

In his wake followed press speculation that he was marrying *somebody*: Barbara? Zsa Zsa? No one was sure. But it was an irresistibly juicy story that was selling newspapers. At airports in New York, Los Angeles, and Las Vegas, Rubi was met with questions about whom and when he would wed. He brushed them off. Zsa Zsa told anyone who asked that Rubi had assured her he was marrying the heiress—she herself had refused him repeatedly and he'd finally given up. "I think Barbara Hutton is very eager to marry him," she continued. "She has nothing else to do. He can take her to lots of parties. They were in Deauville this summer. He was playing polo at his best. Her son is a very good friend of his." And Barbara issued a statement from her suite to the effect that she would not be issuing a statement. "She is resting and reading," as a spokesperson blankly put it.

But clearly Rubi had something on his mind besides Barbara. He was either truly smitten with Zsa Zsa or he was too proud to be refused. Zsa Zsa always contended the latter, and it would certainly be the most sympathetic reading of the moment: He was willing to hold his nose and

* And he dined out on the story of this adventure for the rest of his life. Not three weeks later, screenwriter Nunnally Johnson repeated Sanders's tricked-up version of events—which included shaking hands with Rubi's erect member—in a letter to a New York friend.

marry the neurasthenic millionairess only if his true love wouldn't have him. But even if that was the case, his decision making was uncharacteristically erratic. With no firm agreement with either woman, in the glare of more publicity than he could have imagined, he was genuinely risking all the money that was waiting to be snatched up in New York by rushing out to Las Vegas.

There, as when he joined Danielle Darrieux on the film set in Morocco, his presence was decidedly vestigial. The sisters didn't appreciate having him around while they rehearsed, so he sampled the pleasures of the fledgling little Strip, where a mere handful of small roadside hotels—none with more than two hundred rooms—then stood. He took in shows by Lena Horne at the Sands and Marlene Dietrich at the Sahara. And he gambled. At baccarat. A lot. And poorly.

By Sunday, he was well behind—as much as $50,000. And, as he was on the outs with Trujillo, who had just recently dismissed him from the diplomatic corps because of the ugly divorce scandals in which he'd been named, there weren't very many places he could turn for the money.

He told the casino managers that he was engaged to Barbara Hutton and suggested that they phone New York to confirm that she would stand for the debt. They did, and she said she would, asking to speak to Rubi and reassuring him: "Don't worry, darling. I'll wire them the money at once."

He said he wouldn't sign anything indebting him to her.

"Don't worry, darling," she repeated. "There will be no strings attached."

He had painted himself into a corner. There he was sniffing hopefully around Zsa Zsa's hem, and he had just accepted a hefty chunk of Barbara's money. He would have to return to New York and marry her, unless . . .

=====

The Gabors had finished their final rehearsal for Monday night's premiere when Rubi found Zsa Zsa in her dressing room at the aptly named Last Frontier. With hangdog frankness, he explained himself. "I need $5 million," she recalled him confessing to her, "and she's offered it to me if I marry her. I'm broke, so I have to."

But he apparently held out hope that Zsa Zsa would rescue him from this doom, would leave Sanders and marry him, would conspire with him to forge a life, pay back the money Barbara had lent him, ride off together in connubial bliss.

She wouldn't hear of it. Aside from her increasing awareness that there was something dangerous about tying herself to a man whose principal employment was so vague, who seemed even more likely to be dependent on her than her current husband, the fact was that she still harbored feelings for Sanders, even after all his cruelties, even after that awful Christmas Eve surprise.

"I still love George," she told him.

Booze; anxiety; anger; fear; frustration; desperation; beastliness; lust; dumb habit; all of that and more bubbled up in him and finally burst: He cuffed her.

She took the blow in her right eye. Or maybe she fell away from him in such a way that her right eye hit something. No matter. She'd been rapped, and she had the mark to show it.

"You beast! You've disfigured me!"

He tried to apologize, but she wouldn't have it, and he skulked off, even more desolate than when he'd gone to see her.

She called for a physician. "She has a good shiner," reported Dr. Edgar Compton. "Her eyelid is as black as the ace of spades."

She called for a lawyer. "It appears that my client has been pretty badly hurt," reported Jerry Geisler, who was also handling her divorce. "It could be a criminal action or it could be a civil action for damages. I think my client is entitled to something." One million dollars seemed about right to him.

And, most important, she called for a publicist.

All Sunday night and Monday morning, Rubi kept phoning to apologize, but she wouldn't take his calls. So he went to Los Angeles and from there to New York and Barbara.

Zsa Zsa, meanwhile, took the stage Monday night with her sisters, her eye covered in pancake makeup and partially hidden by a new hair-style. It wasn't an effective cover-up. She would need to wear an eye patch.

But the world would know why.

TWELVE

CENTER RING

**RUBIROSA, SPURNED BY ZSA ZSA,
TO WED BABS HUTTON TOMORROW**

—*New York Daily News*, December 29, 1953

**"DON'T DO IT,"
HER FRIENDS WARN ALTAR-BOUND BABS**

—*New York Post*, December 29, 1953

ubi arrived in New York on Monday night, the twenty-eighth, and walked purposefully past a little clutch of newsmen and photographers waiting to pin him down about his plans. He made his way via limousine to 26 East Thirty-eighth Street, where Leland Rosenberg was letting him bunk in his studio apartment.

The next day, he woke before noon and sent his suit out to be cleaned and pressed. Still wearing his bedclothes, he was visited by Dr. Joaquin Salazar, the Dominican consul general in New York, and at least one reporter, to whom he confessed that he'd proposed to Barbara two weeks earlier and that they were finalizing their plans to wed. As always, he denied ever having intended to do the same with Zsa Zsa. "We have been friends and will remain good friends, I hope. As for marriage, Miss Gabor prefers her career."

By 4 P.M., he was dressed and on his way to the Pierre to work out the details of the wedding and the prenuptial agreement. The ceremony would be held in the afternoon of Wednesday, January 30, and conducted, like his marriage to Doris Duke, on Dominican soil, in this case the New York consulate in Rockefeller Center, with Ramfis Trujillo standing as his best man; to ensure that Dominican property laws would govern the union, the bride would be granted Dominican citizenship by special decree of the government in Ciudad Trujillo—which had suddenly seen fit to rename Rubi to his diplomatic post in Paris. Pursuant to a prenuptial contract, Rubi would receive a lump sum of $2.5 million.

For Hutton's friends and family in New York, it was a nightmare scenario. Twice in the previous year Rubi had been named a corespondent in truly messy divorce cases; just a couple weeks previously he'd been fired by his government for the disgrace he brought on it with his tomcatting; what was more, Barbara herself had practically been an invalid until recently, and it wasn't widely agreed that she was in command of her faculties or was even sober enough to make such a momentous decision. "Barbara is going to fool around this way till she makes money unpopular," groused one acquaintance anonymously. Others, also from under cloaks of secrecy, deemed the upcoming nuptials "horrible" and "degrading"; her ex-husband Cary Grant, her uncle E. F. Hutton, and other friends and relatives urged her not to go through with it. Pointedly, none of Barbara's relatives save Lance—wearing that perpetual moue—would be there. Jimmy Donohue, Barbara's wild-card cousin, politely demurred and then made fun of his own politesse: "They asked me if I wanted to come and I said no, because they wished to have a quiet wedding. Quiet? What am I saying—with 400 newspapermen outside!"

RUBI BLACKED MY EYE: ZSA ZSA

—New York Daily News, page one, late edition, December 30, 1953

I SAID NO, SO PORFY POKED ME: ZSA ZSA

—*New York Daily News*, December 30, 1953

While this tumult brewed in New York, Zsa Zsa called a press conference in Las Vegas. She had a black patch on her eye and a wild story to tell. She was hit "six or seven times"; she had "fierce headaches"; she was X-rayed and the procedure was photographed as evidence; she might have to skip one of her shows and ask Jolie to stand in. Her flak, Russell Birdwell, had raced into town from Los Angeles and immediately turned the ugly little spat into an international headline. "The Sheriff's office here is outraged," he reported. "They say this is the Old West where men do not hit women."

Zsa Zsa was as scathing about Rubi as she had been about Sanders a few weeks earlier. "In Spanish, Rubirosa means a red rose," she announced, "but to me it's a black eye. He said to me, 'If you do not marry me now I will marry Barbara Hutton.' I said, 'That is a smart idea.' He said, 'Why won't you marry me?' And I said, 'If I must tell you the truth, I am in love with George.' And so then Rubi hits me. But I am the luckiest woman who ever lived. He might have broken my head or my nose."

She made light of Rubi's marriagability, explaining that he got angry with her because "it was the first time in his life he couldn't marry the woman he wanted." And she had some backhanded praise for his apparent new bride. "I'm better off than Barbara, even with a black eye," she pronounced. "I think that Barbara's very brave if she does marry him. For a rich woman he's the very best pastime she could have."

The combination of Rubi's quickie wedding to another heiress and a movie star with a black eye was irresistible tabloid fodder. And newspapermen weren't alone in seizing on the outlandish events: The night of Zsa Zsa's press conference, the dancers in Marlene Dietrich's Vegas show turned up wearing eye patches; at several New Year's Eve balls, the cheeky chic wore them as well, some bedecked with rhinestones or even real gems; when Zsa Zsa next flew to New York, she was greeted at the airport by a press corps each member of which sported a patch over one eye. It was no little wonder that Eva, Magda, and even Jolie felt that Zsa Zsa had turned the family's theatrical debut into a one-woman show—and a freak show, at that.

But that was nothing compared to what was going on in New York.

RUBI SEES BABS ON WEDDING

—*New York Daily News*, page one, city edition, December 30, 1953

RUBIROSA HERE, WON'T' TALK;
NEITHER WILL MISS HUTTON

—*New York Herald-Tribune*, December 30, 1953

RICHES? "SOMETHING DIFFERENT"
ABOUT BABS SENDS HIM, SIGHS RUBI

—*New York Post*, December 30, 1953

On Tuesday, as news of Zsa Zsa's shiner made its way around the world, Rubi tried to pretend it was a bad dream and to focus on his wedding plans. But neither he nor Barbara could avoid questions about the incident. Barbara simply declared that she was "a lady" and refused to discuss her rival any further.

That night, Rubi sat with Earl Wilson in a midtown bar in an effort to put his own spin on the story, but there was no point in trying: Gossip about the wedding was everywhere. Barbara had never really recovered from the PR catastrophe that engulfed her during the Depression and the renunciation of her American citizenship. And Rubi, though given a free pass when he married Doris and for all his escapades prior to that, had been splashed all over the papers throughout the year for the Zsa Zsa business, the divorce suits, and the loss of his diplomatic post. Combined, they were a lightning rod. Predictable snipers such as Walter Winchell and Hollywood gossip queens Hedda Hopper and Louella Parsons took their shots, but comedians, too, got in on the sport: Bob Hope, George Jessel, and Eddie Cantor all had at them. A droll aphorism made the rounds: "In America, the poor get poorer and the rich get Porfirio Rubirosa." Even on the street they were hounded: Rubi was making his way to Barbara's apartment in the middle of it all when some New York wisenheimer recognized him: "Next time you'll marry Ft. Knox!"

You would think a couple of foolish kids could just get married in peace. . . .

BABS WEDS RUBI–KEEPS MONEY/SAYS "SÍ"
AS DOMINICAN CITIZEN

—*New York Daily News*, page one, December 31, 1953

RADIANT BABS YEARNS FOR A BABY;
COUPLE PLANNING TO LIVE IN PARIS

—*New York Post*, December 31, 1953

RUBI MOVES IN HIS WARDROBE; HE IS STAYING

—*New York Daily News*, January 1, 1954

EVERYTHING LOOKS BLISSFUL AT PIERRE

—*New York Daily News*, January 2, 1954

On Wednesday, they awoke determined to put a happy face on whatever it was they were doing.

By lunch, word had gotten around that the ceremony would be held not at the Dominican consulate but at Dr. Salazar's home at 1100 Park Avenue. Prior to the event, the couple would deign to sit with the press for a brief while at Barbara's suite at the Pierre.

Leland Rosenberg, now described as an agent of the Dominican government, met the mob of one hundred or so newsmen in the lobby and escorted a party of them upstairs. They milled about sampling a few bottles of booze and trays of canapés, then Rubi strode in, affecting mock surprise at the size of the assembly—hands to his cheeks as in Edvard Munch's *Scream*. His hair, perfection, was combed back in the usual left-to-right part and he was done up in his wedding day best: black suit, light gray shirt with a subtle black stripe, black-and-white-check tie. (Rosanno Brazzi eat your heart out.) He radiated such happy cheer that you could almost start to feel good about the thing.

Then Barbara arrived, and that inkling of joy quickly vanished. She looked drawn and weak. And her outfit—black taffeta Balenciaga dress, deep purple velvet coat, and a black taffeta Dior hat with purple lining—gave her a funereal aspect. She almost stumbled into the room. "I feel as though someone hit me on the head," she exclaimed. (One wag on the scene snickered, "For her fifth wedding, the bride wore black and carried a scotch-and-soda.")

In their brief tête-à-tête with the media, they revealed that they had been in love since Deauville in July. "He told me he loved me," she remembered. "And I didn't believe him. But I'd loved him from the first moment I met him—and I'd known him a long time, really." She couldn't understand, she added, that people didn't believe it was the real thing: "No one will give anyone credit for liking me because I'm myself. And I love him so much." She blamed the press for this perception, branding them "people who crucify people like me," but she admitted, too, to having fed them fodder, namely "all the silly things I've done but didn't think were silly at the time." She seemed genuinely shocked when asked if it was true that the marriage proposal came over the phone—"I don't think the telephone is a very good medium; do you?" Rubi perked up at this, patting the green settee on which they sat, averring that he'd popped the question "on this very sofa."

It all made for a disquieting spectacle. And Rubi didn't exactly lighten it. Uncharacteristically brief with reporters, he categorically denied everything Zsa Zsa said about his slapping or wanting to marry her. (Years went by before he would admit to the incident: "Okay, we used to quarrel. And once, during a tiff, she received a black eye. Then she gave a party to show it off and have it photographed.") Asked about why he had chosen Barbara as his fourth wife, he couldn't find words. "Miss Hutton has brought something into my life . . . ," he began, and then turned to Barbara for a quick consultation in French. She finished his thought: "Call it sincerity."

Perhaps he was ashamed of the scene they were making, or perhaps, as he wrote, he was disturbed by the physical change that had come over her. Just the night before he had bragged to Earl Wilson about what great shape his bride was in: "I don't like skinny girls—and she's all right!" But when she turned up at the wedding, she was visibly altered for the worse. "I regarded her anxiously when I got to the Pierre Hotel," he remembered later. "A new nervousness assaulted her. All the effects of the medical treatment had disappeared."

And yet he remained as committed to the task in front of him as if he were in a polo match or an auto race. With whatever moxie or greed he had, with all his tricks of suavity and his athlete's calm, he would marry her, regardless, despite, in front of everyone: *tíguerismo* on an order to make even Trujillo blanch.

He helped her up and out and through the throngs in the lobby and into a car for the quick trip uptown for the ceremony. There, they were greeted by yet another crush of newsmen—"Tell me," Barbara gasped as she got out of the limo, "is this really happening?" In Dr. Salazar's apartment, they were met by Ramfis Trujillo, Jimmy Donohue, who had apparently changed his mind about the business, a few Dominican officials, and a few friends. Adolescent Lance, suited and scowling, had, like Rosenberg, come along from the hotel.

The ceremony was conducted in Spanish—both principals answered "*Sí*" when taking their vows—and seemed unnecessarily protracted to onlookers unused to the formality of Hispanic rituals. Rubi slid the usual gold band set with rubies onto her finger and a plain gold band onto his own. The entire wedding contract was read aloud and four copies were signed. Barbara was so flustered that she inadvertently put down "B. Troubetzkoy" as her name.

They posed for pictures. Barbara turned to her new husband: "Aren't you going to kiss me now? The press has waited for so long. . . ."

Nice.

They stopped for the press once again in the lobby, and then they went back to the Pierre for a champagne reception, joined by the witnesses, Dr. Salazar and his family, and a few more friends and family members: no more than two dozen merrymakers, or less than a quarter of the press contingent that was waiting downstairs. Jessie Woolworth Donohue—Barbara's aunt and Jimmy's mother—stayed for a decent interval and even allowed the groom to kiss her hand, but she left quickly enough, fulfilling her duty but making her point. Barbara, whom everyone referred to as Mrs. Rubirosa, sipped champagne and repeatedly announced how out of sorts she felt: "I could die I'm so tired!" And she babbled to a guest that she wanted to have a child: "Oh, I would like to have another baby . . . a child for my wonderful husband . . . it would be such a great thrill . . . but I am probably too old . . . I'm 41."

There was little feeling of festivity, and in less than two hours the guests all departed, Rosenberg going downstairs to tell the reporters there'd be no more show that night.

In Manhattan, anyhow.

At airports in New York and Los Angeles, reporters managed to buttonhole ex-inamoratas of both newlyweds, Bob Sweeney and Marianne O'Brien Reynolds; both wished the couple well and moved briskly on.

But in Las Vegas, Zsa Zsa laid on another press conference. With an eye patch and a photo of the wedding as props, she went wickedly to town. "See how unhappy they both look," she laughed. "I give them six months."

On second thought, she reckoned, it would be even quicker: "In a couple of weeks this man will be after me again. He certainly did not jilt me. Ten days ago he sat in my mother's New York shop and begged her to get me to marry him. He even tried to get my attorneys to hurry up my divorce. But I never wanted to marry that man."

And she got in one final slap of her own: "I love George; Rubi loves me; Barbara loves Rubi; but who loves Barbara?"

(That would be Hungarian for "meow.")

MRS. RUBIROSA BREAKS ANKLE

—*New York Times*, January 8, 1954

RUBIROSAS CHARTER AIRLINER

—*New York Times*, January 13, 1954

RUBIROSAS FLY TO FLORIDA

—*New York Times*, January 14, 1954

In the coming days, the Rubirosas sorted out details of their honeymoon and mutual future. They had considered a trip to Ciudad Trujillo, where the swank Hotel Jaragua along the seafront had reserved its best suite (Rubi kept a bungalow there as his only true Dominican home). But they settled instead on Palm Beach, where the social season was at its height, complete with top-flight polo and the auto race at Sebring in which Rubi would drive for the Lancia team. Their base would be the Ocean Drive villa of the maharaja of Baroda, a palace boasting a full-time staff of six. Rent was a cool $10,000 a month; they took a three-month lease.

Before they could get down there, however, Barbara took a tumble in the bath and broke her ankle. Rumors flew: Rubi, blacker of Hungarian actresses' eyes, had beaten her; Barbara, shocked at the spectacle of Rubi's wedding night arousal, had fled and tripped. Whichever: She was in a wheelchair, and travel would be a nightmare. So they rented a plane—a whole eighty-eight-passenger Constellation from Eastern Air Lines, $4,500 one-way—and headed toward the sun, with an entourage that included the talented Mr. Rosenberg and Barbara's miniature Doberman, Cocotte. (Lance had already flown off to California and his classes at Pomona College, declaring to reporters en route that he and his new stepdad "have been good friends for a long time.") One last audience with the press, at Idlewild Airport, and then they were Florida's problem.

Once again, they proved a circus.

They kept different quarters in the maharaja's home and kept to themselves largely (at least one witness to the business suggested that there was no sex, and Rubi would later hint that such whispers were true: "How could I? She was on drugs!"). Rubi played polo, drove, hit the nightclubs, and shopped: By one account, he added several dozens each of suits, shirts, sweaters, slacks, sports jackets, and pairs of pajamas to the trousseau he had assembled at Dunhill's and the $1,370 he spent outfitting himself at the A. Sulka boutique in Manhattan. Barbara barely left her rooms, much less the house, still hobbled by that bum ankle, still rattled by the ghosts she could never shake.

She blamed her injury: "It's disgusting. My husband is going to play polo and I will have to sit and look at the sea." And, indeed, his native restlessness made it virtually impossible for him to sit solicitously by her side, holding her hand. "Darling," he was said to have told her, "I don't drive a car which has a broken wheel or take out a lame horse."

But, truly, he didn't have to convince her to stay home. She had no interest in the sporting life that consumed him, only showing up once to watch him play. (The Trujillos were there, too, both Ramfis and the Benefactor, and the older man wasn't impressed with his former son-in-law's latest conquest. "You're losing your touch," he sneered. "Look at who you've married. She's an old hag." Rubi answered, "Yes, but . . ." and made the universal sign of money by rubbing his right thumb back and forth over his fore and middle fingertips.)

There was some sun in this grim scene. One week after they arrived in Florida they celebrated Rubi's forty-fifth birthday at the Moulin Rouge restaurant. Along with some friends and the Cuban guitarist Chago Rodrigo, who served Rubi as a kind of roving accompanist, they had what everyone described as a lovely evening. The bride's gifts to her husband, echoing those he had received from Doris, included jewelry, a string of polo ponies, a plantation in the Cibao, and, most spectacular, a B-25 even more elaborate and luxurious than the one that Doris had bought him and had been wrecked in New Jersey. With its massive propellers and wingspan, the World War II–vintage bomber was a stunner in its own right. But even more amazing was its interior: All traces of its original purpose had been removed, and it had been retrofitted with brass, mahogany, gilt, leather sofas, coffee tables (one with a built-in radio), green broadloom carpets, reclining arm chairs with beige upholstery, and a bedroom area complete with closet and leather-paneled bathroom. It stupefied people, and, at an estimated $250,000, it better have.

But mostly the honeymoon was given over to Rubi running off and seeing to himself while Barbara fermented in her signature low, anxious hum. Rubi put a melancholy veneer on his account of the times, "This marvelous place, which could make a couple happy, was, for us, a clinic. Barbara failed to follow faithfully the course that had, with discipline, been her treatment. There was no honeymoon. She didn't leave her room. She refused this world of sun, light, sport and happiness. This attitude made a common life difficult."

That was the positive spin—such as it was. The darker version, provided amply by Barbara's old friends in the Palm Beach colony, was that Rubi ran roughshod over her, chasing women brazenly (one glamour gal got a shiner from her husband simply for chatting with him) and bringing them back to a trysting spot that he kept in a discreet complex of garden apartments on Peruvian Avenue. He made quick trips to Ciudad Trujillo and to Miami, where Ramfis Trujillo had repaired after the wedding ceremony to stay on his massive yacht, the *Angelita* (named for his kid sister) and was engaged in polo and epic *parrandas:* booze, music, floozies. This dark Rubi frankly terrified his neurasthenic wife of less than a month: Cobina Wright reported that she found Barbara weeping quietly in a corner at a party. "It's Rubi," the new bride explained. "One of these days he'll do me in."

There was no dramatic explosion of tensions, no epic scene in which this mockery of a marriage burst apart so that everyone could know. One day in February, Barbara simply packed her things and left the house, moving in with her aunt Jessie Donohue, she whose hand Rubi had kissed just weeks prior, at the exclusive Everglades Club.

"Barbara is definitely through with that disgusting man," Jessie pronounced.

Almost. Almost.

―――

Phoenix in the winter of 1953–54: sunny days, cool nights, few locals, fewer tourists, the exclusive suburbs that would in later days draw snowbirding socialites still taking shape: a perfect spot to get away—a quick vacation, maybe, or a project you'd prefer to undertake out of the glare of big city attention.

The latter was what brought Zsa Zsa there in January: a film, *Three Ring Circus,* a gigantic production starring the comedy team of Jerry Lewis and Dean Martin and featuring the Clyde Beatty Circus, which wintered in Phoenix in preparation for its touring season. The film's title could well have described the atmosphere surrounding the shoot: After eight years together, Martin and Lewis had been feuding both with each other and with producer Hal Wallis in the months leading up to their arrival in Arizona, and people were astounded at the hostility they expressed toward one another. It was all Wallis could do to keep the peace.

So perhaps it was the desire to concentrate on her work and her failing marriage and keep clear of the press who were poking around her feuding costars that made Zsa Zsa decide not to stay at the Arizona Biltmore with the rest of the principal cast and crew but to bunk at the Jokake Inn, an upscale dude ranch in nearby Scottsdale. Or maybe it was because she was traveling with tumult of her own in her wake. Rubi, playing at piloting with the same seriousness with which he played at auto racing, hired a copilot and flew his new plane to Phoenix one misty night to conduct a reunion.

Zsa Zsa would later claim that she begged him to stay away. But Rubi found her readily enough and there was already a cover story in place: A room in the name of William Perkins—his old pseudonym—had been reserved at her hotel. That little service was provided by Mary Lou Hosford, a wartime disc jockey and New York scenestress who had, like Joanne Connelley, been "discovered" by Ted Howard (he got her name in the papers by encouraging such stunts as riding a horse to El Morocco). Married to an heir to the John Deere fortune but with her eyes on a bigger prize, namely Cornelius Vanderbilt Whitney, whom she would marry in a few years, Hosford was something of a genius at simultaneously dazzling the press and keeping them at bay. "Tell them everything," she famously aphorized, "but don't tell them anything." She was herself staying at the Jokake Inn while supervising the construction of a winter home in Scottsdale, and she was obviously delighted that her boredom would be interrupted by a bit of glamour, scandal, and skullduggery.

When he arrived, Rubi was whisked from the airport to Zsa Zsa's side. The next day, the two went along with Hosford to watch the sunset and eat a picnic dinner at her home site: chicken, roasted peppers, a bottle of wine: ordinary folks. When they headed back to the hotel it was dark. The women walked ahead on the narrow pathways with Rubi contentedly following.

Out of nowhere, a flash of light, a clamor of voices: a knot of reporters: Word was out.

"Is Rubi here, Zsa Zsa?"

With his athlete's instincts, Rubi bounded into the bushes bordering the path. Zsa Zsa screamed a denial, insisting that she would never allow herself to be involved with a married man. Hosford pushed through the pack of pressmen to enlist the hotel manager's help in getting rid of them—and, more important, in seeing that Rubi wasn't discovered. She and the manager came up with a plan. Arthur Wilde, a publicity man working on the movie, would drive out to the hotel, walk through the lobby, and then hop in a car with Zsa Zsa and Hosford; the reporters, mistaking the dark, handsome Wilde for Rubi, would certainly follow; when they did, the hotel manager would drive Rubi to Hosford's unfinished house.

As the plan hatched, and Zsa Zsa walked along with her little pack of newshounds, Rubi stayed in the shrubbery and got soaked by sprinklers. Eventually, the publicist arrived, and the decoy was put into motion; as predicted, the reporters followed on what turned into a wild-goose chase around the city and the surrounding desert. Rubi and a change of clothes were taken by the hotel manager to the rendezvous, where he had a couple hours to brood over the indignities of the evening.

When Zsa Zsa and Hosford finally shook the press and joined him, he wasn't happy: "Where the hell were you?"

The next day, he got back in his flying palace and returned to Palm Beach and Barbara.

Talk that he'd been in Phoenix didn't die, however. A reporter reached him and he acted utterly dumbstruck by the question. "How did this start?" he asked. "I have just been down to my Dominican farm in La Vega. Be sure to get that right—*La Vega*, not Las Vegas. I've been talking to my wife every day by telephone from there. She wasn't worried."

Zsa Zsa denied everything as well. But the press dug and they pretty much had the story; there was no record of Rubi flying in or out of Miami International Airport, but a man answering his description was confirmed by three Phoenix airport employees to have arrived and departed on a private flight.

Busted.*

RUBIROSAS SEPARATE

—*New York Times*, March 14, 1954

Barbara was back in New York by St. Patrick's Day.

Officially: "We regret that we have mutually decided that it is wisest for us to separate. Our separation is entirely friendly and any public statement giving a different impression is completely incorrect."

That was how she tended to characterize her bust-ups: happy events.

It sat like that for about a week, and then Rubi sailed into town, too, taking a suite at the Plaza, just a block from Barbara's bat cave at the Pierre.

And he called reporters round to share the state of his heart.

They photographed him spooning out a window toward a view of Central Park. "Never again will I marry a woman of wealth," he sighed. "Perhaps it is better that I marry a poor girl. This is what I will do."

He complained gently of the differences between himself and his soon-to-be-ex. "We are very different people. I am very active and I like to go out at night. She wanted to stay home at all times and read books. This is a very boring life. If she had led a normal life, I would have been very happy. But she wanted to stay home all the time. She liked to stay in the house all day, and I like outdoor sports."

* As a silly denouement, Rubi was actually offered a part in *Three Ring Circus* by producer Wallis, who thought he could get a cheap laugh at the end by having Rubi pull up to Zsa Zsa's character at the end of the story and ask her, "How about hopping in and taking a ride with me, baby?" Less vulgar heads prevailed and it never came close to happening. But the B-25 actually *did* appear in a movie. In 1969, its then-owners leased it to the producers of the film of Joseph Heller's *Catch-22*, who required an entire fleet of authentic World War II aircraft; by all accounts, Rubi's was far and away the most luxurious of the lot.

He swore it was all meant to be different. "I married her because I loved her. . . . It may have been conceit, but I really believed I was the man who could change her into the lovely, intelligent, elegant woman she can be. . . . Almost on the day of our wedding I knew it could not be. . . . There was nothing I could do to beat off the sickness and sadness that engulfed her."

He insisted that he'd been faithful to her, that he never visited Phoenix, that he took nothing from the marriage save a framed photo of his wife of less than three months. He wished his new ex-wife well—"She is a very, very nice girl, and I hope she can find a man she can keep around the house"—and ended with words of wisdom: "Don't marry too young. A man should be 35 before marrying. I was but 23 when I began. It was too young."

It would be the deepest his thinking on the matter would get. But it wouldn't be his final word.

That, amazingly, would come in a huge newspaper story at the end of March, a confessional ghostwritten by James D. Horan and Jeffrey Roche of the *New York Journal-American* and the *Los Angeles Examiner,* two of the chief outlets of the Hearst media empire.

In it, Rubi once again anatomized Barbara's condition: "I do not think that Barbara is a sick girl, but for some reason she does not want to participate in an active life." But this time a note of revulsion seeped in. "I am horrified at the thought of a healthy person who stays in bed all day as Barbara did. I like to go out with my wife and enjoy life."

He hoped she could be cured of her malaise: "I truly wish that my wife, Barbara Hutton, would abandon her way of life. Then with her poise, beauty, education and enormous wealth she could well become one of the leading ladies of her country."

And he declared himself to be outraged by suggestions that he had been anything but a loyal husband: "This, of course, is to throw the lies back into the mouths of the gossips and the whisperers who insisted that I was spending my evenings with ladies other than my wife. Let me emphatically emphasize at this time that this was not true. . . . I am sure that there are plenty of people who would prefer to believe that I escorted beautiful young ladies to chic night clubs and that I left Barbara home while I led a very gay life." But that wasn't it at all, he said. "It was simply a case of a vigorous life failing to fit in the pattern of a quiet one. Surely it has happened before to other people and undoubtedly will happen many times to still other people."

In the end, he invited the world to blame him for the whole thing. "For my final word, let me say that I am sorry. Let's say it's all my fault. But I couldn't trade the polo field, the excitement of the racing car competitions, the open air and the zest for a full life—for the reclusion which she preferred."

Of course, he could afford to take the blame. They had been married about seventy-five days. He had the $2.5 million cash payment, the plane, the plantation, the clothes and jewelry, the polo ponies, plus incidentals. Call it $3.5 million (about $24 million today).

It was disgraceful. And it was an audacious success: Having publicly and crassly latched on to Barbara and her money, he was, for all purposes, immune to every possible drag on his progress. He could live with the ill repute he had cultivated in certain circles because he had the money and, frankly, the standing. He had hurt Barbara, probably, but she had been warned amply and, besides, he was hardly the first. He could even afford to sit with the press and muse about the whole business with a poker-faced brass that any politician would envy. No *tíguere* ever had such gall, reach, and fortune.* And on top of it he was world famous.

If there could be said to be an acme of his profession, he had reached it.

═══

Meanwhile, across Fifth Avenue, Barbara wore her exorbitantly expensive outfits and sat in darkened rooms, chain-smoking, sipping drinks, gossiping in a low voice, sobbing, making plans: a broken thing.

* Well, there was Leland Rosenberg. Having passed from Lance Reventlow to Rubi, he attached himself to Trujillo, who deemed him an extraordinarily helpful fellow, gave him Dominican citizenship, and appointed him to a series of governmental and diplomatic posts, including a legislative seat and the ambassadorship to Iran. In the course of his work for the Benefactor, Rosenberg grew wealthy, and Rubi was once overheard asking him for a taste of the bounty he'd accrued on the strength of the introduction to the Trujillos Rubi had made for him.

"Now everyone thinks I'm crazy," she told a reporter. "Do you think so?" And then she drifted into disconnected thoughts about her son, her previous marriages, an old flame.

By late June, she was traveling as Barbara Hutton and he was in Ciudad Trujillo placing the public newspaper notice that was the requisite means under Dominican law of initiating a divorce proceeding. It wasn't entirely clear that Dominican courts had jurisdiction over the union—technically, they may never have *officially* been married—but as everybody simply wanted the thing to go away, that was that. A year later, at the end of July 1955, they were entirely quits.

She wasn't done with that yearning search of hers. There were affairs—one with James Dean, she claimed, about a year after Rubi. There were two more marriages—homosexual German tennis champion Gottfried von Cramm (never consummated) and Raymond Doan, a bizarre, inscrutable Laotian artist for whom she purchased the title Prince Vinh Na Champassak—and another grand home, a folly: an authentic Japanese palace in Cuernavaca.

Lance, ever the kid turned on to fast cars by Rubi ("he seemed like a terribly nice guy," he swore), became a pretty good gentleman amateur racer in an era that was faster and more competitive than Rubi's. His mother was sickened by the danger, and she offered him opulent bribes to quit the sport, one of which was an L-shaped house in Beverly Hills with a then-one-of-a-kind indoor-outdoor pool. (He was twenty when he got it; he also owned a farm in Surrey.) He shared Barbara's poetic restlessness but had a ripple of his father's steel in his heart; it suited the occupation he shared with Rubi: oblivion through speed, competition, and women. He married Jill St. John in 1960, and they split three years later, and then he married a former Mouseketeer. He ran with the fastest crowd on the Sunset Strip in its frothiest days, and he financed the legal defense fund of the kids arrested in the Sunset Strip riots. He formed a company to build his own car, the Scarab; it won a big race once at Riverside.

His Cessna went down in Aspen in 1972. He was thirty-six.

Barbara was living mainly in hotels by then. She had never paid a lick of attention to her finances, and, in her indifference, leeches, some with the most genteelly beguiling aspects, bled her white. When she died at the Beverly Wilshire Hotel seven years after Lance, she had her homes and precious objects, and her name and repute, but there was a mere $3,500 in cash in the bank: at age sixty-seven, picked bare.

She always hated when people called her "poor little rich girl."

Turned out it was true.

=======

With the charade of Rubi and Barbara's marriage over, it was left for Zsa Zsa and Sanders to throw in the towel on their own farcical union. In January 1954, Zsa Zsa had counterfiled against Sanders, charging him with inflicting "grievous mental cruelty, distress and anguish" on her. On April 1, their fifth wedding anniversary, she sat in Santa Monica Superior Court and convinced Judge Stanley Mosk to approve an uncontested divorce. Wearing a black veil, Zsa Zsa testified for ten minutes to the effect that Sanders "does not want to be married; he wants to be a bachelor." She explained that he had several times moved out of the house or gone to Europe without her "because I spoiled his fun." When her attorney, Jerry Geisler, asked her if Sanders maintained a separate residence throughout the marriage, she finally broke down sobbing: "He says he had to have some independence." (To be fair, at least one newspaper reported that she was already in tears as she posed for photos before entering the courtroom.) Also testifying was her secretary, Cathy Kalt, who corroborated her employer's words and described Sanders as "very moody." Sanders himself didn't appear, and after about twenty minutes Judge Mosk granted the divorce request, announcing that it would become effective, per California law, after one year.

Her third divorce in a decade secured, Zsa Zsa wiped away her tears and headed to Cannes for a film premiere—via New York, where Rubi was still ensconced at the Plaza Hotel pouring his heart out to the press. She decided that she, too, had best hold a press conference so that the world would know that she had no designs on him.

Would she be seeing him in New York? she was asked. That wasn't her intention. What about France? "I don't own the airline," she replied. "I can't control who the passengers will be. I don't know whether he will be in Europe. How do I know if I may bump into him in a nightclub." (He had his own way of addressing the matter: "My marriage is finished and certainly I cannot be expected to stay home alone!")

Of course, they were together already. Jolie had vacated her apartment and helped Rubi sneak in, giving the couple several days alone. When reporters got wise and started camping out on the doorstep, he was trapped. Jolie devised a ruse: She left and returned to her house several times in a large overcoat and concealing hat, as if she was trying to avoid prying eyes; then, against his protests, she dressed Rubi in the same get-up and he was able to skulk in drag through the pack of photographers unmolested.

The following week, Zsa Zsa was in Paris, and he was right behind her. And she called yet another press conference—so that the world would know they were still together. "When he married Barbara it was easy to predict the marriage wouldn't last," she said. "Now he is coming back to me." And would they marry? "Who knows whether I will marry him. I don't know myself. I am still sore from this divorce I just had with George. It cost me a fortune. It hurt my feelings besides. If things between us stay as they are a year from now, we'll get married. He loves me more than I thought he did. He always comes back." But what about the shiner she got in Vegas? "That was a publicity stunt that went too far," she confessed. "I fired my publicity man after that. [True.] Especially as it inspired a lot of silly people to imitate me. One starlet even wrote to me suggesting that I get into a fight with her which would give us both publicity."

Rubi dove into the thing unbridled, with enough of a nest egg that he didn't especially care how it looked. "Was it callous of me to rush at once to the lovely Zsa Zsa?" he asked a reporter. "I suppose so, but that's the kind of man I am. If a thing is over, it's over. That's how it is, whether it's a marriage, a love affair or a business deal."

On April 9, just eight days after her divorce hearing, they were out on the town, hitting all the usual spots. When they arrived at Jimmy's, his Montparnasse haunt, they had a full coterie of reporters and photographers in tow. He got testy with them: "You will not take any pictures of me with Miss Gabor." That wasn't, apparently, the way she saw it. She posed; they had words; she cried; he hollered, "Get out! I don't need you!"; she raced away. The next day, with all the tabloids in Paris splashed with accounts of this fracas, they rode horses together in the Bois de Boulogne: all better.

They went to Cannes; they went to New York. When they got off the plane there, reporters noticed that Zsa Zsa was wearing a diamond ring; the story went out on the Associated Press wire. She insisted they weren't engaged: "When we are free, then we will be engaged." Someone asked Rubi if they'd marry. "I hope," he said. "Why not?" And Zsa Zsa chimed in: "We don't speak of marriage. We're petrified of marriage." So, a reporter wondered, is this just "a nice platonic friendship?" The two of them burst out laughing.

On to Los Angeles, where she had to shoot the pilot for a comic TV western tentatively titled *Zsa Zsa the Kid* (as she had been warned by her agent, film offers were drying up because of the adverse publicity she was garnering with Rubi). They landed in the B-25 in Burbank after a twelve-hour voyage that included stops in Memphis and Phoenix (Rubi had listed Zsa Zsa as a "stewardess" on his flight manifest). As their twenty pieces of luggage were unloaded, Zsa Zsa explained that the jewelry that everyone was asking about was her "working diamond" and not an engagement ring. "We're engaged," she said, "but we cannot speak of marriage because neither of us is yet free."

In fact, all they did was speak of marriage, and it was all anybody else seemed to talk about. Edith Sitwell, the avant-garde English poet and eccentric, was living in Los Angeles at the time and somehow bumped into the couple. She thereafter gossiped about the affair with surprising zest. "He must be a charming man," she surmised to a reporter. She called him "Porfirio the Persecuted" and compared him to Lord Byron as a figure of unwarranted public rebuke. "What a pity he doesn't read more," she concluded. (Rubi, who prided himself on his vast knowledge of the life of Napoleon, took great umbrage on hearing this: "How the hell does she know how much I read?") In a letter to another reporter she declared of Rubi; "What an appalling man! So awful as to be enthralling!"

(So awful, too, as to be chasing other women still: Jimmy "the Weasel" Fratianno, the Mafia stoolie, recalled a competition with Rubi at this time for the affections of one Celine Walters, a New York socialite, would-be actress, and amour of Paul, King of the Hellenes. "This Rubirosa was trying to fuck Celine but she wouldn't give him a tumble," the Weasel said. "Rubirosa can't give her the royal treatment I give her in these joints. All this bowing and scraping, these broads eat it up. They like the best table, to be with somebody who's respected. That Rubirosa's a big shot, but he don't get this kind of reception.")

In June, Rubi and Zsa Zsa flew to New York, shaking off a gaggle of press men at the airport. "It is unfair to come out to meet us so early in the morning," Rubi mewled.

From there, they went back to Paris and then down to Le Mans for the Grand Prix, during which Rubi's codriver crashed their Ferrari in only the fifth lap; prior to the race, Zsa Zsa had been hanging around in the pits, causing one French mechanic to hoot admiringly, *"Et voilà un chassis!"*—"Now, *there's* a chassis!"

Then they flew back to Los Angeles on a commercial jet.

Thousands of miles and scores of hours in airplanes in a matter of weeks. They had ample time to put their heads together and make plans. And what did they come up with? A movie plot. Inspired, perhaps, by *Zsa Zsa the Kid*, they decided they would make a western together.

Zsa Zsa set about commissioning a script from Andrew "Bundy" Solt, a family friend from the Budapest days who had become a screenwriter with such pictures as *The Jolson Story, In a Lonely Place*, and *Little Women* to his credit. *Western Affair*, as his finished work was dubbed, was a story about love between rival saloonkeepers in Deadwood Gulch, South Dakota—a French showgirl and a Spanish nobleman.

In Los Angeles, Rubi dedicated the summer to perfecting a western twang, practicing quick draw tricks with pistols, and learning how to act under the tutelage of Michael Chekhov, a nephew of Anton Chekhov and an actor and acting guru in his own right. He did cowboy bits wherever he went; when he met Gary Cooper at a Hollywood party, he greeted him with "Howdy, pardner," to which the actor replied, "Why you ol' ornery buzzard!"

"I had never seen him so enthusiastic," Zsa Zsa remembered. "Somewhere inside him was a man who desperately wanted to achieve something for himself." (Years later, she reflected, "He hated being a kept man. George Sanders wanted to be a kept man, but Rubi hated it.")

Insanely, Republic Pictures, the B-movie studio where so many cookie-cutter westerns had been made through the years, thought enough of the project to throw a little development money at it and sign Rubi to a contract for $1,500 a week—*if* he could get a work visa out of the Immigration and Naturalization Service. In July, through attorney Michael Kohn, Rubi sought a special disposition that would allow him to make the film. His request was denied, according to Herman R. Landon, the INS district director in Los Angeles, because "the conditions that would permit such employment have not been met." But Landon was, by his own admission, leaned upon by morality watchdog groups who didn't want to see the likes of Rubi sully America's movie screens. "There have been expressions of opinion against Mr. Rubirosa and his plan to make the film," he said. "While these protests were not the controlling and deciding factor in the case, they were considered in the decision to reject Mr. Rubirosa's request."

Rubi's lawyer appealed the decision. "We're just shooting in the air with our appeal," Kohn admitted. "We have no knowledge of the reason why the request was denied, but our brief will take into consideration the reasons similar applications have been turned down in the past— lack of unique ability and the possibility that an American actor will be deprived of a job." But it was for those reasons precisely that, in September, the INS issued a final denial of the petition.

That ended the film as far as Republic was concerned. For a few months, Zsa Zsa kept alive the tiny hope that it could be made, perhaps in Mexico, where the work visa would not be an issue; she even got it into her head that they could get surrealist auteur Luis Buñuel, who was then living in Mexico and whom she seemed only to know for his recent

film of *Robinson Crusoe,* to direct the thing. But—perhaps justly, perhaps to posterity's loss—it was never to be.

By then, she was en route to Germany to make a film (in which Rubi
was rumored falsely to have been offered a small role) and they were
still dropping hints to the press about marriage. But their hearts didn't
seem in it quite so much. The back-and-forth between Paris and Los
Angeles kept interrupting their work responsibilities, such as they
were.

"In Paris now they are having their last farewell," Jolie Gabor confided to a journalist in the spring of 1955. "She can't marry Rubi, the
darling boy, because he's so jealous. This time it's over. She will be a
very big shot in Hollywood and in television. She would have to give
that up to marry Rubi. He is so jealous of Zsa Zsa he is even jealous
of me."

And they themselves would constantly reveal a deep-seated ambiva-
lence about tying the knot. "Marriage could not increase our happiness," Rubi said, fairly enough. "I am going to have to start running
because I don't want to get married," Zsa Zsa told a friend, only half
joking.

He was, as ever, looking at other women: He was linked in the coming months with Ava Gardner, Empress Soraya of Iran, and Gregg Sher-
wood Dodge, the onetime pinup girl who married an heir to the
American automobile fortune. He was back in Los Angeles in October
1955, and again two months later. Reporters caught him at the airport
both times.

But in the spring of the following year, Zsa Zsa announced her engagement to building magnate Hal Hayes, who sealed the deal with a
20-karat diamond ring. Deeply moved by this new love, she—what
else?—called a press conference. "I heard from Rubi about a week ago
from Florida," she said. "He calls me all the time. He wanted to marry
me but I never wanted to marry him. Rubi lives an entirely different
life. He lives all over the world and I like to live in Hollywood and act.
I like hard work and being an American." A week or so later, she sat
with reporters again: "I was in New York last week and Rubi was in the
same hotel. He was very broken up and he wanted me to forget Hal and

marry him. He is a wonderful man—much nicer than the newspapers picture him. But I could not marry Rubi. He wants me to give up my career and live with him in Paris. I could never give up acting. It is my life."

And that was about it: three years, two marriages, a mountain of newspaper clippings, at least one disastrous holiday eve, an airplane, a pile of eye patches, an ocean of gossip, a true love that was truly not meant to be.

Jolie, who counseled her daughter repeatedly not to forge a union with Rubi, took all the credit. "It is my fault that they never married," she boasted. "I was dead against it although I liked Rubi very much."

Zsa Zsa went on to appear in B-movies and TV shows and sit beside Merv Griffin and Johnny Carson countless times—and to marry again and again and again: Six poor souls followed Sanders to her side at the altar of marriage.*

Rubi, for his part, was philosophical and perhaps even wiser. "Zsa Zsa is very gay and wonderful company," he mused to an interviewer. "She will make the right person a good wife. But I am going to think very hard before I marry again."

* Sanders, perhaps even more befuddled, married Zsa Zsa's older sister Magda in 1970, for about six weeks; he killed himself in Barcelona two years later, leaving behind a note that read, in its gist, "I am bored."

THIRTEEN

CASH BOX

CASANOVA

"Must a man be assertive?"

"He must never paw a woman. A woman does not like to be
pawed. She likes to be . . . ah . . . liked."

"What happens when you meet a girl? Does she look at you
and do you look at her and—zing?"

"Yes. Zing!"

"Then what?"

"I ask her out. If she likes me, she says yes."

"Do you send her flowers the next day?"

"Yes. I send her flowers and a little note."

"A love note?"

"No. Something like 'Thank you for last night.' "

"And when you take her to dinner, is it a fancy one? Are you
a gourmet?"

"Yes, I love good food. If she likes that, we have a good dinner. But some girls don't care. If she likes hot dogs, I buy
her a hot dog."

"How about dancing?"

"I take them dancing a lot. Women like to be gay. I like to be gay.
   They want to be happy. I try to make them happy."
"Does it require something special to marry a wealthy girl?"
"No. They are like everybody else."
"Would you marry a poor girl?"
"Yes. Rich girls are too difficult."

—Radio interview, 1955

It was the Eisenhower 1950s, mind, before Elvis and the Rat Pack
and JFK. Some things were not done. And Rubi did them, frankly, in
public, for money, with a smile and a smooth word. He became a real
fascination, and the facts were as exciting as the whispers.

The day after Rubi married Barbara, Jimmy Jemail, the Inquiring
Photographer of the *New York Daily News,* walked around midtown asking random passersby, "What does Porfirio Rubirosa have, anyway?"

"Latin charm," advised Karal Lindbergh, a (female) Manhattan cos-
metics executive, "is appealing to many Anglo-Saxon women."

"He is a diplomatic Mike Hammer," bubbled Kim Wiss of the ad biz.
"It's like the fascination of the cobra."

Confided Cornelius Joyce, a racetrack official from New Hampshire,
"My doctor friends tell me it is a form of atavism" (he neglected to add
why he had sought medical insight into the question).

And Susan Webb, student of Glen Cove, sagely opined, "It seems to
be human nature for women to be attracted to the wastrel. He seldom
has any trouble getting along. Women go out of their way to help him.
Rubirosa is in this category. He has charm and physical appeal. He'll
go through life without any trouble."

Thanks to Barbara, he had been named one of the Tailors Guild's Ten
Best-Dressed Men just that winter, his youthful love of handmade uniforms having evolved into a mature, internationally recognized eye and
sense of style. Oleg Cassini would, shortly, solicit Rubi's opinion on the
design of men's shirts; fashion-conscious European and Caribbean acquaintances would often admire some detail of his formal or, especially,
informal wear and adopt it as a look: jeans and a sports coat; shoes without socks; ascots; a crimson polo helmet that made its owner impossible

to miss amid other players' bobbing white heads. His physique in his mid-forties was still lean, firm, narrow-waisted—drenched, his five feet nine inches never topped 170 pounds—he could still race and ride and swim and fence and play tennis and dance and be up all night and do whatever else was required (he took judicious naps to maintain this rigorous schedule). He was careful with his skin, wearing broad-brimmed hats in the sun and applying lotions and even honey to his face when he played polo. His hair was impeccable: tastefully flecked with gray, immaculately groomed by such high-end crimpers as Jerry Spallina at Madison and Fifty-seventh in Manhattan. He was considered such a connoisseur of women that he was twice selected as a judge in the Miss Universe pageant, in 1954 and 1958. He had improved on the guitar and drums. He could speak at least five languages, three fluently.

He was an ideal of the part, the very image of the Latin lover. And the world ate it up.

His operatic folly with Zsa Zsa and Barbara may have been played out beneath the cloud of American censoriousness: McCarthy, Hoover, the Hollywood Production Code. But it found its way into the mass consciousness not only through the mainstream press but through a new breed of publication that was beginning to seep through the wall of censorship meant to keep decent Americans from accounts of such men and such deeds: *Whisper; Hush-Hush; On the Q.T.; Inside Story; Exposed; Uncensored; Exclusive; Sensation;* and the biggest and boldest of them all, *Confidential.*

They offered their readership—a curious coalition of aficionados of movie magazines, men's true-life stories, girlie mags, and women's romances—a blend of celebrity gossip, rumors about international society, political smears, news of the weird, and, on occasion, real journalism: muckraking articles about airline safety, the Red Menace, the dangers of cigarette smoking, and the fixing of TV quiz shows. Monthlies composed with low-fi graphics on cheap paper, they screamed out to readers with titillating headlines:

"THE SKELETONS IN RED SKELTON'S CLOSET"

"WHY SINATRA IS A TARZAN OF THE BOUDOIR"

"ARE GALS MAKING GLEASON GO-GO-GO FOR BROKE?"

"THE STRANGE ORGY OF SHELLEY WINTERS"

"THE IMMATURE WORLD OF VICTOR MATURE"

"OPERATION HOLLYWOOD: CUSTOM-TAILORED BOSOMS"

"THOSE PHONY BEGGING NUNS"

Sometimes based on scuttlebutt that had been around for years but never printed, sometimes being told for the first time by sources such as private eyes, hookers, hotel maids, and others shocked or disgruntled by their brushes with the rich and famous, these stories were written with a terse, lingo-rich voice cribbed from the likes of Mickey Spillane and Walter Winchell, writers whose through-the-keyhole style and attitude the scandal rags avidly appropriated. Articles referred to women as "chicks," "pigeons," "dames," or "dishes"; gay men were "limp-wristers"; prostitutes were "pay-for-play" or "loot-for-lovin'" girls. And much of the writing was done pseudonymously by their small staffs or by otherwise legitimate writers out for a quick payday or unable to unload some especially salacious story anywhere else: A cursory once-over of a representative selection of tables of contents reveals such outré noms de plume as Jacques du Bec, Truxton Decatur, Harper Genus, Horton Streete, J. Shirley Frew, and Chumley Yorke.

Confidential, a virtual blueprint for the others, was founded in 1952 by a crew that included a publisher of such soft-core girlie mags as *Titter* and *Wink,* an editor from the *Police Gazette,* and another editor who had made a name for himself as a repeated friendly witness for Senator Joseph McCarthy's Red-baiting Senate committee. The magazine took a famously heedless tack against movie publicists, politicians, and the social elite, publishing every damning thing it could and daring those it exposed to sue. It operated under a ruthless cloak of practical necessity: When, famously, *Confidential* amassed proof of Rock Hudson's homosexuality, its editors struck a bargain with Universal Pictures,

Hudson's studio, which provided in exchange for their silence on Rock the dirt on Rory Calhoun, a lesser star who had amassed an extensive criminal and jail record as a juvenile in Oklahoma. By the mid-1950s, the lawsuits started coming—Doris Duke filed a big one for the magazine's insinuations about her relationship with an African prince—and the Hollywood community was trying to encourage prosecution for charges ranging from obscenity to what would in a later day come to be known as stalking.

By then, *Confidential* and its brethren had made a mainstay of Rubi:

"CASH BOX CASANOVA"

—*Confidential*, March 1954

"SECRETS OF A SUCCESSFUL LOVER"

—*Bold*, June 1954

"THE GIRL WHO SAID 'NO' TO RUBIROSA"

—*Sensation*, July 1954

"RUBI'S GREEK SECRET!"

—*Exclusive*, August 1954

". . . UP IN ZSA ZSA'S BEDROOM"

—*Confidential*, September 1954

"THE GLAMOUR DEB WHO MADE RUBI RUN"

—*Confidential*, January 1955

"HOW RUBIROSA PROCURES HIS WOMEN"

—*Inside Story*, April 1956

(and much later, but irresistibly)

"WHO DONGED THE DING-DONG DADDY?"

—*Confidential*, April 1962

A surprising amount of the material these magazines dug up on him was true and even newsworthy: the story of the Bencosme murder, complete with photos of the rat-faced Chichi Rubirosa; the story of the Aldao jewels; the story of brother Cesar's woes in Greece; George Sanders's amazing Christmas Eve raid on Zsa Zsa's house. Some was of far lesser interest and intensity—accounts, mainly, of women who got away. And a good deal of it was merely punched-up versions of his well-rehearsed life story, such as it could be researched, confirmed, and written on minuscule budgets of time and money.

In January 1957, when they were still feeling their oats sufficiently to publish articles like "Joan Crawford's Back Street Romance with a Bartender" and "Girls! Beware of Elvis Presley's Doll-Point Pen," the editors of *Confidential* found a new way to work Rubi into their pages. "The Vine that Makes You Virile," screamed the headline on the cover, teasing an article about a tropical elixir called Pega Palo. According to the story (written by the magazine's editor A. P. Govoni under his actual name), Pega Palo grew abundantly and was widely and cheaply for sale in the Dominican Republic. One simply had to clean it, chop it into chunks, and steep it for a few days in liquor; after that, a mere jigger of the stuff worked as both an aphrodisiac and a pick-me-up; the beneficial effects, it was said, could last two days; Rubi, it was said, enjoyed two jiggers a day—there was even a photo of him with a glass in his hand.

The whole business was news to Rubi. "The photo was taken in some bar somewhere," he remembered, "and what I was drinking was without any doubt an 'Americano'—a whisky." In fact, he said, he wasn't interviewed and had absolutely no idea what Pega Palo was or how he came to be associated with it.

The stuff called Pega Palo was actually known more commonly as *funde (digitaria exilis* or *digitaria iburua)* and was originally brought from West Africa into the Dominican Republic, where it grew abundantly, back in the Columbus days; it was imported as a cereal for porridges. But now, with the inadvertent imprimatur of the world's greatest stud, it was enjoying a new currency in the American marketplace of chatter as a liquid aphrodisiac. Indeed, currency was the key word; not long after *Confidential*'s Pega Palo article, the vine was being bottled in the United States as Fortidom, a wild night in a bottle.

Made with Dominican *funde,* packaged and sold by the Bridges Company of Houston, Texas, Fortidom was, out of the gate, a $1 million business—and, as Rubi knew, nobody could do business on that scale in the Dominican Republic without the significant involvement of Trujillo. Soon after the article appeared, Rubi was in Ciudad Trujillo trying to finagle a slice of the deal. He approached the minister of health, who was all wrapped up in the business. "How can you use my name in all these deals," he wanted to know, "without asking my permission and without offering me any participation?" The bureaucrat gave him a look that indicated that they both knew how it had happened, and declared, "You know who the only person is who could give such orders."

As it turned out, the Dominican source for the Bridges Company's *funde* was a plantation and refinery owned wholly by Trujillo, who had ingeniously devised a moneymaking scheme out of his former son-in-law's sexual notoriety. Rubi was beaten at this particular game before he'd even sat down at the table, and he knew it. "I went to Paris," he said. "A few days later, I received generous compensation in the form of a dozen trial bottles of Pega Palo."

There was an additional irony in the crossing of the interests of Rubi and the Benefactor in the pages of *Confidential.* In the United States during the heyday of scandal rags, celebrity gossip served as a kind of cognate to the more chilling sort of whispers and lies associated with McCarthyism and the Red Scare—lips loosened in the direction of select ears could and did sink lives. At the same time, in the Dominican Republic, gossip was used even more brazenly as a tool of civil control. And, as in so many other things, Trujillo was a master at the nefarious business of death by scuttlebutt.

Listín Diario, then the most important daily newspaper in Ciudad Trujillo, was, like every other key component of Dominican life, controlled, through puppets and discreet dodges, by Trujillo. And its public letters page, the *"Foro Publico,"* was used by the dictator to cow, denounce, and expunge anyone who fell short of his approval—and not just in their work, but in their private comportment as well.

Trujillo was one of those fastidious sadists who placed the highest premium on personal grooming, polite manners, and moral uprightness. Never mind that he was the sort of tyrant who preyed on young girls throughout his country (legend would have it that some Dominican families deliberately hid their daughters away or even scarred them so they wouldn't in mid-puberty be set upon by the Benefactor); everyone in his circle had to conform to his courtly ideals of appearance and decorum.

His punctiliousness puzzled and frightened everyone—in no small part because Trujillo literally had the power of life and death over his countrymen. By the 1950s, some twenty years into his reign, he had massacred and raped and emptied the pockets of tens of thousands. He had a secret police force, the SIM, run by a half-German, half-Dominican named Johnny Abbes García, a pudgy, vicious killer who oversaw a variety of operations of intimidation, extortion, murder, and torture both at home and abroad to protect *trujillismo* from its oceans of enemies (the SIM killed with both an electric chair and a block-and-tackle suspended over a vat of boiling oil). And he had, as well, his pen—and access to all media distributed in the country. With the tools of physical and psychological terror, he forced the entire country to knuckle under. And it would be hard in some cases to say whether the tortures inflicted by Abbes García or the genteel tyranny of the *"Foro Publico"* were more degrading.

Each day in the pages of *Listín Diario* there would be letters from a variety of citizens who had only the best interests of the nation and its people and its leadership at heart. Some of these would be praising this or that bit of modernization and progress. And perhaps rightly so: If nothing else, Trujillo certainly brought the Dominican Republic into the twentieth century, constructing for the first time in most of the nation such basic public works as roads, sewage systems, electricity, waterworks, telephones, schools, hospitals, and the like, not to mention profitable industries that, to be fair, were so monopolized by him and his inner circle that they constituted an entrepreneurial rather than a national empire.

But the majority of these letters were of the poison pen variety—and were certainly more widely and carefully read than any of the accompanying paeans to macadam roads and flush toilets. Correspondents to the *"Foro Publico"* would wonder aloud what the world was coming to when this or that minister or military officer or bureaucrat was drinking too much at a social occasion or speaking inappropriately about something or other or was seen going into a house not his own in the middle of a workday. Readers would pore over these missives with their sweet teeth bared and the hollows of their stomachs poised to tighten. Because as everybody knew, the author of most of these censorious letters was Trujillo, writing under a variety of pseudonyms, male and female. Those whose ways had offended him found themselves criticized and, often, stripped of position or livelihood or liberty or even life itself, as if the very hand of God had wrought a gossip column that did double duty as an inventory of the damned.

Rubi made his sole appearance in the *"Foro Publico"* in this period, when his international fame had eclipsed Trujillo's to a degree that the dictator couldn't abide.

In the spring of 1955, the famous playboy sat in the choicest bungalow at the Hotel Jaragua, the most modern and luxurious resort along the Malecon, Ciudad Trujillo's charming seaside boulevard, and spoke with a journalist from *Listín Diario*—one of the few truly in-depth and far-ranging chats he ever had with a reporter. He was happy to offer his opinions to a Dominican organ, he said, because the media in that country was so decent to him, particularly in comparison to the American press. "In Paris, the journalists don't bother you like in the U.S.," he explained. "I arrive in Paris? One photo and it's done. North Americans meet you in a mob and ask the most ridiculous questions. This is why I come here. Here I can really have a vacation."

He spoke about Zsa Zsa and the movie project, *Western Affair*, about his impending divorce from Barbara Hutton, about Danielle Darrieux's visit to his posh internment camp at Bad Nauheim, about his law school days. He discussed motor sports and polo and cock fighting and his taste in food and wine and his love of history and the fine arts ("I like French and English theater. The Italian cinema has reached a surrealism that's beyond reason. You want to dream a little. Mexican cinema is beautifully shot"). He griped a little bit about being too much in the sun of the media. "I don't seek publicity as you might think," he said. "Any woman whatever can call a journalist and say she has been with me and they'll publish it!" And he insisted that he was not a fortune hunter: "I don't divorce to acquire millions. If that's what I wanted, it's logical that I wouldn't divorce."

Fluffy, harmless stuff.

The next day, the *"Foro Publico"* lashed out at it.

He hasn't done the least thing to make known in the outside world—and as little here—the prosperity, progress and improvement that in all ways, material, moral and cultural, this country has enjoyed in this luminous Era.

I was also surprised to read, a few days ago in "El Caribe" [a competing newspaper], a caption under a photo of Rubirosa, declaring his statement that he had never before seen a cock fight, whereas in the hallways of his paternal home in San Francisco de Macorís there were [cock fighting implements] celebrating the victories in the nearly daily battles.

If "El Caribe" is so fond of the figure and words of Porfirio, I suggest they interview Cesar, the other Rubirosa, about his experiences in Egypt and Greece.

"Idleness is the mother of all vices" . . . how true!

Pure Trujillo, attempting to put Rubi in his place by emphasizing his reputation as a profligate, his common origins, and the disreputable behavior of his brother.

The note might have had some impact on the readers of *Listín Diario*, who perhaps thought slightly less (or maybe *more*) of Rubi after reading it. But it had none on Rubi, who left the country the morning it was published to play polo in Palm Beach and then returned to Paris. Indeed, it was more than a month before he saw the column and cabled a response from France:

I read the Foro Publico of April 12 which says that I have contributed nothing to the external or internal knowledge of the progress our country has made in this luminous Era. I wish it to be known that as a great admirer of the great works of Generalissimo Trujillo I have told and continue telling more than anyone about the great works that our beloved leader has realized.

If Trujillo didn't believe a word of Rubi's letter, he nevertheless allowed it to be printed. The public slap was meant more for Dominican eyes than as a genuine upbraiding. Indeed, as the exchange demonstrated, Rubi was unique among Dominicans in being granted the temerity of standing up to Trujillo, even if only in this modest fashion, because his international fame and éclat were true assets to the dictator and his regime. He was so celebrated and ubiquitous that he was suspected to be something more than a mere playboy—a key conspirator, surely, in some byzantine scheme of the Benefactor's. There was an element of truth in this, to be sure, but not in the way that the mainstream press surmised. *Argosy* magazine sent a query directly to Trujillo's office asking, "Will you either confirm or deny that Porfirio Rubirosa, while posing as a glamour figure of the international set, is actually a 'hatchet man,' as has been charged, in direction of a worldwide counter-movement against the Caribbean Legion underground?" This was a truly hilarious claim: If Rubi had had any role in countering the Caribbean Legion, a loose organization of mercenaries who hired out against various despots in the region under the rubric of freedom fighting, it wouldn't have been the sort conveyed by the term "hatchet man"—unless there was some use for a hatchet in a nightclub or on a polo pitch. A functionary drew up the government's incredulous response: "Congratulations. This is the 52nd time this question has been asked me, but this is the first time I will expose Rubi for what he is. Yes, Porfirio Rubirosa's pursuit of well-heeled broads is actually a mere cover for his real role as head of our Anti–Caribbean Legion underground Boudoir Brigade."

Trujillo felt entitled to such a mocking stance because he was in the midst of celebrating himself in a massive jubilee marking the twenty-fifth year of the era that bore his name. A huge fair was planned with his youngest child, Angelita, as its queen and representatives from nations all around the world converging on the Dominican Republic for an exposition of the nation's progress and achievement. Books were published—epic poems, histories, biographies, even an entire encyclopedia of *trujillismo*—and hundreds of thousands of dollars poured out of the national treasury into infrastructure improvements and beautification of the area around the fairgrounds. It was a mammoth expression of the Benefactor's cult of personality . . . and a colossal failure. Though there was representation from elsewhere in the world, it wasn't a diplomatic A-list, and the tourism that the event was meant to generate never materialized—and this at a time when Cuba, the neighbor island from which Trujillo always feared a hostile invasion, was becoming a favored vacation spot for big-spending, freewheeling Yankees.

It was a hard blow against Trujillo, and he had worse coming. Just as he was indulging himself in monumental accounts of his triumphs, the Caribbean was turning into a tinderbox of cold war intrigue and international subterfuge. Trujillo had effectively squelched all opposition within his borders, but he was ever alert to the possibility that exiles and outside agitators could threaten his realm. He gave Johnny Abbes García and his cadre of thugs and saboteurs free rein to go after enemies of the regime, whether they were hiding in Cuba, Costa Rica, Venezuela, Guatemala, Honduras, or Nicaragua—and even to pry loose hostile governments, right from the top if necessary.

And he continued to do away with anyone who criticized or fomented against the regime in the United States. In the fall of 1952, Andrés Requena, a dissident novelist and newspaper editor living in Manhattan, was lured to an unfamiliar address and gunned down in a dark hallway when he got there; no one was ever arrested for the killing. More spectacularly, four years later, Jesús de Galíndez, a Spaniard who fled his homeland after supporting the losing side in the civil war and who then spent years in the Dominican Republic working first as a bureaucrat and then quietly agitating for reform of Trujillo's government, disappeared.

Galíndez wasn't, like Angel Morales, the intended victim in the Bencosme killing, a potential usurper of Trujillo's seat. Nor was he, like Requena, a semipublic figure, rabble-rouser, and man-about-town with the ability to draw publicity to the anti-Trujillo movement. Rather, he was an egghead, the sort of malcontented wonk whom Trujillo would normally dismiss as not having hair on his chest. But he had been at work for years on a book—it would serve, in fact, as his dissertation at Columbia University—that tirelessly and exhaustively examined Trujillo's abuses of power, human rights, international law, and economic justice. He had submitted it to his doctoral committee in February 1956, and had made plans to publish it, in Spanish, later in the year. Trujillo tried to buy him out—he offered him $25,000, much more than publication would have netted him—but Galíndez refused. On March 12, he gave a lecture on Dominican affairs at Columbia, accepted a ride to Central Park South from some students, waved good-bye at the top of the subway steps at Fifty-seventh Street and Eighth Avenue, and was never seen again by anyone friendly.

It was a few days before the quiet Galíndez was missed, and by then, of course, police were working from cold clues. But more than one investigator, news organization, and diplomat connected the dots between the vanished scholar and the Dominican despot, and the case quickly drew attention in more exalted places than the NYPD missing persons bureau. There was a rumor of a Dominican ship docked in Manhattan on the night of the disappearance, of a large parcel—perhaps a human body—being thrown into the boiler; it didn't pan out. Another line of investigation, the possible involvement of Galíndez in intrigues involving the Basque separatist movement and the CIA, also turned out to be a dead end. The little bit police had—notes found in Galíndez's flat, principally, and fears he had expressed to his friends—suggested a Dominican connection to the disappearance, but there was far too little to go on.

That slim thread grew significantly more easy to follow, however, in the fall, when a car was found abandoned near an abattoir in Ciudad Trujillo. Its owner, Gerald Lester Murphy, a twenty-two-year-old American pilot, was missing and presumed dead by Dominican investigators.

But Murphy was far more connected to the world than Galíndez had been. He had parents back home in Oregon who were sure there was more to his death than mere misadventure. He had a fiancée, a Pan Am stewardess, who had been in the Dominican Republic with him not long before he vanished. And he had a big mouth: He had been on a toot in the last few months, bragging about his newfound wealth, partly earned, he said, in his new job with the Dominican national airline, and partly earned, he hinted, after a secret mission he'd flown the previous spring—airlifting an invalid from Amityville, New York, to Ciudad Trujillo.

The Murphys' scrappy congressman, Charles O. Porter, spearheaded an inquiry into the incident—and, by extension, of Trujillo's rule and the support Washington had given it; a lengthy investigation began into the United States' policy in the Caribbean and the sorts of regimes which were benefiting from the American impulse to keep the peace in the region. At the same time, Galíndez's book was published in Spanish throughout Europe, South America, and the Caribbean. Trujillo tried to explain away Murphy's death with an unbelievable cover story—the pilot had been driving along with a Dominican army officer and made a homosexual pass at him, whereupon the officer killed him; ashamed at his action, he later hanged himself in his jail cell. The story naturally failed to mollify the Yankees and, worse, had a deleterious impact at home, where the friends of the dead soldier began mumbling about a coup. The Benefactor was being boxed in, and his enemies were encouraged.

═══

Rubi, on the other hand, had never been more free.

Barbara's money, Doris's house, Trujillo's imprimatur in Paris, the cars, the ponies, the clothes, the antiques, the plane (which always gave him trouble—grounding him once in Shannon, Ireland), the fishing interests in Africa (he never failed to mention these) and real estate in the Cibao, the worldwide reputation, the skills of diplomacy, seduction, sport, and high living all perfected. This was the sort of life that Hugh

Hefner had in mind when he published that first issue of *Playboy* magazine a mere two months before the hurly-burly of Zsa Zsa/Barbara–gate. This was the male ideal that hadn't been yet overtaken by the surge of rock-and-roll and teen culture that would soon swamp the world. This was what suburban men envied and their wives fantasized about, the mystique behind *"¿Que Es Lo Tuyo Rubirosa?"* Movie stars, sports heroes, heads of state: None of them could get away with what he could because he was uniquely allowed to enjoy at once the reputation that accrued to a scandalous life *and* the sort of earthly rewards those who lived above reproach secretly yearned for. He was playing life with house money—piles of it—and he was sufficiently deft to be resented for the fact only by prigs.

And, of course, there were still the women. Always there were the women. Barbara wasn't the end, after all, nor was Zsa Zsa. By the time he and his Hungarian soul mate ended their mad intercontinental caravan of sensations, he had dallied among the likes of Eartha Kitt and Ava Gardner and Rita Hayworth and Empress Soraya of Iran.

Eartha was in Paris dancing for choreographer Katherine Dunham when Rubirosa came backstage to pay his respects to the artistes; she stood with her back to the wall in a narrow hallway while he passed her, grinning politely. "Handsome?" she remembered, "God, was he handsome!" The next night, a note in her dressing room: "I will pick you up tomorrow night after the show for dinner at Maxim's." The following morning, a phone call from his valet confirmed details. Fearing Miss Dunham's jealousy (she herself had dated Rubi), Eartha tried to beg out by explaining she had nothing to wear. Not a problem: "Mr. Rubirosa has given me instructions to take you wherever you want to go shopping for anything you want—at his expense, of course." She chose Pierre Balmain and a little black silk dress with matching shoes and handbag. At dinner, a rose, a string of pearls, champagne, caviar, violins. "I felt the heroine of a romantic novel," she recalled. And then he took her home. "Now came the payoff, I thought." But no: a gallant good-night, she said, and another invitation every day or so for a couple weeks, another dress, another night on the town, another chaste *adieu.* He called her, she remembered "Fire and Ice." And he drifted off after a while, upon which Orson Welles (who also didn't touch her, she swore in her implausibly chaste memoirs) started squiring her around.

Rita may have only been the invention of gossip columns, but he was her type, for certain, and they certainly knew one another when she was previously married to Aly Khan. They were spotted together at parties and such, just enough to start word circulating that there had been more between them. The rumor was that Rubi didn't go through with it because Aly said he'd consider it a favor if he didn't. That was the rumor, anyhow. . . .

With Ava it would be harder to say. They were seen together at least twice and there was talk they would be seen together more when she was finally free of Frank Sinatra. (Her love of Spanish men had even been enacted in one of her most famous films; in *The Barefoot Contessa* she was involved with a fellow of the Rubi sort, an Argentine millionaire and sportsman.) She denied the whole thing up and down: "There is absolutely no truth in the report that I am to marry Porfirio Rubirosa. I met the gentleman once in Madrid and dined with him on another occasion in Paris with other people. These are the only two occasions on which I have ever seen him." And Rubi backed her up, phoning Louella Parsons from Rue de Bellechasse: "I scarcely know her."

Perhaps. The thing was, so many famous and not-so-famous women had passed through his hands that he became a synecdoche for playboyism itself and fact and gossip about him blurred into a cocktail—and he did nothing to dissuade anyone from trafficking in what amounted to free publicity for his way of life.

======

At the height of this season of fame and celebrity, a new girl came into sight. Sometime in the spring of 1956, he got a gander at her on the cover of *Paris-Match*. She was nineteen, with a wide smile, almond eyes, freckles, voluptuous curves, a mod hairdo: a chic, Left Bank sort of girl. She was a student at the Conservatoire National d'Art Dramatique along with older classmates Jean-Paul Belmondo and Jean-

Claude Brialy. Twice she had slipped the censorious eyes of her school-masters to make films under a stage name—one starred Brigitte Bardot and was shot in Vienna; the other starred none other than Danielle Dar-rieux.

She was born Odile Berard—her paternal grandpa Jean Berard was a renowned physician in Lyon. She didn't want to sully the name—or let the officials at the Conservatoire know that she was taking paying jobs—and so the acting trade was coming to know her as Odile Rodin.

Odile had come to Paris at age five when her mother remarried after the untimely death of her first husband: another distinguished doctor, named Dupuy de Frenelle. There was a younger sister and a still younger half-sister. Even compared with the teenage Flor de Oro, there wasn't much back story to her: She was a pretty, up-and-coming young girl of the stage, better bred and prettier than most, saucy, vital, spry.

At a party after a polo match in Paris, she met Rubi, his neck still in a steel-and-leather brace after a nasty fall on the polo pitch. "I have heard a lot about you, Monsieur," she told him as he kissed her hand. "None of it good."

He laughed at her high spirits and they chatted. "She was so young and fresh, so pretty," Rubi remembered, "with a certain mystery in her gaze. I immediately monopolized her. I spoke of my country, the Caribbean, the sun beating down on the coral, the coconut groves. She listened to me smiling. The miracle is that she wasn't ashamed, didn't mock, didn't ask if I spoke like this to all the girls who fell in my path. On the contrary, when I asked her questions, she spoke gently."

As she remembered, "I found him attractive, but I was not com-pletely fascinated like the other ladies. He wasn't good looking, but he had charisma. He was not very tall, not very perfect. He had a magne-tism."

He proposed dinner. There was another night out and maybe even a third: dancing at the Elephant Blanc and New Jimmy's (the old Jimmy's, his haunt of choice, had relocated and was now being run by the famous hostess Regine). Her mother wasn't happy about the business, warning her daughter away from the man she had read about so often in the scandal sheets. Rubi invited Mme. Dupuy de Frenelle to dine with them one night, and the older woman let him know frankly of her disapproval. "Odile is in the springtime of her life," she told him. "You, on the other hand, are past your prime. You will never be able to keep up with her, and you will be made most unhappy in the end." But Rubi easily deflected that salvo and countered with his patented brand of charm. "After she danced just one slow dance with him," Odile recalled, her mother relented—or at least kept her reservations about the relationship to herself.

Maybe she just reckoned it would fade away. Odile had snagged a plum stage role: The great playwright and director Marcel Pagnol had glimpsed her first on the screen and then in a café in Paris, where the sight of her eating a piece of fruit captivated him. "I was fascinated by the dainty way she was peeling that apple," he later said. In his new play, *Fabien,* the story of a fairgrounds photographer out to seduce his wife's sister, Odile would star as the object of lust. Rehearsals for the September premiere would keep her in town and busy while Rubi followed the racing and polo seasons.

But during the summer holidays they wound up together on the Riviera. Rubi was staying with the Dubonnet family of distillery fame in their seaside villa at St.-Jean-Cap-Ferrat and Odile had been invited to stay with industrialist Paul-Louis Weiller and a large party that included Charlie Chaplin and his family. On the town in St.-Tropez, she learned that Rubi was around. She dumped her hosts, hopped into a motorboat, and sped off to surprise him at the Dubonnet house. And what a surprise! She showed up with her already sheer summer wear drenched by sea spray. "I made quite an entrance," she recalled. "I must have looked like Ursula Andress!" Rubi snatched her up for the rest of her stay, sending a car to fetch her things from the Weillers' house.

This was where the romance really blossomed, she said. "During those ten days he revealed how he truly is: attentive, always happy to get going as soon as he awakes, capable of going out 10 nights in a row but equally capable of staying at home to read or watch TV. Rubi is a man who is deeply interested in the women he takes out. He isn't satisfied merely to make a date, take her to some trendy restaurant, the theater and a cabaret. He discovers her intimately."

But what was he discovering? Pretty young girls he could have whenever he liked—he had the money, the cars, the clothes, the house, the name, the legend, the moves. . . . Odile's family had no money; there would be no dowry of plantations and aircraft. Maybe—always the dark "maybe" with him—he needed a wife to keep his diplomatic posts, a beard, as it were, for his real behavior, a screen to make him seem more reputable than he really was. Or maybe she simply made him feel young. She was brash and newfangled in that postwar way that first caught on in France and Italy before popping up in England or the States. She was truly a breath of fresh air—particularly necessary in the wake of Zsa Zsa's perfumed haze and Barbara's medicinal gloom.

Back in Paris, they kept the romance kindled but relatively hush-hush. Rubi made a visit to Ciudad Trujillo, where his older sister, Anita, was dying of colon cancer at age fifty-four. "It was a melancholy separation," Odile remembered. "I was very much in love. He too, I believe, because as soon as we were apart he didn't stop calling me, writing me, sending me telegrams as long as novels."

He made it back home in time for the opening night of *Fabien*. "Porfirio was more nervous than me," Odile said of that debut. "Always so optimistic, he was sad. He told me later he feared the worst catastrophes: memory lapses, tripping, prop failures, cabals." But she was a hit, as was the show, and the cast, crew, backers, and friends of the play were out celebrating at Drouant's when Rubi pulled up and whisked her away for a private dinner at Maxim's. Not long after that, Odile moved out of her family home and into Rue de Bellechasse.

"I was a baby," she remembered. "I wanted to have fun. I didn't want to get married. I wanted a career. But by the end of one month I was totally fascinated by him."

In early October they called in a few friends from the press to announce their engagement.

"Miss Rodin and I have decided to get married," Rubi declared. "The wedding probably will take place within one month. It will be quiet and, I hope, secret. That's all I have to say."

Odile chimed in: "I'm lucky in the theater, and I'm lucky in my private life. Now, I'm so happy."

They were questioned about the rumors that they were shacked up. "I have been living here with Rubi for the past week," Odile admitted. And when she was asked why she sported a bandage on her hand, she explained, "I cut myself when I changed his razor blades this morning."

No, she didn't cook for him, she said, and she started to explain what the servants did when Rubi interrupted, "Please, Odile." Then to the press: "There will be no more questions. We are going to marry soon and, believe me, ladies and gentlemen, you will not be invited."

On the way out, a reporter asked, "Will it last?"

"Sure," Rubi said. "I love her."

It wasn't what her mother had been hoping for. When the press caught up with her, Mme. Dupuy de Frenelle would only say, "That is my daughter's personal affair. She has gone her own way for quite some time."

Talk, of course, was everywhere.

Rubi had been so rapacious in his dealings with Barbara that he had no chance of marrying another fortune, gossips said. And Odile was simply climbing her way into a sensational position: Why not marry a vigorous man twenty-eight years her elder if it meant international attention, not to mention sharing the life of luxury he had created for himself through years of marrying up.

At the end of October, after a performance of *Fabien*, she mentioned backstage that she was getting married the next day, but nobody took her seriously. After all, none of them had been invited to a wedding. But, true to her word, on October 27, she and Rubi stood in the *mairie* of Sonchamp, a village some thirty miles southwest of Paris, and exchanged vows before a small contingent of friends that included Aly Khan, fashionista Genevieve Fath, the duke of Cadoval, Count Guy d'Arcangues, and shipbuilder Armand Boyer, Rubi's polo buddy and best man. The groom gave the bride the usual gold band speckled with rubies. They went back to town for a small champagne reception, and she made her curtain that evening.

"That night," she remembered, "I presented myself at the theater as if nothing had happened. But I must confess: the discipline I had put into *Fabien* had left me." She told her producers that she was feeling unwell, a cold, and then raced off to London with Rubi for a weekend getaway. While they were dancing in Les Ambassadeurs, one of the producers walked in, gave Rubi the fisheye, and said dryly to Odile, "So this is the cold."

As he had with Zsa Zsa, Rubi pressed her to choose between marriage and a career, and lacking the Hungarian's mettle, she caved. "Rubi made me cancel my contract with my impresario," Odile remembered. "He told Rubi, 'You are doing the most foolish thing because Odile would have a great future.'"

But leave she did, going with Rubi to the Dominican Republic for a honeymoon. They stayed on tropical beaches, walking, swimming, riding; he cooked Creole food for her and started teaching her Spanish. He had plucked her from one stage, but he was determined to groom her for another.

FOURTEEN

THE STUDENT PRINCE
IN OLD HOLLYWOOD

H e was looking at fifty.

He had money in the bank.

He had a beautiful young wife and lots of friends and fast cars and horses and a lovely house and plenty of clothes; gossip columns referred to him by instantly recognizable nicknames; Groucho Marx told jokes about him.

He was a star; he had no worlds left to conquer.

And his symbolic daddy, Trujillo, had similarly maxed out and perhaps leveled off—and might even be said to be in decline. His attempts to export his strong-arm tactics around the Caribbean were blowing up in his face, and the U.S. government was still interested in finding out just what had happened to Jesús de Galíndez and Gerald Lester Murphy. Trujillo was even older, of course, than Rubi, with all that that implied in physical decay and the stiffening of prejudices, fears, and resolve. But he was defiant in maintaining his rule—just ask anyone who'd had a visit from the SIM, which patrolled neighborhoods with listening devices, ever at the ready to swoop down on dissent. And he had hopes to extend his reign through means that Rubi could never emulate: namely, dynastic succession.

Rubi had his women and his polo and his theme song.

Trujillo had Ramfis, his replacement-in-training, the scion who would carry forth the Trujillo name and dynasty into a new century, a chip off the old block, an apple that hadn't fallen far from the tree, the living image of his father in act and deed.

Except he wasn't.

Where Trujillo was the raw stuff of a *tíguere*, clawing his way to the top, scratching his ascent over a pile of dead men and live women, nimble and cunning and ruthless, Ramfis was a despondent drag, a pouty brat who took pleasure only in the releases of *parrandas* and polo. Where the father was all comportment and propriety, Ramfis was a debaucher. Where the father calculated his progress through the world with steely precision, Ramfis was given to mood swings and lethargy. Trujillo could respect someone like Rubi, whose life, outwardly, Ramfis seemed to emulate: Rubi, like the Benefactor, rose in the world through discreet application of his ruthlessness and talents. Ramfis, on the other hand, was weak, uncertain, childish; had he been any other man's son he would have lived out his days in ignominious obscurity.

But he wasn't any other man's son; he was Trujillo's—and, moreover, his firstborn. He was going to be groomed for excellence, respectability, and greatness even if nothing in him suited the role. A colonel at age four (with a $350-per-month salary), he had been promoted to brigadier general at age nine. Graciously, he was demoted to cadet upon entering the Dominican military academy at fourteen, but he continued his meteoric rise after his aborted schooling: lieutenant colonel at twenty-one, colonel at twenty-two, and then, that same year, general once again. He was given a law degree. He was named commander of the tiny Dominican air force— even though he couldn't, at the time, pilot so much as a crop duster.

In most regards, he was a disappointment—not that Trujillo or anyone around him or, indeed, in the country would say so. While attending school in the United States as a ten-year-old, he fell into a depression and was sent to a psychiatrist; at the time, the diagnosis was simple homesickness, and he returned to Ciudad Trujillo. But it was the start of a lifelong routine of mental health care. In his manhood, he was taller than his father and more slick in appearance, but his weak chin and tiny mouth tended to give him the aspect of a pimp—and the way he did up his wavy hair and dressed far too finely for almost every occasion only bolstered that impression. He was a little musical; he would often break into song during an evening's festivities. And he was said by those sympathetic to him to have a retiring nature—which, however, was usually read by outsiders as diffidence and even contempt.

At eighteen he wed the pretty Octavia Adolfina Ricart, and they produced a brood of six children within the first decade of their marriage. But domesticity did nothing to keep him from whoring or drinking or ignoring his home life or building around him a coterie of pampered sons of privilege, among them Rubi's nephew Gilberto Sánchez Rubirosa and Luis León Estévez, the cocky little colonel who married Angelita Trujillo and was snickered at behind his back as "Chesty" for his full-of-airs mien.* With this posse of sneering upstarts, Ramfis had no time or interest to spend on his nominal duties, preferring to play polo (he was said never to have lost a match in the Dominican Republic—imagine!) and visit Miami and Palm Beach for orgiastic holidays.

He was, in short, something like the combination of the worst of his father and the worst of his former brother-in-law, Rubi, who introduced Ramfis to many of the pursuits that consumed him but stayed a judicious distance from him as well. One Trujillo at a time, Rubi learned from his first marriage, was plenty. He steered Ramfis with a ginger hand but rarely wedged himself into a place alongside him; the one sure way to reap the Benefactor's wrath was to meddle in his plans for his golden child.

Chief among Trujillo's boasts was Ramfis's reputation as a soldier. As evinced by the absurd string of promotions Ramfis was granted without ever serving a day in any branch of the service, Trujillo was infatuated

---

* Angelita gave birth to the couple's first child less than six months after her wedding, prompting one of Trujillo's most impressive acts of reshaping the perceptions of the world around him. Presented with his grandchild, the Benefactor declared, "How rare a thing this is! It's extraordinary that a five-month baby would live!" No one ever dared challenge his suggestion that his daughter was pure when she wed.

with the trappings of military glory. (His own official list of titles, honors, and citations ran to several single-spaced pages.) In 1957, he determined to initiate Ramfis into the elite echelons of the global military fraternity by enrolling him at the Command and General Staff College at Fort Leavenworth, Kansas, an advanced training school for the highest-ranking officers from around the world. It was a grueling course in logistics, strategy, theory, and even nuclear policy designed for senior soldiers from the United States and its allied countries, and admission was strictly limited to those invited by the U.S. government. As the Dominican Republic was seen as a stable friend in the Caribbean in the view of those who implemented the Eisenhower administration's Good Neighbor Policy, Trujillo was extended an invitation to fill a position, and he naturally chose Ramfis for the role.

The American government wasn't too terribly thrilled with this decision. A State Department memo of a few years earlier described the younger Trujillo as "a logical product of the environment in which he was raised . . . very spoiled, headstrong, and utterly ruthless with anyone who opposes his whims. He has a close group of friends who act in the nature of a gang of bodyguards. The group as a whole is carefully avoided by persons who do not feel inclined to be completely subservient to Ramfis." Another document told the extraordinary story of how Enrique García, one of Ramfis's circle, fell out of favor at a *parranda:* "When García fell asleep in his chair, Ramfis poured a glass of brandy down his throat, and García, reacting instinctively, swung on Ramfis and connected beautifully. Ramfis's bodyguards then gave García a working over so thorough that they had to take him to a hospital for repairs. García, upon recovering consciousness, escaped from the hospital and sought to take asylum at an undesignated embassy. He was unsuccessful in doing so. He is now reported to be under detention in a local hospital."

It was with these sorts of reports in mind that the State Department denied the request from Ciudad Trujillo to grant Ramfis diplomatic status during his matriculation at military school. Rather, upon arriving in Kansas in September, Ramfis enrolled as a colonel (as a general he would have been the senior officer in the whole facility, an anomaly even Trujillo couldn't support). But that would be virtually the only concession he made to protocol or propriety. For his nine-month sojourn, Trujillo gave Ramfis a gift of $1 million plus another $50,000 in monthly allowance.* His retinue included the usual gang of secretaries, aides, and hangers-on, as well as Octavia and the five oldest children. They all lived in a $450-per-month rented house in Leavenworth (gussied up with air-conditioning and hi-fi equipment) and, on weekends, in $100-a-day accommodations in Kansas City—the entire top floor of the town's best hotel. He had a full-time staff of seven; the Student Prince of operetta fame was a parvenu in comparison.

Ramfis had everything, it happened, save the slightest bit of interest in the work he'd been sent to Kansas to do. His course was a six-hour-a-day grind with copious amounts of reading and writing involved. His English was sufficient to the task and so, by the accounts of his instructors, was his aptitude. But he had no *ganas,* no desire: He skipped classes or busied himself writing letters during lectures. He didn't get along well with his fellow students; "he made everyone feel as though he thought we were after his dough," said one. He rarely smiled or chatted, didn't rise from his chair when introduced to fellow officers' wives, walked about in his absurdly elaborate Dominican uniforms as if encased in a protective shell.

He seemed rude, but mainly he was mopey, so much, in fact, that he started seeing another psychiatrist, probably one connected to the Menninger Clinic in Topeka. Through interviews with Ramfis the doctor reckoned that the young man's father was an outright psychotic and that several relatives on both sides of the family suffered mental disease. Ramfis was diagnosed with clinical depression and mild hypomania and put on a regimen of medication: among the pharmacopoeia, Miltown for his nervous anxiety and Doriden for his sleepless nights. (The former proved so useful to his son that the Benefactor sped its intro-

---

* Those sums didn't include the cost of the round-the-clock protection that Ramfis required. Trujillo was afraid that reprisals would be visited on Ramfis by the fiancée of slain American pilot Gerald Lester Murphy, who happened to hail from nearby Wichita. As a result, Ramfis never walked to his classes like the other students but came and went in a motorcade of armored Cadillacs. Security ran the Dominican government some $3,000 a day for two scores of armed guards, surveillance equipment, alarms, fortified cars, cameras, guns, and the like.

duction into Dominican pharmacies, declaring it "the happiness pill" and creating a fashion for it among the tiny elite of the country.) Ramfis, heedless, habitually chased his diet of pills with his father's favorite sedative, Spanish brandy, which amplified the effects of his medication in some ways and negated them in others. He was given to broody, boozy torpors; he was a mess.

When the school shut down for Christmas, he went home to Ciudad Trujillo with Octavia and the children; then he left them there and returned to the States to finish his course of study in a slightly different style. The first sign of change arrived in the form of the single most unlikely visitor to the Great Plains: Rubi. Perhaps sent by Trujillo to see what was bugging young Ramfis, perhaps alerted by his nephew, Gilberto, to the wingding that was sure to ensue in the absence of Ramfis's wife and kids, Rubi showed up and helped jump-start the party. The rented ranch house was already the scene of late-night drinking bouts, with loud music and raucous laughter keeping the neighbors up. But Rubi pointed Ramfis toward yet more fun and distraction: Why waste so much energy on Kansas, he counseled, when America held far more glittering attractions?

Rubi dressed him for the part—some $7,000 in fine clothes from a New York tailor—and then provided a truly invaluable service: He called Zsa Zsa in Bel-Air (like the decadent former lovers in *Les Liaisons Dangereuses,* they remained friendly after their affair had died) and asked her to introduce Ramfis to Hollywood, in particular to some of the actresses over whom he'd been swooning in movie theaters recently, dropping the piquant detail that Ramfis was thinking of divorcing Octavia and seeking a bride—perhaps minting a Dominican Grace Kelly in the process.

Zsa Zsa had met Ramfis on a trip she'd made to Ciudad Trujillo with Rubi and then again in New York. She reckoned she could be of help. She suggested that Ramfis come to Hollywood so that she could throw a party, and he immediately dispatched Gilberto to California to lay the ground for his arrival. When he visited Zsa Zsa, Gilberto insisted that she get on the phone to Ramfis in Kansas and reassure him that everything would go well.

"I die here," he moaned. "I don't know a soul. I am like a fish out of water. I can hardly wait to come there."

She told him of her plans for a big bash.

"Will I meet all your friends? All the stars?"

"Of course you will."

"I have a terrible crush on Kim Novak. Will I meet her?"

"She's one of my best friends," Zsa Zsa ad-libbed. "Of course you'll meet her."

The two made further plans. Ramfis had ordered that his yacht, the *Angelita*, be sent to Miami so that he could use it as a base during his school breaks. Zsa Zsa helped him pass those holidays by arranging for a guest to meet him there: Joan Collins, then known leeringly around Hollywood as the British Open, a sex kitten currently between marriages, love affairs, and movie roles. "He was good looking in a glossy, black-haired, olive-skinned Latin way," La Collins recalled. And he was catching her at just the right time. "I had never before slept with anyone unless totally carried away by passion or love. This time my motivation was mental and physical exhaustion, mixed with gratitude for a consolation missing from my life for months." As a token of his esteem, Ramfis gifted her with a choker from Van Cleef and Arpels—about 25 karats total. She protested that the $10,000 bauble was too much. But she kept it.

A bit later, the *Angelita* was docked in New Orleans and Ramfis invited Zsa Zsa herself to come join him for Mardi Gras, which she did. She, too, stayed aboard the boat. And when she got back to Los Angeles, she, too, found herself the recipient of a surprise gift: a $5,600 red Mercedes convertible roadster with black leather interior. (She never protested its richness.)

Back in Kansas, Ramfis was barely attending to his studies and finally complained to his superiors that he had developed a problem with his sinuses. They suggested he see a military doctor but he applied for and received two months' leave to see a specialist.

In California.

═══

The ensuing circus began, literally, with a splash.

A sometime actress named Lynn Heyburn—pretty, slender, twenty-three—came by the house that Gilberto had rented for Ramfis at 243

South Mapleton Drive in Holmby Hills, the celebrity enclave adjacent to Beverly Hills (the rent—on top of what he was paying in Kansas—was $2,500 per month). She had made a movie in Ciudad Trujillo a few years prior, she said, and she thought she could make contact with a niece of Trujillo's who befriended her there if she paid respects to Ramfis. On her first visit, she was met by Ramfis's spokesman, Victor Sued, along with Gilberto; they told her that Ramfis was still indisposed with the ill effects of his sinus treatment; they invited her to a party that evening; she declined. She came back the next day when, she claimed, Gilberto and his uncle Rubi met her and led her into the backyard—where they pushed her into the deep end of the swimming pool. A young woman who was apparently staying at the house ran to help her and found her a towel to wear while her own clothes dried; she holed up in a bedroom while, she claimed, Rubi and Gilberto tried to get in to see her. Her clothes were ruined; her dignity was dented; she would sue—or at least have a chunk of the Dominicans out of court. It all dragged on for months until a quiet settlement was reached.

The Benefactor would never have countenanced such capricious cruelty—not to mention the publicity it generated once the story emerged. But the set around Ramfis was far more goonish than the crowd with which Trujillo surrounded himself. Rubi increasingly kept a polite distance, sensing that Ramfis was less than in control of himself and his posse. But there was no way Rubi was going to miss the bash that introduced Ramfis to Hollywood society.

In April, Zsa Zsa orchestrated a truly all-star gala. Everybody, but simply *everybody*, was there: the Jimmy Stewarts, the Gary Coopers, the James Masons, the Robert Taylors, the David Selzniks, the Kirk Douglases, the Charles Vidors, the Robert Mitchums, the Van Johnsons. On hand were two of Rubi's rivals in the international playboy sweepstakes: Jorge Guinle, the Brazilian hotel heir, and Baby Pignatari, the Brazilian mining tycoon. There were swell dames: Shirley MacLaine, Jeannie Crain, Maureen O'Hara, Ann Miller, Kathryn Grayson, Rhonda Fleming. There were odd couples: Along with her ex, George Sanders, with whom she had recently acted in the *film à clef, Death of a Scoundrel,* Zsa Zsa invited Rubi and Odile (a photo of Rubi trying not to notice while Zsa Zsa and Odile greeted one another with plastered smiles would appear in *Life*). And there was Kim Novak, Ramfis's dream girl, beside him for much of the evening in a floral gown while he wore a big dumb grin atop his tuxedo.

Ramfis and Kim had already met before the big night: Zsa Zsa had arranged a dinner at her place. They had begun dating, making him the latest in the string of amours, public and private, that had been part of the publicity machinery concerning the rising star. She had been linked to Frank Sinatra and John Ireland (and, secretly, Sammy Davis Jr., until Columbia Pictures boss Harry Cohn had his mob buddies threaten him away for risking her career to a miscegenation scandal); there had been a fling with Aly Khan and another with Italian tomato magnate Mario Bandini; there had been directors and doctors and businessmen. She was, sigh, famously unlucky in love. And now there was the son of a dictator—a prince in all but title; it was something of a dream come true. They dated regularly; they drove about in his coupe; and he even came *thisclose* to proposing marriage. He carved their initials into a tree in a Beverly Hills park one night to prove his sincerity.

Ramfis once again combined courting with shopping. He gave Kim a lavender $8,500 Mercedes (lavender was her color, per Columbia's publicity campaign, down to the rinse in her blond hair), as well as a $3,500 diamond-and-black-pearl ring, a set of $1,500 diamond earrings, and the promise, it was whispered, to back a Broadway show in which she would star. Zsa Zsa, for her work as hostess and matchmaker, got a knee-length empress style chinchilla coat valued in newspaper reports at $17,000 (she was just about to buy it for herself, she said; *imagine* her surprise when the furrier told her that Ramfis had picked up the bill!).

All this spending could get a fellow noticed—and not just by salesmen at car dealerships and jewelry shops. There was the little matter, recall, of Jesús de Galíndez and Gerald Lester Murphy and the ire incited by their disappearances in Congressman Charles O. Porter. While Ramfis was busily buying up cars and jewels and furs for Hollywood honeys, Porter and his colleagues were investigating the actions of the Trujillo government and, in particular, the money the United States annually gave the Dominican Republic in aid pursuant to the two nations' joint Military Assistance Treaty. Congressional investigators had gotten word from Kansas about Ramfis's spending, and now they were reading in the gossip pages about these even more gaudy instances of his free way with money. In fact, some people involved with the inquiry began to wonder aloud whether Ramfis's spending in the United States wasn't exactly equal to the amount of money that the United States had sent to his father's government.

In May, Congress was set to debate a $2.95 billion foreign aid bill representing disbursements to more than one hundred countries, including $600,000 in military equipment and training personnel for the Dominican Republic (down from $1.3 million in similar aid in preceding years). Porter and his Republican colleague Wayne L. Hays of Ohio were determined that the money wouldn't get to Ciudad Trujillo without a full inquiry into the operation of the government there—and of Ramfis and his cohorts in the United States.

"The fact that Trujillo gave his boy a million dollars a year to play with while attending the U.S. Army Command and General Staff College is not only ridiculous," fumed Porter, "it is downright humiliating to America." He was just getting started: "Perhaps this federal aid should be paid directly into the bank accounts of Zsa Zsa Gabor and Kim Novak. At least that way we could get taxes on the money. Those ladies, at least, are U.S. citizens. Wouldn't it be better than paying them through General Trujillo?"

Hays (who would resign in disgrace from Congress eighteen years later when it was discovered that he kept his mistress, Elizabeth Ray, on the federal payroll) thundered particularly against Zsa Zsa, taking to the floor of the House to decry her as "the most expensive courtesan since Madame de Pompadour." When it was argued to him that money sent abroad helped create goodwill, Hays countered, "It seems to me that young Trujillo is restricting his goodwill to too small a clientele." Yet another congressman, Barrett O'Hara of Illinois, chimed in, "If it can be established that foreign aid funds are being used to buy mink coats or fancy automobiles for anyone, it's wrong, and any girl who accepts and is bragging about it is certainly indiscreet."

Among the allies of the Dominican regime in the United States, Walter Winchell was particularly keen to defend the Trujillos, for which the Benefactor sent him a telegram of gratitude (and, likely as not, a check). But for the most part, editorial writers and politicians piled on the little nation, demanding to know what was going on down there with the fruit of American's generosity.

The outbursts caused genuine concern in Ciudad Trujillo, where the government was quick to issue the sort of explanations of Ramfis's fortune that merely served to raise more questions. "He is one of the wealthiest young men in the world," said a spokesman, "and he will continue to spend his money as he wishes. It is his own personal money. He owns sugar mills and has a dairy farm." What's more, another statement continued, "the Dominican Republic has never received any outright cash grants from America." The contretemps got so out of hand that the Benefactor began looking into the hiring of an American public relations firm to repair the damage and put a bright face on his rule and his land.*

In Hollywood, the responses were equally hasty and panicked. Zsa Zsa, characteristically, shot right back at these attacks. Her attorney released an angry statement: "I would like to challenge Representative Hays to come out from behind the Congressional walls of immunity and repeat his statement. . . . I will sue him." A few weeks later, she was in Washington for a nightclub engagement and reporters asked her what she would say to Hays if she met him. "First I have to see if he's young and handsome," she replied.

More quietly, she sat at a desk at Conrad Hilton's Hotel Statler and wrote a letter to Ramfis's mother, Doña Maria, assuring her that media accounts of the situation were simply out of control. First of all, she insisted, she and Ramfis weren't involved with one another. "You also must understand that I am not in love with him, nor is he with me. Our relationship is more that of a brother and sister. And I can only tell you one thing. If I should ever have a son, I could only wish that he would be exactly like Ramfis." And second, she should understand why Ramfis was being spoken about so harshly by the press: "A man like Ramfis, handsome, intelligent, and having wonderful parents like you, is bound to arounse jealousy in many small people. On the other hand, the right people, the ones that we are concerned with, admire him greatly."

---

* There was nothing they could do about the brief craze among the young women of Los Angeles for bumper stickers reading "This car is *not* a gift from Trujillo."

Zsa Zsa's mother, Jolie, didn't have to be so careful about the business. Reached for comment on Ramfis's munificence at her jewelry shop in Manhattan, she replied, "So what do you expect—for him to send flowers to a girl like Zsa Zsa?"

Rubi, who'd returned to Paris before the storm hit, issued no statement but sent Ramfis a telegram upon hearing reports of the younger man's notoriety: "My god, you have replaced me!"

And Kim—Kim blundered big time.

The story broke when she was in San Francisco to promote Alfred Hitchcock's *Vertigo*, which was shot there. The publicity office of Columbia Pictures, where she was a contract player, whisked her back to Los Angeles, where the press managed to find her almost immediately. First, she said that the car was Ramfis's and she was just keeping it safe in her garage. Told that the vehicle was registered in her name, she acted shocked, shocked: "It must be some kind of a secret gift. Honestly, I know nothing about it being mine. Anyway, a gift like that to Rafael [she used his given name] is like a trinket to other men, like a bracelet, I mean a novelty bracelet." She then went on to anatomize his qualities to the assembled gentlemen of the press. "Everything he does is of international importance," she explained. "He is a goodwill ambassador for his country. He is a wonderful gentleman and an honor to his great father, who is doing a world of good for his country. It is a shame to bring his name into a story like this about giving cars to all the pretty girls in Hollywood. Let them pick on movie actresses, but don't let them pick on such a goodwill ambassador as General Trujillo."

Then they told her something that Ramfis hadn't mentioned in their many chats—namely, that he was married. She excused herself from saying anything more.

Columbia Pictures, still cross with her for the way she had carried on openly with Sammy Davis Jr. the year before, whisked her off to New York to do publicity for *Bell, Book and Candle*—which wasn't supposed to open for another seven months. She sat in a hotel room and received visitors from the press—and refused to talk, pointing toward a nearby Columbia spokesperson whenever she was asked a question.

She returned to Hollywood and two weeks of dodging questions.

Ramfis holed up in his house and refused to speak to the press, either, claiming he was still laid up with the sinus troubles that had brought him out west. Good job, too, as he would have had more embarrassments than ever to address. Seven members of his entourage had rented a Pan Arn jet to fly from New York to Los Angeles at a cost of $15,000 (which included gourmet food and drink service) and had filled the plane with wrapped packages. The same day, his spokesman Victor Sued was stopped for erratically driving a new Cadillac late at night in Torrance, south of Los Angeles, and booked on a drunk driving charge; he tried to claim diplomatic immunity out on the roadside, and the cops slapped the cuffs on him.

Finally, Ramfis had to go back to school—by train, he explained as he boarded a private railcar at Los Angeles's Union Station, because his sinus condition wouldn't allow him to fly. Kim came along to bid him adieu and was swarmed by paparazzi. "Goodness," she declared as the lightbulbs popped, "I'll probably get fired for this!"

When Ramfis arrived back in Kansas on the Super Chief, though, it was, ironically, he who was given the boot. He was told that he hadn't met the requirements for his military course and wouldn't be able to make up what he'd missed. If he wished, he could attend the graduation ceremony and accept a Certificate of Attendance, which nobody in the audience would be able to distinguish from a proper diploma. Instead, he thanked the officer who gave him the news (and to whom he seemed to be on the verge of tears) and made plans to leave Kansas once again for Los Angeles, where the *Angelita* would meet him and serve as a movable home away from home.*

He tried to see Kim some more, to explain that he and Octavia had filed for a divorce in Mexico (which may or may not have been true) and

---

* Trujillo got his revenge for this slight on his son: All thirty Dominican military cadets studying in the United States were withdrawn, future American financial aid was rejected by a unanimous vote of both houses of the Dominican congress, Trujillo threatened not to allow American forces to use the missile base and listening stations they manned on the island, and the Dominican ambassador to the United Nations deliberately failed to attend a speech by President Eisenhower later in the year. The fact that Ramfis didn't *deserve* to graduate didn't seem to factor into his father's thinking.

to insist that she was still the queen of his affections; he gave interviews to the press in which he professed his love for her. But the studio once again sent her to New York, where, this time, she was allowed to speak and managed with some grace to slip out of the whole tawdry thing. "I don't know if I'll ever see him again," she sighed. "If I'd been asked a couple of months ago whether I planned to date him I'd have said, I'd be delighted, I can't wait to see him. But now that he's been painted as a villain it has spoiled everything. Our romance was stopped before it had a chance to get started. If I went out with him now people would say we were going to get married. All the publicity has ruined the whole thing."

If she was done with Ramfis, Ramfis wasn't done with Hollywood. First Zsa Zsa announced that she was throwing another party for him, and the papers all went to town. After she'd gotten headlines with the story for a few days, he recognized her for the bad news she was and cut her off. Then he gave up the lease in Holmby Hills and moved onto the *Angelita*.

If that was meant to dissuade people from noticing him, fat chance. The *Angelita* was no mere pleasure vessel but a four-masted, 350-foot museum of luxuries, with fireplaces, marble, king-sized beds, hi-fi equipment, bars, a bandstand (a twelve-piece orchestra was available at all hours, along with a crew of dozens); it was probably the largest privately owned ship in the world, originally built in Germany in 1931 for (circles within circles) stockbroker E. F. Hutton and his wife Marjorie Merriwether Post, Rubi's erstwhile aunt and uncle by brief marriage. Because it carried a pair of small deck guns, which it used for ceremonial salutes and to launch landing lines, it qualified as a man-of-war and didn't have to pay harborage fees in American ports; Ramfis saved a cool $380 a week through this bit of frugality.

Throughout the summer, the *Angelita* was the scene of loud, debauched parties, of girls driving up in taxis late in the night or being whisked away by other taxis early in the morning, of a fake bomb scare phoned in by a drunken longshoreman who thought the cops guarding the pier looked bored and needed something to do. It traveled between Santa Monica, San Diego, Catalina, Long Beach, and various Mexican ports, drawing a bevy of pressmen and rubberneckers wherever it docked.

Ramfis stayed on the boat, growing sullen with booze and boredom. He managed to rouse himself to make a stab at another Hollywood starlet, Debra Paget, who came aboard with her mother and listened to his plans to produce a film of *Don Quixote* and cast her as Dulcinea; he drank the whole while until his thought muddled and he scared them off. Other, less well-known young ladies came by to be assessed for the role of the Dominican Princess Grace.

Finally he got lucky.

Lita Milan was a few years into being groomed by the Hollywood machine when she boarded the *Angelita* in a red dress and dark veil and set off a frenzy of pressmen trying to figure out who she was. She had been born twenty-five years earlier as Iris Lia Menshell to a Hungarian furrier and his Polish wife in Brooklyn; she'd been schooled some in Europe and attended some college and had a knack for languages; she spent time as a Vegas showgirl and saved her dough to move to Hollywood. From the get-go, she was lucky in landing jobs: With her long black hair and pretty, peasant girl aspect, she was described as "Magnani-esque" and often cast as a Latina or Native American. In her first three years in town, she appeared in eleven movies and ten dramatic TV series episodes, rising with such speed as to play the female leads in films as diverse as the psychological western *The Left Handed Gun* (opposite Paul Newman) and the crime story *I Mobster* (opposite Steve Cochrane). Studio publicists depicted her as a quirky bohemian who surfed, designed fabrics and furniture, did her own cooking, dug modern jazz, read existentialist novels, and disdained makeup, high fashion, and old-time mores. A *Look* magazine feature story published in the spring of 1958 depicted her reading poetry to jazz accompaniment at a Hollywood nightclub and doing scene work in an acting class with a fellow student named "Steven" McQueen.

After several visits to Ramfis on his yacht, Lita was clearly marked as a favorite, and when she flew with a girlfriend to meet the boat in Mazatlán, it was even rumored that they tried to marry but were frustrated because the prospective groom couldn't offer evidence of having divorced his first wife. There were several more cruises—Mexico, Catalina, San Diego; Ramfis kept declaring that he was leaving town and then turning back to California. Finally, he issued a statement to the press and left. "This talk of romance with professional actresses leading to possible marriage is nonsense and very insulting to me and my nation," he protested. "When my divorce is granted, then I shall seriously consider taking a wife. But she must be suitable to my position and acceptable to my father, the Generalissimo."

The *Angelita* departed. Lita waited a few weeks and then flew to Nicaragua to join it on the final leg of its return voyage to Ciudad Trujillo. Somewhere en route, on the high seas, they were married by the captain of the ship, taking no pains to confirm whether the wedding was, in fact, legal.* When the yacht finally arrived at its home port, the Benefactor planned to meet his son with an elaborate ceremony at the dock. Formally uniformed, with full official entourage, he boarded the vessel for the ceremonial reunion. In the ship's salon, he found Ramfis and his comrades so plastered on booze and whatnot that they couldn't rise to greet him; Ramfis needed a shave and fresh clothes; the ship looked like it had passed through a squall. Trujillo walked wordlessly to a table, poured himself a glass of brandy, and made a toast: "I drink to man's labor, the only thing that dignifies humanity and brings it close to God." Then he turned on his heels and left; he had no further use for such a son.

The following year, Ramfis made one more awful splash. In June 1959, two groups of invaders landed on Dominican soil—expatriots and freedom fighters from around the Caribbean determined to remove the dictator Trujillo from his perch. The attack was easily repelled by a military that had been trained for decades to expect just such an incursion. As it was the Dominican air force that had been chiefly engaged in the battle, the dozen or so survivors of the invasion were brought to the San Isidro Air Force base for interrogation. Ramfis, as commander of the air force, had them tortured and executed; he was himself a party to the

---

* Ramfis finally divorced Octavia in 1960, up to which time Lita was his constant companion and, in effect, common-law wife. They eventually had a family together and she never acted again.

cruelties and murders. And then he ordered the roundup and execution of anyone in the country who might have had a hand in abetting the invasion.

Trujillo took note of this savagery bubbling up in his son—dirtying his hands with deeds best left to henchmen—and prudently sent him off to Brussels for yet more psychiatric care (there were rumors of electoshock), the dynastic dream indefinitely deferred.

═══════

Rubi, of course, had no claim to the line of succession that Trujillo imagined would be his glory. And he was, in some part, to blame for the dissolution of Ramfis—not only by setting an example that the younger man couldn't emulate but by introducing him to the women who were, through no fault of their own, his downfall. But—and particularly in the face of the evidence of Ramfis's uselessness—Rubi was still arguably the most valuable asset the Dominican strongman had on the world stage. No Dominican had more or better contacts in Europe or the United States. Rubi, even as he settled into something like the role of aging lion, was still invaluable.

He had associates, for instance, in the world of public relations and the media, and he profited from the introductions he facilitated even when the relationships that ensued from them failed to bear fruit. In 1958, for instance, when Trujillo felt he had a need to polish his nation's reputation in the United States, Rubi introduced him to the fellows at the Mutual Broadcasting System, one of the largest news and entertainment networks in North America. Rubi's contact at Mutual was Alexander Guterma, a financial rapscallion of the highest order who had spent the latter months of 1958 and the dawn of 1959 unsuccessfully ducking a series of bankruptcies and indictments connected to his myriad investments. Through his controlling interest in Hal Roach Studios—the same folks who brought the world the filmic adventures of Laurel and Hardy and the Little Rascals as well as TV's *Blondie* and *Amos and Andy* series—Guterma had purchased Mutual in 1958, and now that he was hemorrhaging money on fines and legal fees he was in dire need of cash flow.

Need, assets, and opportunity all combined when Guterma met Rubi, who suggested that Mutual would find a useful client for its services in Trujillo. In January 1959, the Benefactor proposed that Mutual broadcast uncensored, unedited "news" about the Dominican Republic on its air in exchange for a cash infusion: 425 minutes of propaganda per month for eighteen months for a grand sum of $750,000. It was a lot of money and a lot of promise; some in the Dominican government counseled Trujillo that it wasn't worth the risk. But Rubi, according to one palace official, argued avidly in favor of the deal: "He lobbied and buttonholed. He fluttered and hovered around the power-that-was. . . . He projected that high-voltage Rubirosa personality."

His campaign succeeded; The money was delivered—Rubi took a $50,000 taste off the top for his services as matchmaker—and at least some of Trujillo's material was actually aired. But Guterma and his companies were under a withering assault by U.S. authorities throughout the year; by summer Mutual itself was declaring bankruptcy; by fall, the trail from the company to Trujillo was discovered by auditors—who also noted that Guterma and his fellow executives Garland L. Culpepper Jr. and Hal Roach Jr. had failed to register, as the law required of them, as agents of a foreign government. They were indicted on that charge in September. Guterma, hammered from all sides, pled no contest to the indictment and received an eight- to twenty-four-month jail sentence.*

Maybe Trujillo was losing his touch. Maybe he was so busy with the dozens of intrigues he had in motion that he couldn't worry about past trespasses. Maybe he was, after all this time, genuinely fond of Rubi. Or maybe he just didn't have anyone else that he could trust for certain types of work. For whatever reason, as the Guterma deal ground slowly forward, Rubi was already serving in a new diplomatic post for Trujillo,

* Rubi tried the trick once again soon after, introducing Trujillo to another man who claimed to represent a major North American broadcast entity; this fellow arrived in Ciudad Trujillo less interested in talking about propaganda than stocks, namely, the certificates he had in his luggage and which he wanted to sell to the Benefactor for $700,000. Trujillo bit—on what turned out to be forged securities.

the most sensitive, in fact, that he had occupied since he'd left Buenos Aires more than a decade earlier. In September 1958, Rubi had arrived in Havana and presented his credentials as ambassador to the government of Fulgencio Batista. He had been charged with representing his government at ground zero of what was emerging as the most explosive episode in the modern history of the Caribbean.

He had been in Havana the previous winter for the Grand Prix of Cuba, the last car race that Odile would allow him to enter, the one that achieved legendary status when a group of bandits kidnapped the great Juan Manuel Fangio just beforehand and released him just after. The kidnappers turned out to be a group of rebels living in the hills—the Twenty-sixth of July Movement, led by a charismatic guerrilla named Fidel Castro; so unknown was the group and its leader that headlines about the kidnapping in American newspapers wondered aloud if they might possibly have communist leanings. Interrupting the auto race turned out to be Castro's debut on the world stage. And now that he and his comrades were engaged in outright revolution, they would have Rubi as an eyewitness to their progress.

Trujillo had come to rely, curiously, on Rubi's contacts, renown, and blend of palaver and charm as tools of diplomacy. Few people inside the Dominican Republic reckoned much of Rubi's abilities, but few of them shared his singular gifts: the international name, the ease among the wealthy and powerful, the personal charm, the familiarity with the peccadilloes and secrets of the sort of people on whom Trujillo needed to keep tabs. Indeed, the very triviality of Rubi's fame—the high living, the skirt-chasing, the glamour—was an advantage: Who could believe that such a superficial fellow was actually an important cog of Trujillo's machinery of power? It was a guise that made Rubi invaluable to his former father-in-law.

In Havana, Trujillo counted on Rubi to use his cunning and his cool demeanor to make peace with both sides in the simmering conflict. He was, for instance, intructed to offer to sell arms both to Batista, who had been cut off by the Americans, and to the rebels (cannily, Trujillo would only sell to the government for cash but was willing to extend credit to Castro). At the same time, he was to gather any intelligence that he could from all parties, including the U.S. ambassador, Earl E. T. Smith, who, along with his wife Florence, would become a boon friend to Rubi and Odile in the coming years. Among Rubi's contacts were Dominican exiles who were unfriendly to Trujillo; he was to sound them out as gingerly as he could to determine what, if any, activities were under way that might threaten the Benefactor's regime.

And Rubi had personal interests of his own. In June 1958, he had started another business, this time with Emilio Tagle, a Chilean of independent means who raced cars and played polo and ran in chic circles in Palm Beach, where he met Rubi during the fiasco of the Hutton honeymoon. Along with two members of the Batista government, these two poured money into a mining venture in the Cuban city of Mantanzas, and Rubi hope to milk the maximum from the venture by being on the scene.

As soon as Rubi hit Havana in September 1958, he sussed out some important changes that needed to be made to secure Dominican interests there. "I intend for our embassy to have a key place in the social life of Havana," he wrote to Trujillo.

> To that end it is vital to refurnish and make over the residence of the embassy, which I have found in a disastrous state. It's a magnificent building, and it's incredible that it has been furnished in the way it has and that it has been allowed to fall into this state of decay and filth. I consider it shameful to receive important guests in these rooms. I have given immediate orders to paint the walls, rearrange the furniture and clean the rugs—steps that have already cost more than 2000 pesos. I believe we must get rid of all the furniture and lighting in the reception and dining areas and decorate them in an appropriate manner.

It wouldn't be a long stay, but it was vivid. "Havana at this time was the wildest place in the world," remembered Odile, who met Senator and Mrs. John F. Kennedy at a party at the American embassy there soon after arriving and liked to brag decades later that she was the youngest ambassadress in the world when she arrived in Havana. She and Rubi partied at the city's nightclubs and casinos; they posed for pictures at the Dominican embassy—one even showed Rubi sitting at a desk strewn with papers, a strangely thought-free expression on his face. Rubi took up yoga—yet other photos would show him attempting a variety of poses under the tutelage of an unnamed guru—and he kept up his polo, his boxing practice, his *parrandas*. He was still a famous figure: When he visited a doctor for some intestinal pains, word got out that the famous Rubirosa would be visiting the clinic, and he had to pass through a crowd of gawking admirers to keep his appointment. It was almost like Paris, specifically—given the revolution brewing in the mountains and the air of panic that infused Havana—the Paris of the prewar 1930s that had so excited him.

Following orders, Rubi met with Batista, however briefly. The president, Rubi reported to Trujillo, had "very kind words for the Dominican Republic and Your Excellency. He told me he would like to get to know the Dominican Republic and he would visit. When I asked him if I could relay these intentions to Your Excellency, he responded, 'Yes, yes . . . tell Generalissimo Trujillo that I will come to the Dominican Republic.' "

That visit would have required a thaw in Cuban-Dominican relations—the two dictators always kept uneasy eyes on one another—or something even more unexpected. On December 31, the unexpected came to pass. Rubi and Odile were dining at the U.S. embassy and, as Odile remembered, "Ambassador Earl Smith told Rubi that something was going to happen: 'You are going to maybe have a problem. Whatever happens I'll call you later on in the evening and let you know. But be ready, something is going to happen.' " The Rubirosas left the Smiths' very late in the evening and found themselves in a Havana under siege: Rebel troops led by Che Guevara had entered the city. When Rubi and Odile got to the Dominican embassy, the phone was already ringing. "Earl Smith called Rubi," Odile recalled, "and said, 'Listen, come over now to my embassy. Batista left the country and he just landed in the Dominican Republic.' "

This was a real crisis. Nobody in Ciudad Trujillo knew much yet about the rebels or their intentions, even though Rubi had made efforts to sound them out. Nor had Rubi alerted Trujillo that Batista and a number of high-ranking officials of his government would be imposing their presence on him. (Not that he could have known; Batista fled at the last minute, originally headed for Florida; when the Yankees rebuffed him, he only naturally thought of his esteemed neighbor Trujillo.) But if Trujillo was angered by all this, he would have to hold it in: Rubi and Odile remained trapped for days at the American embassy, where Smith had arranged temporary asylum for them as they determined what to do next.

"We packed at five in the morning," Odile said of that anxious episode. "We took my jewelry and the dog. . . . We were stopped by Fidel Castro's guerrillas a couple of times on the street. Thank God they didn't recognize it was Rubirosa!" As it happened, Earl Smith, still able to liaise with both the rebels and the outgoing government, had arranged for Rubi and Odile to have safe conduct between the Dominican and American embassies. As nobody knew the rebels' politics entirely, much less how they felt about potentially hostile Caribbean neighbors, it was a prudent precaution.

Given the flurry of activity in those first hours and days after the fall of Havana, it's not surprising that a number of contradictory stories about Rubi's activities survived. In one account, he helped a squad of Trujillo's SIM goons steal their way into the city and put them up at the Dominican embassy; in another, he waltzed freely about the city, stopping for a drink at the Havana Hilton on New Year's Day and spending an afternoon a few days later in a café, drinking and chatting amiably with Fidel Castro's brother, Raul; another story had him hunkered down at the Swiss embassy and sending Odile off to safety in Miami; yet another suggested that he was more preoccupied with getting his polo ponies out of the country than himself or his wife.

Odile painted a picture of the weeks following the rebels' victory that was at once pedestrian and sensational, a combination of domestic routine and martial excitement.

We stayed at the American embassy for a week but then went back to the Dominican Republic's embassy. We went through hell.

They were yelling outside that Rubi was a murderer. I couldn't understand a thing that was going on. I couldn't speak Spanish or English. One night we were watching television and all of a sudden there was this boom. I thought the embassy was falling apart. There were a couple of cars outside and they threw hand grenades—and they weren't small hand grenades. They made a hole in the patio and they were shooting through all the windows of the embassy. The guards were playing cards in the garage. They didn't hear anything. We couldn't go out any place. For four months, until we broke relations with Cuba, it was very hard for us.

During these weeks, relations between the new Cuban government and the regime in Ciudad Trujillo were volatile. Castro wanted Trujillo to cough up Batista and his cronies, but the Benefactor, who had given Juan Perón sanctuary in 1955 when he was booted from his despotic seat, wouldn't comply. Rubi remained a curiosity for Castro, who once sat quizzing the Dominican ambassador about Trujillo and his means of holding on to power. But the bombing of the embassy—in April 1959— was pretty much the final straw. By May, Rubi and Odile had left Cuba for good.

The revolution, of course, spelled the end of the mining business Rubi had entered with Emilio Tagle. Soon after the new year, the Castro government got word to Rubi that all agreements made with the Batista crew concerning the deal were null and void. Tagle tried to get some American money to keep the venture afloat, but when he arranged to meet some backers at the Hotel Nacionale, he was greeted instead by Castro's cops, who whisked him off for three hours of questioning— mostly about Rubi, his attitude toward the new Cuban government, when and how he had left Havana, and whether he was helping Trujillo plan an invasion. Tagle knew nothing, and was given leave to go, only slightly mussed, after three hours.

But Rubi would, perhaps, leave one last remembrance for the Castro regime. In March 1960, an explosion roiled Havana harbor, killing scores of sailors, longshoremen, and passersby. The *Coubre,* a freighter loaded with arms intended for Castro's militias, was sunk in a series of explosions that were caused, investigators surmised, by devices loaded onto the ship when it sailed out of France with a load of weapons purchased from Belgian concerns. Castro and his government immediately accused the United States, specifically the CIA, of this act of sabotage; many historians would come to see the *Coubre* incident as a decisive turning point in the Cuban decision to ally with the Soviet Union. But the American government denied stridently any involvement with the explosion.

There was another explanation, though, having to do not with the United States but with Trujillo. The ship, remember, had sailed with its Belgian cargo from France. And, according to insurance investigators associated with Lloyds of London and CIA informants including Cesar Rubirosa, there were two people there who might have been able to arrange for the ship to be booby-trapped before it crossed the Atlantic, abetting Trujillo by seeing that his dangerous new neighbor didn't get any stronger but doing it from a discreet remove.

One was General Arturo Espaillat, once the Dominican Republic's ambassador to the United Nations and, by the time of the Cuban revolution, Trujillo's secretary of state security.

The other was Rubi, who had been named ambassador to Belgium just one month after leaving Havana.

As in the Bencosme murder, his fingerprints were nowhere on the operation. But, then, the new Cuban regime couldn't get its hands on him to fingerprint him.

FIFTEEN

BETWEEN

DYNASTIES

On November 21, 1958, mere weeks before the rebels took Havana, the Dominican ambassador to Cuba and his wife attended a philanthropic "Cuba Gala Night" at the Waldorf-Astoria Hotel in Manhattan. They were seated at the affair at the same table as Mr. and Mrs. Nicolas Arroyo—the Cuban ambassador to the United States and his wife.

It was a late evening, and when they returned to their suite at the Plaza Hotel, the Dominicans were horrified to discover that they'd been burgled in their absence: Gone were a $7,000 mink, a $500 watch, a $200 pearl necklace, a $150 tie clasp, and $1,500 in cuff links and studs. But all of that was nothing compared with the $23,000 diamond-and-ruby necklace and earring set, purchased only the month before. Detectives gave the room the once-over and chatted with the couple: He remembered some fellow in the hallway looking right at him earlier in the evening, but there wasn't much else in the way of useful information. On Sunday morning, the theft was front-page news in the *New York Post:*

"RUBIROSA ROBBED AT THE PLAZA."

The episode was little more than a curiosity—hotel heists were a huge racket in New York for several years before and after this one. And the fact that the Rubirosas hadn't bothered to entrust their valuables to the hotel safe, while indicative of a certain naiveté, may have been due simply to the fact that they had only flown in from Havana a few hours before the gala.

No, the most interesting thing about the story was the company the couple kept: ambassadors and their wives, financiers, high-echelon politicians, bluebloods. For decades, Rubi's main society had been musicians, party girls, sportsmen, playboys, and denizens of the night; now he and Odile were likelier to hang out on the fringes of the Social Register than in the dark alleys of the Left Bank. At fifty, representing a government that was under pressure from within and without, sizing up the dynastic heir as his next potential patron, he was becoming an eminence grise, and, graying, showing the slightest hint of thickening, he looked the part. (He *always* looked the part. . . .)

It had been years since he had last chased a movie star or heiress around the world; he was no longer racing cars; he had even ceased to live in Paris proper. The house on Rue de Bellechasse sold in 1959 to a Rothschild for a cool sum reckoned by friends to be as high as a half-million dollars—figure five times that in today's money. Rubi spent about half of what he recouped from the sale on a large house with a garden at 12 Rue Schlumberger in Marnes-la-Coquette, a simple suburban village where Eisenhower had headquartered during the war and which had since then principally been known as the home of Maurice Chevalier—whom Rubi might even have seen perform way back between the wars.

He was that sort of fellow, now, the sort who could remember the days between the wars—*before* them, even; you didn't meet many his age in the hot spots that were starting to pop up, the sorts that Odile enjoyed so well. There was friction between them now, friends noticed: Whatever had made Rubi marry her in the first place there was now, four years into their relationship, a new dimension to it. Early on, it was tutor-tutee: He knew a world into which she would, with the proper cultivation, easily ascend, and he taught her what she needed to know. But once her place was assured, she may have proved a handful for him. Acquaintances don't remember quarrels so much as absences: Just as Rubi had not been a stay-at-home husband, so Odile, it was whispered, liked to be out and about. "He has taught her so much that she has outdistanced him," Ramfis Trujillo declared. A New York gossip columnist was more explicit: "It's an old story that he and his too-young wife have not been a thrilling love match for some time now," wrote Aileen Mehle (aka Suzy), adding that Rubi was particularly distressed by Odile's "continual devil-may-care attitude, . . . her obvious disinterest in the Dominican ex-playboy and just as obvious interest in any number of his men friends."

This sort of deflating scuttlebutt, of course, was far from Rubi's public image, the idea that he was the center of attention wherever he went, the glow that ensured that he was still an asset to the tottering regime in Ciudad Trujillo. He was still Rubi, still out partying, still playing polo, still looking like a million bucks, still able to grab hold of someone, man or woman, still always filled with good spirit. He learned to dance the Twist; he liked it. All that exercise and yoga had kept him limber.

A woman who met him at around this time remembered him as still a vital, charming presence. "He had an almost feline grace," she said, "wavy graying hair, quizzically arched eyebrows that could be mocking, amused or exquisitely languid, an irresistible wide smile that gave his otherwise too-handsome face a disconcerting air of sincerity."

And it wasn't just society women who were impressed by him. "He had the qualities that seemed to justify his career and reputation because of his outgoing charm," recalled Alfredo Vorshin, a Dominican diplomat who also met him at this time. "Very generous, his door was always open to any Dominican of any social class; many drank his wine and ate at his table including opponents to the regime."

It was true about his kindness to his countrymen: He never came across any of them partying in Paris without quietly arranging to pick up the tab. He enjoyed meeting high-spirited young Dominicans, like the poet he met at a roadside café who told him, "I want a life like you: drinking, dancing, fucking. . . ." Rubi laughed. "But you want to take over my job!"

At the same time, he could be philosophical, as when some other Dominicans—students and journalists exiled in Paris—told him about their grievances with Trujillo. He heard them out sympathetically, responding finally, "I'm a *trujillista,* but for me the *trujillistas* have nothing to offer. You do, on the other hand, because in the future you will govern the land. My only tie is to Trujillo. It's a friendship that has passed many difficult tests, such as when Trujillo was so hard toward me because I married his daughter."

Such savoir faire! Such dispassionate wisdom! Such cunning preparation for an uncertain future should the wind suddenly turn against the Benefactor!

He was good, Rubi was, and polished to a perfect sheen.

But he couldn't control his fate, tied as it was to the machinations of truly giant figures on the historical stage.

=====

From the vantage of his new post in Brussels, Rubi could see clearly that the Trujillo dynasty was toppling. He'd been sent there in July 1959, not so much to handle diplomatic chores as to keep an eye on Ramfis, who was there to undergo a barrage of psychoanalytic treatments after slaughtering all those rebels. Within the year, the Dominican heir apparent was released from his physicians' care and given reign over Dominican affairs in Belgium, which he handled with predictable tactlessness and crudity. Surrounded by his posse of swell-headed upstarts, including his brother-in-law Chesty Estévez and Rubi's nephew Gilberto, Ramfis acted even more grandly in Europe than he had in the United States, bolting from city to city on whims, cruelly punishing hangers-on who didn't comply wordlessly with his wishes, drinking to excess (a habit that only exacerbated the side effects of his medication), pouting, spending money. By the spring of 1960, his father had given up all hope that Ramfis could represent the Dominican Republic in the diplomatic corps—"Hell, that one's no good for anything," Trujillo railed when it was suggested that his son be given an appointment to the European Common Market. And so Ramfis holed up in a house in Neuilly-sur-Seine, right next door to Aly

Khan's digs and not far from where Rubi was living; the two Dominican sportsmen played polo regularly—virtually their only connection and one of the few healthy habits in which Ramfis willingly indulged.

Back home, the Benefactor had more pressing matters to attend to. Rightfully fearful of another invasion (perhaps from Cuba, perhaps from Venezuela, perhaps from Costa Rica—he'd aggravated them all into justifiable enmity), he simultaneously grew harsher on domestic dissenters and exported his own brand of counterinsurgency, the latter of which climaxed in a botched attempt on the life of Venezuelan president Rómulo Betancourt, who was perceived as a chief agitator against Trujillo's rule. With this provocation, the Catholic church abandoned its long alliance with his government, assigning Archbishop Lino Zanini, whom Juan Perón had always blamed for his own downfall, as the new Papal Nuncio to Ciudad Trujillo. Not long after that, the hemispheric diplomatic council, the Organization of American States, began proceedings to bring sanctions against the Dominican Republic, including an embargo on exporting petroleum, petroleum products, trucks, and spare automotive parts out of the country. And then the United States declared void a treaty that allowed for a bonus to be paid for sugar imports from the Dominican Republic—a deal that had regularly netted the Benefactor and his interests more than $13 million a year.

Of course, the Dominican Republic was of increased concern to the United States. Having lost Cuba, officials of both the outgoing Eisenhower and incoming Kennedy administrations—as well as careerists at the CIA and Department of State—kept watchful, even frightened, eyes on the country. It was a dicey time: Dominican opponents of the Trujillo regime were given at least inklings of encouragement, while the regime still commanded support in Washington. There was fear, naturally, that Trujillo's cruelties would incite a rebellion that the United States couldn't control, and those fears led to conversations between American interests and members of the Dominican government and military who—along with so many of their countrymen—had suffered personal losses and wanted to see the regime crushed. But at the same time, many in power in the United States felt that it would be too easy to pull the wrong string in Ciudad Trujillo and see the whole thing unravel and another Cuba so dangerously close.

The whole business was a mess, and Trujillo seemed to be doing his best to make it as bad as possible. By August 1960, the Eisenhower administration cut its diplomatic ties to the Dominican Republic, closing its embassy, recalling personnel (including CIA operatives), and leaving behind a single representative, Henry Dearborn, who was as connected to the American intelligence community as he was to the diplomatic corps. Dearborn made contacts among Dominican dissidents—a group that included some high-ranking officials and even some members of the extended Trujillo family, all of whom had suffered slights and worse at the Benefactor's hand. Dearborn told Washington that there was a strong sense throughout the country that Trujillo had to be removed, by whatever means necessary. That drastic tack didn't yet have the blessing of the White House, but Trujillo was increasingly being seen in Washington as one of the world leaders—including Fidel Castro, the Congo's Patrice Lumumba, and South Vietnam's Ngo Dinh Diem—whose continued rule ran contrary to American interests in the Cold War. The walls of history were closing in on Trujillo, and everyone knew he would fight to the death before he allowed himself and his regime to be crushed by them.

——————

Despite the clouds that had gathered to threaten his patron, Rubi was still chiefly engaged in the pursuit of pleasure. On January 30, 1960, he took possession of a new toy, a Ferrari 250 GT Pinin Farina Cabriolet Series II sports car, serial number 1561GT—silver with red leather interior and black convertible top, one of only two hundred of these little rocket-powered beauties the factory ever made.* He picked it up in Belgium (as in other of his automotive purchases, a tax dodge may have been involved); it must have been a joy to drive back to Paris.

He had returned to France full-time. With Ramfis no longer under the care of Belgian doctors, there was no more call for Rubi to be in

* One of the others appeared, driven by a jewel thief wearing a gorilla suit, in the film *The Pink Panther* (1963).

Brussels. Trujillo, increasingly investing him with trust, couldn't be sure where or when he'd need him next, so he invented a new position for him—inspector of embassies, a kind of carte blanche post that allowed him to present himself anywhere his singular services were called for without the formality of having his credentials recognized by the host government.

To be back in Paris was a treat and a relief: polo, night life, the social ramble. Especially the social ramble.

On the night of May 12, Rubi and Odile were at a dinner party in Ville-d'Avray, a suburb of Paris not far from Marnes-la-Coquette. They had taken the new car and looked forward to an enjoyable evening with hosts Gerard and Lorraine Bonnet and their fellow guests Baron and Baroness Guy de Rothschild, Baron Elie de Rothschild, Stavros Niarchos, and Aly Khan, accompanied, as usual, by his longtime sweetheart, the fashion model Lise Bourdin Bettina. It was a sophisticatedly late party, but when Aly failed to arrive by nine-thirty, his hosts were worried. Then a phone call: There had been an accident; Aly had crashed his Lancia sedan in nearby Suresnes and had been killed.

Rubi had already seen several friends die behind the wheel. Fon de Portago, the dashing Spanish nobleman, had been killed along with a dozen spectators in a catastrophe in the Italian village of Cavriana, near Verona, during the Mille Miglia race in May 1957. Four other of Portago's Ferrari teammates died similarly within eighteen months, including Rubi's former racing rivals Peter Collins and Mike Hawthorne. And, of course, there had been Jean-Pierre Wimille. But those men were race drivers and were killed in the heat of competition—a hazard that went with the glamorous profession. Aly was simply a zestful man going out to dinner: His girl was along for the ride, as was his chauffeur (useless in the backseat). It was a senseless death. And the very next day, Harry Schell, another of Rubi's racing chums, was killed in a practice run in Northamptonshire: a sickening coincidence.*

* Another odd coincidence: In January 1960, another pillar of Left Bank life, a sporting man from a colonial country, would die in an auto crash about forty miles southeast of Paris: the Algerian-born novelist and philosopher Albert Camus.

Odile had only just managed in the last eighteen months or so to keep Rubi out of auto racing. Perhaps this string of tragedies would turn him off the sport for good.

═══

He still traveled to keep up with the polo season. Winters brought him to Palm Beach, Florida, with its mild weather, fabulous shopping and night life, and, of course, proximity to seats of power of both the Dominican Republic and the United States.

Palm Beach remained a terribly social scene for him. His old Cuba friends, the Chilean sportsman Emilio Tagle* and the former American ambassador to Havana, Earl Smith, had retired there and were always happy to host Rubi and Odile. The polo crowd was on hand, as were acquaintances he'd made and kept as friends from that tumultuous season with Barbara Hutton. Although Rubi might be shunned by the older members of the set centered around Barbara's lordly aunt, Marjorie Merriwether Post, the younger and more daring socialites were still happy to know him. He met Barbara's niece, Marwee Durant, at a party and made a play for her. As she remembered, "My girlfriend says to me, 'You know who that is? He's supposed to be the greatest lover in the whole world!' And I say, 'No kiddin'? Hell-lo!' " He drove her home to the family estate Mar-A-Lago and her grandma hit the roof: "Under no circumstances do I ever want you to ever talk to that man again, Marwee, let alone see him." She sneaked out and saw him anyhow, claiming later that it was all chaste: "I didn't want to sleep with him; he was out of my class. Like an amateur playing with a pro."

Equally delicate was Rubi's relationship with Jimmy Donohue, Barbara's cousin who had carried on all over the world since Rubi first met him as the companion and, apparently, lover of the duchess of Windsor—this despite his homosexuality and her very-much-aware-of-it-all husband. In May 1961, Rubi and Odile had ringside seats at the Convention Hall in Miami Beach to watch Floyd Patterson defend his heavyweight boxing title in his third fight against Ingemar Johansson;

* Tagle would himself die in a car wreck in Mexico in 1961.

along with such others as Frank Sinatra, Joe DiMaggio, Milton Berle, and Debbie Reynolds, Donohue was there with a campy retinue with whom he had rented an entire floor at the Fontainebleau Hotel. After the fight, Rubi and Odile tagged along to the hotel for a drink, and Rubi found himself being uncomfortably cruised by several of Jimmy's gay chums, who had all, naturally, heard all the whispers about him. Rubi was so rattled by the scene—some rooms had been given over to an orgy—that he insisted on being chaperoned when he had to use the rest room. "Not you, Jimmy!" he made sure to add when he asked his host for some help in the matter.

Rubi had yet one more particular friend in Florida, a true spiritual kinsman who proved a connection to a world that Rubi—and, indirectly, Trujillo—very much wanted in on. Since his escapades with Zsa Zsa and Barbara Hutton, Rubi had been a fast friend of Igor Cassini, the gossip columnist who wrote under the pseudonym Cholly Knickerbocker for the Hearst newspapers. Cassini, known to chums as Ghighi, wrote an immensely popular jargon-rich three-dot column that aimed a degree or three higher in social rank than those of such rivals as Walter Winchell and Ed Sullivan; he wrote about New York's—and, indeed, the world's—top families with the same intimacy with which he covered show biz; he was widely credited with coining the phrase "jet set" to describe his subjects and their swell ilk.

The two met when Rubi was still married to Doris and first enjoying the delights of New York night life. Cassini, already well en route to his own string of five wives, found in Rubi a perfect comrade-in-arms; the two fell in with one another instantly, and Rubi would become a frequent source and subject for Cassini during the next two decades, just as he would become a consultant to Oleg Cassini, Igor's older brother, when that noted designer of women's fashions decided to try his hand at a line for men.

The kinship of Igor and Rubi was based as much on personal compatibility as on the coincidence of their usefulness to each other. Cassini had been born in Sebastopol, Russia, to an Italian countess and her White Russian diplomat husband, probably some half-dozen years after Rubi. (Like the Gabors, the Cassinis could never be ascribed specific ages; the records of their births were lost to the vagaries of history and a penchant for self-mythologizing.) With the rise of the Bolsheviks, the family left the fatherland for the motherland, settling in Florence, where father, Alexander Loiewski, took the name of mother, Marguerite Cassini, and settled into a life of cursing the Communists and chasing women while his wife set up a profitable dressmaking business.

After formal schooling in the gentlemanly pursuits of riding, fencing, skiing, tennis, dancing, etiquette, languages, and the rudiments of the liberal arts (among their classmates was Oleg's future friendly rival in the rag trade, Emilio Pucci, or, more properly, the Marchese Emilio Pucci di Barsento), the brothers separated. Oleg went to Paris and art school, quickly segueing into fashion design; Igor went to New York and Columbia University. By the mid-1930s, they were known on two continents as gay blades with wit, verve, style, and talent. By the end of the decade, they had wed American socialites and had launched professional careers.

Several marriages followed for each Cassini, and sensational professional episodes to match. After a disastrous first union, Oleg was married for more than a decade to Gene Tierney and made his name as a designer with the gowns he produced for her to wear in such films as *The Shanghai Gesture, The Razor's Edge,* and *The Ghost and Mrs. Muir.* Igor first made a splash when, as a rookie columnist for a Washington, D.C., newspaper, he so ran afoul of prominent local families that he was beaten by thugs in their employ. By the mid-1940s, he had assumed the Cholly Knickerbocker column from its originator, the viperous Maury Paul, and was wooing eventual wife number three, Charlene Wrightsman, the daughter of oil baron and scion of New York and Palm Beach society Charles Wrightsman. The two brothers' careers coincided in 1948, when Igor identified as his "Deb of the Year" Jacqueline Bouvier and became friendly with both the girl and her family, including her future in-laws, the Kennedys. Oleg, of course, went on to become Jacqueline's favorite designer, but Igor became a true friend: The Palm Beach estate owned by his father-in-law was adjacent to the Kennedy grounds, and Igor was a regular golf partner of papa Joe Kennedy and his more sporting sons, Joe Jr. and Jack.

By the 1950s, the Cassinis were ubiquitous, Oleg with his prominence in the world of fashion, Igor with his column and, for one mad winter, a TV series, *The Igor Cassini Show,* on which he chatted with celebs and swells. The brothers both had a visionary side that turned their passions into business opportunities: Oleg dreamed up and created the Sugarbush ski area in Vermont, and the two brothers collaborated in opening Le Club, one of the first European-style discotheques in New York City. But their careers were crucially different: Whereas Oleg had to judge precisely the tastes of his clientele and the fashion press, Igor soared on gusts of his own words, opinions, connections, and legend; he had an estimated twenty million readers; he was a newsmaker and a star.* And perhaps that was why he saw nothing wrong when he branched out from writing about newsmakers to shilling for them: In August 1956, he began a new enterprise, Martial & Company, Inc., a public relations firm.

Yes, that's right: a newspaperman with his own flack factory.

Over the years, Martial's clientele would include such diverse entities as the Brazilian Coffee Bureau, the Tourist Bureau of Mexico, Fiat Automobiles, the Patrolmen's Benevolent Association, the Lanvin perfumery, Harry Winston jewelers, Buitoni pasta, and, of course, Oleg Cassini Inc. Wisely, he rarely took on individual personalities as clients—that would have been an obvious conflict of interest for a man whose bread and butter was writing gossip about famous names. Rather, he concentrated on corporations and foreign countries. "That," he reflected years later, "was where the money was."

The intricate dealings of Martial weren't always easy to sort out. Because some accounts weren't seemly for him to assume, Cassini diverted them to a second company created for the purpose and run by a close family friend, attorney Paul Englander. Among these dicey accounts was, for a one-year contract signed in 1959, the Dominican Republic, which had tried several means of improving its image in the

---

* Producing a column of that sort was a labor that no one person, not even a Cassini, could handle alone. Among his assistants over the years would be a young journalist from Texas named Liz Smith who always remembered her dervish of a boss with fondness.

United States since the Galíndez-Murphy case and Ramfis's tear through Hollywood. At the time the deal was struck, Martial was doing business with a number of anti-Trujillo interests in the Caribbean and South America, and Cassini felt it would be best if the Benefactor's PR campaign be handled by Inter-American Company, the subsidiary that he vouched for but neither operated nor profited from directly.

The contract didn't get renewed after the first year, but during negotiations for it and throughout its tenure, Cassini became familiar with Dominican affairs and the Trujillo family. And that, in all likelihood, was why over dinner not long after John Kennedy was elected president, Rubi spoke to Cassini about his concerns for the state of his country should the Trujillo regime—as looked increasingly likely—tumble. Soon after, playing golf with CIA director Allen Dulles, Cassini mentioned Rubi's fear that the Dominican Republic might go Red (as the sons of a White Russian, the Cassinis were staunchly anti-Communist). And that chat was immediately followed by a conversation between Cassini and Joe Kennedy, who promised to alert his son, the president, about the situation and then immediately changed the subject to Rubi, whom he'd met briefly on the Riviera the year before: "Is he really the stud they say he is?"

Whatever Igor told the old goat worked, because almost immediately Rubi became a Kennedy family favorite. Well, a favorite of all of them but Bobby, the prig, who was always looking down his nose at friends of his father and brothers who shared those spirited gentlemen's tastes, and Jackie, who didn't care, frankly, for the cut of Odile. "Only once did I see Jackie lose her composure because of another woman," remembered Bobby's lifelong friend Lem Billings. "It was over Odile Rodin." As Billings recalled, Igor had introduced Jack and Rubi, and the two bonded: "They had one thing in common: a burning interest in women. They became friends; Jack and Odile became better friends. Rubi, never particularly prone to the vagaries of jealousy, didn't seem to mind; Jackie minded a great deal." She certainly had opportunity to mind: Rubi and Odile had the habit of popping up around them almost from the time Jack won the White House. On New Year's Eve, for instance, just weeks before the inauguration, the Rubirosas and the

Kennedys and a couple hundred other merrymakers attended a big Palm Beach bash. A photo of Odile twisting the night away appeared on page one of a local paper the next day—and no mention of the presence of the first couple–elect was made; Jackie noticed.

But far more important than a potential catfight between their wives was the acknowledgment by Jack Kennedy and his advisers that Rubi was right: The Dominican situation was a potential firestorm of trouble, and it seemed to be getting worse as the weeks wore on. A pirate radio station had been set up to broadcast antiregime propaganda. A cadre of conspirators kept asking Henry Dearborn for CIA aid in removing Trujillo and received caches of American weapons that had been shipped into the country under the guise of diplomatic material. In the spring of 1961, Thomas Reilly, an aging, American-born bishop newly installed in the Dominican Republic, drafted a Pastoral Letter decrying the greed and cruelty of the Trujillo regime and ordered parish priests to read it aloud at masses. The Benefactor had then tried delicately to silence dissent from the church, but eventually he lost his patience: In April, plainclothes military officers and policemen raided Bishop Reilly's church and rectory in San Juan de la Maguana and fairly trashed the place; Reilly, charged with incitement of treason, fled to the safety of a girls school in the capital and steadfastly continued to defy Trujillo's will and rule. It was a tinderbox that could easily turn into another Cuba, which nobody in the United States wanted to see.

Rubi thought that Trujillo could be swayed into liberalizations by a direct appeal by President Kennedy or, barring that, his father: old goat to old goat. But both scenarios presumed too cozy a picture of the relationship between the two governments. Rubi subsequently proposed a meeting between Ramfis, as his father's representative, and the new American president. No dice. Rather, in February, the White House called on Robert D. Murphy, a legendary figure in diplomatic circles who had liaised with the Free French during World War II and served as the first American ambassador in postwar Japan and then as undersecretary of state in the Eisenhower administration. Murphy had recently retired from public service and was working as vice president of the Corning Glass Company. But he was also an unofficial adviser to the new administration on foreign intelligence, and he seemed like a good choice to shuttle between Washington and Ciudad Trujillo.

In March, Ramfis was in New York and met several times with Murphy, who explained to him that the U.S. government would only reestablish financial and diplomatic relations with the Dominican Republic if a series of economic, legal, and social reforms were begun. If genuine progress was made in these areas, it wouldn't be necessary for the Benefactor to leave the country or resign from office (indeed, as he hadn't actually served as president for more than twenty years, during which time he managed the country through puppets, he didn't have an office to quit).

Murphy's hopes didn't exactly materialize. In part this was because the veteran diplomat really didn't grasp Caribbean affairs as well as he did European and Asian matters. And in part it was because Ramfis had left Ciudad Trujillo after yet another angry falling-out with his father, this time over some military appointments that didn't go to the chums Ramfis had lobbied for. Ramfis and his entourage wouldn't return to the Dominican Republic to convey Murphy's counsel but rather headed to Paris and the spring polo season. And the fact that his father had looked old and frail to him at one of their last meetings—"I told my mother that I had a presentiment that I wouldn't see him alive again"— did nothing to stop him from going off in a snit.

No, if the Kennedy administration was to deal with the Dominican situation, even if through a back channel, it would have to be in the person of the Benefactor himself. In April, the White House sent Murphy to Ciudad Trujillo to convey its desire for reform to the government. And, unofficially, bizarrely, Igor Cassini went along for the trip.

For two days, Murphy and Cassini met with the then-current puppet president, Joaquín Balaguer, and other officials; by their account, Trujillo only dropped in once, briefly, to taste the flow of the discussion. Murphy explained the American government's belief that reform was necessary to ensure a smooth transition in power upon the sad eventuality of Trujillo's giving up the reins—whether through retirement or, God forbid, illness or death. Trujillo cagily insisted that it was Balaguer who was running the show, not he. But he was sufficiently realistic about his perilous situation to listen to the diplomat's advice and cut a new deal with Cassini to produce more positive press for his country—with a bonus written into the contract should the United States once again recognize the Dominican Republic as a result of the publicity campaign. Murphy and Cassini came back to Washington to report that progress seemed possible and that even more good could be expected if the president or his father were to meet with Trujillo.

Unfortunately, nobody in the White House was listening to them. On the very days that the unlikely American emissaries were trying to broker an entente with Trujillo, a ragtag army of American soldiers and intelligence officers and exiled Cubans had attempted to overthrow the regime of Fidel Castro by launching an invasion on La Playa Giron—the Bay of Pigs. In the wake of that unmitigated military, diplomatic, and public relations disaster, the Kennedy administration lost its stomach for nation-building in the Caribbean. Cassini, who stood, at least indirectly, to gain from seeing warmer relations develop between Washington and Ciudad Trujillo, sought to reassure the Benefactor that there was hope of good news from the White House. But in reality the Dominican situation had been put on the back burner.

It wouldn't stay there long.

On May 30, the American president and his wife boarded a plane for Paris and a state summit that would mark a major step in the cultural and political renaissances of both Europe and the United States.

Rubi and Ramfis were already in the French capital, enjoying a particularly successful run of polo matches with Rubi's Cibao–La Pampa team; on the thirtieth, they claimed their fourth victory in a row, a 6–4 win at the Bagatelle over a team called Mousquetaires. The celebration was relatively low-key, not a full-scale *parranda*. Rubi had some drinks in town with the boys and then went home to rest up for a horseback ride he and Ramfis had planned for the following morning. Ramfis retired to Neuilly-sur-Seine and a night of boozing with his crew, which included his brother Rhadamés (who was in town but kept his own digs and didn't play polo), the mysterious Leland Rosenberg (by then the

Dominican ambassador to Iran and husband to a niece of the shah), Rubi's nephew Gilberto, and a few other polo-playing soldiers and relations from back home.

The next day, Rubi arrived promptly at 10 A.M. wearing a black riding outfit.

The house was buzzing with dark energy. Earlier in the morning, first Rhadamés and then Ramfis had been awakened by agitated phone calls from their mother, Doña Maria, urging them to return home but not saying why. Ramfis had reacted by calling his brother-in-law, Chesty Estévez, in Ciudad Trujillo, whom he found equally vague and adamant.

"Is everything under control?"

"Everything is under control."

"Where is my father?"

"You must come home immediately. Everything is under control, but your presence is absolutely necessary. Do you understand?"

Ramfis wasn't *sure* sure, but he knew. He hung up the phone and turned to Lita Milan: "They've killed my father."

He had no idea how it had happened or what the condition of the country was or whether the man to whom he had just spoken could be trusted. But by the time Rubi arrived, the decision had been made that a small group of them would go to the Dominican Republic: the Trujillo brothers, Rubi and his nephew, Leland Rosenberg, and the other Dominican soldiers on hand. Rosenberg had been sent with a bag of cash to lease an Air France jet and crew (at a cost of $27,000) to transport a total of seven of them to Ciudad Trujillo.* They arrived at Orly Airport not long after Air Force One alit with its cargo of Kennedys.

Rubi was still in his riding clothes. When he'd left the house, Odile was at the hairdresser's, and he hadn't yet been able to reach her. He managed to make contact before the plane took off. "When I arrived at Orly I called her at our home," he told a reporter. "She had just arrived and immediately broke into tears when I told her where I was going. I

* The airline balked at first, not sure about the economic or publicity ramifications of cooperating with a Trujillo—or, for that matter, a country on the outs with the OAS—but a combination of Ramfis's money and Rubi's personal connections prevailed.

could not wait for her—or do much explaining. The plane was leaving."
By lunchtime, the nine-hour flight home had commenced.

They sat in first-class, dined lightly, refrained from drinking, focusing their attention on the cockpit radio, which they could hear through a door that they insisted be left open. As they crossed the Atlantic, they heard a bulletin: Pierre Salinger, the spokesperson for President Kennedy, had announced that Secretary of State Dean Rusk wasn't in France but had stayed in Washington to monitor the situation in the Dominican Republic following the death of Generalissimo Trujillo.

Now they knew. But none of them could say what the situation on the ground was. As they neared Puerto Rico, air traffic controllers there tried to force them to land, declaring the airspace over the Dominican Republic unsafe for an unregistered charter flight. The pilot wanted to put down in San Juan, and Rubi tried to persuade Ramfis that it would be a wise course. But Ramfis switched off the radio and insisted that they press on to Ciudad Trujillo. As they approached the airport there, they reopened communications and found Chesty Estévez installed in the control tower and reassuring them that it was safe to land. The pilot passed over the landing strip, which was lined with tanks and columns of troops, and changed his mind. "You may have paid $27,000 for this plane, but it's worth $8 million," he told Ramfis. They nevertheless convinced him that the amassed forces were friendly, and he safely put them down.

With their hands on their sidearms, Ramfis and Rhadamés stood by as the door to the plane was opened. "We didn't know if there would be shooting, shouting or worse," Rubi remembered. Rosenberg made as if to step forward first, and Ramfis grabbed him by the shoulder. "In this place, I go first." He stepped out and descended to be greeted by Estévez and a coterie of military aides and drove off to find a uniform and take control of the situation.

═══

It had been an ambush, and though the job got done it had been a botch: A group of perhaps a dozen conspirators had plotted to gun the Benefactor down and then take the palace with a cadre of the army under the control of General Román Fernández, husband of one of Trujillo's sisters. They'd been goaded by decades of repressed anger, the proddings of the Catholic church, the encouragement of the CIA, and, in many cases their own advancing age, which lent a now-or-never urgency to the plot. They had planned to assault the generalissimo in an isolated location along the seaside road that wended out of the capital westward toward the Benefactor's country estate, Estancia Fundación, a cattle ranch dominated by a dark, grotesquely furnished home known as Las Caobas. On the night of the thirtieth, after hurried preparation, eight of the conspirators, several of whom were high enough in Trujillo's military and security forces to know all of his movements, lay in wait for the chauffeured Chevrolet bearing their quarry.

The first shots hit the car from the side of the road about a mile outside of the city. Trujillo's driver heard the report of the guns and sped up, but he was chased down by a second car, which also opened fire. He turned to see the back windows shattered and Trujillo in obvious pain.

"Please stop, I'm wounded," the Benefactor told him.

The driver could see another car approaching his directly. "It's better to turn back. There are too many of them."

"No! Make a stop now! We have to fight!"

The driver did as he was told, and he commenced firing from the front seat with his own machine gun, wounding at least one of the assailants. Despite being wounded himself, he managed to crawl out of the car and roll toward the side of the road and the safety of cover. Behind him, Trujillo stumbled from the backseat, to be met with a hail of gunfire from two directions. The driver watched as Trujillo shot wildly with a .38 pistol and was staggered by a rain of bullets. The assassins, forgetting in their panic the chauffeur, dragged away their wounded companion and sped off.

By sheer, dumb coincidence, another high-ranking military officer came across the scene soon after and alerted authorities, cutting crucially the amount of time the assassins had counted on to execute the second part of their plan—the actual coup. By an even more dire coincidence, that same officer went directly to the home of General Fernández, the conspirator who had intended to take charge of the country, to tell him the awful news and rally him to the palace. Fernández was thus rendered completely incapable of performing his portion of the plan, and it all began to unravel gracelessly. By the time Ramfis and Rubi stepped off their plane, several of the conspirators had been captured or killed, the others, desperate for their lives, were scrambling for places to hide, the SIM was ransacking the city looking for anyone potentially connected to the tyrannicide (some thirty thousand–plus homes were eventually searched), and General Fernández was sitting amid the extended Trujillo family trying to conceal his involvement in the plot.

In the coming days, power remained divided between Balaguer, the puppet president of surprising mettle and determination, and Ramfis, the presumed hereditary heir with control of the more substantial portion of the military, an immense war chest, and, most of all, the power inherent in the name Trujillo: Not a soul in the country wasn't to some degree terrified by the very word.

On the morning of June 2, the man who'd built the power behind that name was buried in his hometown, San Cristóbal, amid an enormous display of pomp lent considerable tension by the massive military presence. Partly it was a show of intimidation; partly it was one of fear. No one was sure, after all, that the rest of the Trujillo family wouldn't be targeted for death. Rubi attended in a blue linen suit, a panama hat protecting him from the sun, standing a little bit away from them, reflecting his status as an ex–son-in-law but also suggesting the tenuousness of the bonds existing between him and the family. (He was so far from the heart of things that he was cropped out of most newspaper photos of the funeral.)*

That afternoon, a reporter in New York got him on the phone and asked questions about the situation in Ciudad Trujillo. Rubi played it

---

* Conspicuously absent was the Benefactor's eldest child. Flor de Oro. Estranged from her father and living in exile in Canada at the time of his death, she hadn't been able to attend the funeral because authorities there and in the United States refused to allow anyone named Trujillo passage to the Dominican Republic; by the time she was granted a visa, her father had been buried.

cagey, offering vague assurances and saying nothing, really. The following day, at a press conference with Ramfis and Balaguer, he stood silently while the latter explained that Rubi would soon be going to the United States to liaise with various concerned parties there.

The next day, he was in New York. Officially, he was an ordinary citizen on his way home to Paris. That was what he said and that was what Balaguer, still president after all, told the *New York Times:* Rubi's visit was "absolutely private," and anything he did in America would be "on his own."

But, of course, with or without Balaguer's knowledge or blessing (but probably with), Rubi was there in hopes of keeping up contact with the Kennedy administration and maintaining the possibility that a Dominican government rid of the Benefactor could be recognized by the United States. Too, in all probability, he was lobbying for Ramfis. Having been so long associated with the Benefactor's regime, he couldn't suddenly start speaking for an as-yet-unformed post-Trujillo government. Moreover, his official function was too ill-defined for him to have any authority in speaking for the current government, and he had no especially close relation with Balaguer, a poet and historian in whose copious memoirs Rubi never figures, not even anecdotally. What was more, the Trujillos had him by the purse: In the previous year, the Benefactor, pursuing another profit-making scheme, had requested that Rubi sell him his land holdings in the Cibao in exchange for shares in a new corporate scheme he was organizing; Rubi complied and was now tied in to the fortunes of the Trujillo dynasty to the sum of $200,000. He had a mission, all right: to see after Ramfis's interests and, by extension, his own.

━━━━━

He played it like the pro he was, sitting down with Igor Cassini for a private update and a public Q and A that was published in the Hearst newspaper and ran the gamut from serious talk of statesmanship to details of his personal situation to questions about his reputation as "the great Romeo and Playboy extraordinaire" (*"Incroyable!"* Rubi exclaimed).

"We have no single boss today," Rubi told Cassini's readers. "The Generalissimo is dead and no man has succeeded him, and no one person intends to succeed him. President Balaguer heads our government, and General Trujillo commands the army, which supports the government."

As he popped vitamin pills in his rooms at the Stanhope Hotel, he assured the world that the Dominican press had been freed from censorship, that political prisoners would soon be granted amnesty, that no accords existed between Ciudad Trujillo and Havana, that the streets of Dominican cities were safe, that there had not been mass arrests after the shooting, and that free elections were desired by all parties. He especially emphasized the immensity and sincerity of the people's mourning of their Benefactor. "All you had to do was watch television to see the spontaneous outburst of grief registered by the people," he said. "But I was in the streets, and even as a Dominican I can tell you I was overwhelmed at the feeling of sorrow demonstrated by the people."

Mostly, he seemed intent on putting the world's mind to rest regarding Ramfis. "I can assure you, first of all," he said, "that General Trujillo doesn't want to perpetuate the so-called Trujillo dynasty and that he, personally, has no political ambitions whatsoever. . . . Ramfis agreed to head the armed forces only after I and other friends urged upon him that he was the only man in the crisis who could maintain cohesion and stability with the military. . . . He has stated categorically that the Army will be used only to maintain order at home, and will positively stay out of politics. The Army will be used to support any duly elected government, and not to enforce any sort of dictatorship."

As it happened, Ramfis probably didn't want to run the country. He preferred his idle life of wealthy leisure, drinking, screwing around, playing polo, toying with lackeys, making the scene at nightclubs; his family saw him as their savior, but in the immediate aftermath of his father's murder he drank and he shut himself up and he worried, sincerely, that he couldn't handle the massive job of restoring order to the country and rejoining the community of nations as an equal.

———

The article containing Rubi's reassuring words was published on June 7. That same day, John F. Kennedy, back from Paris, was briefed on what Rubirosa and Cassini had told Robert Murphy. If he wanted to, the president could have learned a lot more: From the moment his plane touched ground at Idlewild Airport three days earlier, Rubi was under the constant surveillance of the FBI. The Bureau and its voyeuristic director J. Edgar Hoover had been keeping tabs on him since his marriage to Doris Duke; in late 1953, the Department of Justice, guarding Barbara Hutton's millions, requested anything the FBI had on him and was told that, as there had never been an official investigation, there wasn't much. In 1960, as signals from the Dominican Republic became more ominous, Hoover's agents began asking questions about him again, casually, and with the director's explicit orders that they have "no direct contact with Rubirosa." As late as March 1961, however, the Bureau seemed to feel that he wasn't worth watching too closely; a memo that month from New York to Hoover declared "it is not believed that any investigation is warranted at this time."

That all changed with Trujillo's death and with Rubi's arrival in the States as an agent of shuttle diplomacy between the tenuous new Dominican government and people with connections to power in Washington. A more formal investigation was requested, and for the next three years Rubi couldn't pass through an airport, make a phone call, buy a shirt, or get a haircut in the United States without somebody making note of the fact somewhere and sending word to Hoover's office. Coordination was established among the FBI, the Department of State, the Bureau of Narcotics, the New York County District Attorney's Office, and the Immigration and Naturalization Service, all of whom had an interest in Rubi's comings, goings, and activities. Phone records were traced; acquaintances were interviewed; banks, shops, hotels, and airlines were asked to provide information. In January of the following year, when Attorney General Robert Kennedy requested a copy of whatever Hoover knew about Rubirosa, he was delivered a file thick as a medium-sized city's phone book.

He was informed, for instance, that Rubi's visit to New York in the wake of Trujillo's funeral was followed by a quick trip back to Ciudad Trujillo and a second flight to New York, this time with an official passport and not a visitor's visa like the one he had used only a few days earlier. It was learned through interviews that Rubi had left New York that first time with good news for Ramfis and Balaguer: Through the efforts of Igor Cassini and Robert Murphy, an open hearing would await the Dominican government when the form of it was finally settled. He managed to get the PR contract with Cassini's friend's firm to be extended (probably taking a finder's fee), and he made an unofficial deal with Ramfis and Balaguer that he himself would get $250,000 if his work resulted in restored recognition of Ciudad Trujillo by Washington. Agents were concerned that Rubi might be a bagman, shuttling money from Dominican sources to people with influence in Washington, but they were assured by a confidential informant that "he never heard of Rubirosa paying anyone off inasmuch as Rubirosa had a reputation for taking all he could for himself."

To press for a diplomatic result that would also benefit him financially, Rubi spent the summer cozying up to the Kennedys, with and without the help of Cassini. In August, Rubi and Odile were invited to join a Riviera cruise on a 175-foot steam yacht with a whole cadre of their new Kennedy-circle friends: Peter Lawford and his wife, Patricia, the president's sister; Frank Sinatra; Dean and Jeannie Martin; restaurateur Mike Romanoff; agent Milt Ebbins; songwriter Jimmy Van Heusen; and Texas oilman and Sinatra drinking buddy Bob Neal, who had leased the ship and stocked it with the best food and drink. It was a star-crossed plan: Sinatra threw a hissy fit about some perceived insult, swore off the cruise, and went to Germany with Dean and his missus. The boat, to which the rest of the party repaired, along with old Joe Kennedy, who joined them at Antibes, turned out to be a particularly ugly craft, "the worst-looking damn vessel you ever saw," according to Neal. "It was beautiful inside," he added. "They'd really done a great job refurbishing the thing." But when shipping tycoon Stavros Niarchos invited them all for lunch at his villa they actually anchored it where it couldn't be seen.

The following month, there was a second cruise, at Hyannis Port, the Kennedy family playground on Cape Cod. One Friday night in late September, Rubi, Odile, Pat Lawford, Ted Kennedy, and Sinatra flew from D.C. to New Bedford, Massachusetts, on the president's private jet, the *Caroline* (like the *Angelita*, named after the head of state's daughter).

They landed in a thick fog and hired a brace of taxis to drive them to the compound some fifty miles away. Frank bore a trove of gifts for the president and his father: Italian bread, champagne, and coolers filled with ice cream. In the pea soup weather, the little caravan took a few hours to make the trip, stopping at a dive bar where, according to taxi driver Roger Paradise, "Sinatra bought the whole place a drink. He was talking to everybody and didn't want to leave. He asked to take the drink with him but they said no. He said something really nasty." By the time they arrived—Peter Lawford bounded out of the house to greet them—Sinatra's mood had lightened and he tipped each driver $10. Rubi and Odile went with Ted Kennedy to his home on Squaw Island, about a half mile away, while Sinatra stayed in Joe's house and the president retired to his own cottage. The following day, they all reunited for larks in the sun, capped by a three-hour cruise of Nantucket Sound aboard old Joe's fifty-two-foot yacht, the *Marlin*. The next day, all the guests departed.

It was a couple of weeks before news of this little gathering made uncomfortable headlines for the White House. Sinatra, then at the height of his ring-a-ding-ding, thumb-a-nose-at-propriety Rat Pack phase, was enmeshed in a series of skirmishes with the press over his, cough, alleged ties to organized crime, and wasn't deemed fit by much of the country to be chumming around with the president. Pierre Salinger explained away his presence in Hyannis Port by saying that he was a guest of old Joe's and was in town to discuss a souvenir record album of the inaugural gala that Frank and Peter Lawford had produced.

What was worse, though, was Rubi's presence. Again, Salinger explained that the Rubirosas were guests of the president's brother, but that didn't wash among those who carefully monitored Caribbean affairs. The sight of the president and his family rubbing shoulders with a man so closely associated with a past—and, potentially, future—Trujillo regime added to anxieties in the Dominican Republic and among groups in the United States, including some in the government, hoping for a peaceful democratization of the island. Fidel Castro went so far as to broadcast radio accounts of the Rubirosa-Kennedy friendship into the Dominican Republic in an effort to make citizens there suspicious of Washington's intentions.

In fact, it was *Rubi's* intentions they should have been monitoring. On the one hand, he had the attention of the Kennedys, who were respectful enough of his knowledge of the situation to listen to him if not take his word as gospel. On the other hand, he had Ramfis, growing more and more sullen and dangerous in Ciudad Trujillo, not really wanting to be there, impatient for a resolution, quietly securing the family fortune (estimated at $800 million in 1961 dollars) and, to keep himself amused, torturing the conspirators in his father's murder. A tribunal would later learn of electric shocks to the genitals, eyelids sliced off, sodium pentathol injections, beatings; one of the rebels was served a stew made of the flesh of his rebel son; told what it was he was lapping up, he died immediately of a heart attack.

Ramfis expected quicker results from Rubi and was angered by the slow progress that he was making with the Kennedys. (Too, his mother had warned him from Paris not to trust Rubi and his plans.) He could spin into a fury when he read in the Dominican newspapers that Rubi was in Dallas at the end of October to open a new polo pitch there and break bread with Texas oil baron William H. Hudson. And he spoke extremely bitterly of the machinations of Rubi and his chum Igor Cassini. "If they know Rubirosa in the U.S., it's thanks to the $10,000 he pays Cassini to mention him in his columns," he groused, characterizing Cassini as a man "who sells his services, his connections, his columns and would sell his body if he could. He's a pawnbroker who sells only gossip. But you don't have to pay him more than you think it's worth."

Rubi heard about these sorts of outbursts secondhand and knew that the string he was playing was getting shorter and shorter. By the first week in November, certain that the impatient signals he was getting from Ramfis spelled trouble, he insisted to his contacts in the Kennedy administration that they move to recognize one or another government in Ciudad Trujillo or risk seeing Ramfis move in with the army and take over. He might be able, he said, to keep Ramfis from moving for a week or two, but no more. They promised a response, and Rubi went down to the Dominican Republic, where he was to take part in a parade and polo tournament, to wait for it.

On November 15, the ceremonial paraders included Rubi, his

nephew Gilberto, a variety of military officers loyal to Ramfis, and a selection of government officials riding up the Malecon, the very road along which Trujillo had been gunned down. The following day, Odile watched as Rubi played polo on the pitch beside the Hotel El Embajador. A journalist asked Rubi if he'd heard anything about Ramfis and the rest of the Trujillos leaving the country. "No, not yet," Rubi said.

But he was wrong. During the previous night, Ramfis had finished his business with his father's assassins, personally executing the several who were still alive, including his traitorous uncle. At the same time, the Benefactor's body had been removed from its crypt, and Ramfis's house in the beach resort of Boca Chica had been emptied. The family had fled in a series of secret airplane flights, and the yacht *Angelita* was dispatched to follow them laden with Trujillo's remains and millions in cash, jewels, artworks, and securities. Dominican authorities managed to get enough cooperation from their Caribbean neighbors to force the *Angelita* back to a home port. But the Trujillos had escaped.

Rubi was livid: In the face of the Kennedys and the world he had been made to seem a liar, a puppet, a dupe. He gave an angry interview in the Dominican papers decrying Ramfis as a coward and repeated his outburst in the English press: "I won't ever see him again in my life. He is not my friend. He betrayed me." When he came home to Paris, he was still angry. "He was calling Ramfis all sorts of names," recalled a friend. " 'These guys are no good, they're fucking cowards.' " Ramfis, who would spend the next months shuttling between France and Spain looking for safe haven, never responded publicly and never spoke to Rubi again.

========

With no prospect of recouping his investment money from Ramfis or cashing in on the bargain he'd made with him to win the country back its good name in Washington, Rubi cooled his jets in Palm Beach, waiting patiently to see what shape the new government would take and how he might figure in its plans.

It didn't take long for him to learn. On January 2, 1962, the seven-man Council of State, a newly established interim government that was to help the Dominican Republic make its way toward free, democratic elections, met in its inaugural session.

As its very first action, the council sought not to address relations with Washington or Havana or the OAS, not to settle questions about the military or the economy, not to seek the extradition of the Trujillos or the fortune with which they'd absconded, not to change the name of the capital back to Santo Domingo.

As its very first action, the Council of State fired Rubi from his post as inspector of embassies.

After thirty years of pomp, travel, machinations, and skulduggery, he was truly done with the Trujillos—and, more than likely, with his homeland.

SIXTEEN

FRESH BLOOD

A reporter with a pencil and a pad: "Hey Rubi, don't misunderstand this question, but did you ever kill anybody?"

A pause, a quizzical look, a forced smile, a bark of laughter: "No! Oh God, no!"

Dozens of reporters and photographers and cops and standers-by were watching. Another show, another unlikely pass.

January 9, 1962: Subzero temperatures had been punishing New York for a week, and Rubi had ridden in a taxi from the St. Regis Hotel to the Criminal Courts Building in lower Manhattan. He was, for the second time in four days, attending to the bidding of New York County district attorney Frank Hogan, whose office was putting questions to him about the deaths and disappearances of various Dominican exiles in the city.

Hogan's men had pounced on Rubi within twenty-four hours of his loss of diplomatic privileges. Egged on by anti-Trujillo voices in the city, encouraged by State Department reports, they had two murders and a missing persons case they thought he might know something about: Bencosme, Andres Requena, and Galíndez. And they had waited years—decades—to grill him. Back when he was splashed all over the newspapers beside Barbara Hutton, Rubi had sent an attorney to the DA to say that he was willing to answer questions under the cover of his diplomatic shield, but Hogan's men had balked; they wanted him unprotected or not at all. Now, however, he had no special privileges and he could be made to talk or suffer penalties for his silence.

On January 2, Rubi was staying with his old Cuba pal Earl E. T. Smith in Palm Beach when a U.S. marshal appeared at the door with a subpoena demanding his immediate presence in New York. He signaled his availability and made plans to travel north straightaway. "I am sure I can clear myself of any suspicion," he told a reporter. "I know this is an attempt by [Dominican] opposition people to create a scandal." He explicitly denied any accusation of involvement in the Bencosme murder: "I had nothing to do with that. I know they used it in an attempt to embarrass President Trujillo when I was his son-in-law. I don't know why it has come up now. I hope to find out."

He flew to New York with Odile, checked in at the St. Regis, and reported to Hogan's office on January 5 in a chauffeur-driven Rolls-Royce, begging off reporters' questions as he made his way to his appointment.

They put it to him for three hours. When he emerged, the press asked him what he had told the DA's men. "I could not tell them anything because I don't know anything," he said. "As far as I'm concerned, the matter is finished." He hopped back into the Rolls and drove away.

Privately, Hogan had already told the FBI that "they really didn't have anything on Rubirosa but he was not very well liked and they were going to question him further." The DA's office wasn't happy with Rubi's testimony, telling the Justice Department that he "was not cooperative and answered questions at best in a vague, non-specific and uninformative way."

Reporters learned from Alexander Herman, the assistant district attorney in charge of the Homicide Bureau, that the matter was far from over: After dancing around questions all afternoon, Rubi had been handed a subpoena to appear before a grand jury in three days.

This time Rubi arrived in a taxi—and again without a lawyer. He walked into the Criminal Courts Building without a word to the press, and reporters settled in to see what sort of fireworks would result.

It wasn't a long wait: Ten minutes after he arrived, Rubi was dismissed.

Hogan's people had wanted to question him on the record and under the condition that he waive his immunity against self-incrimination. In their scheme, anything that he said could be used against him in a potential future prosecution. Rubi refused to sign the waiver, signaling his defiant determination to risk prosecution for perjury or contempt or obstruction of justice. As a result of his truculence, he was told by Alexander Herman, "In that case, you're excused. You can leave."

Outside the courthouse, his hatless head exposed to the biting cold, Rubi declared that he was "offended" that the DA's office wouldn't accept his word as a gentleman that he had nothing to do with any of the cases they were investigating. "I felt it was an insult," he said of the subpoena. "I told them Friday the truth. Why should I have to repeat it before a grand jury?"

A reporter wondered if he was truly done with questions. "I cannot stay here all my life," Rubi said. "I must leave to my home in Paris in the next two or three days. I know nothing. I have absolutely nothing to fear. I can't waste time here. They should believe what I say. They should take my word."

And then some joker in the press asked him if he'd ever killed anyone, and he looked shocked and amused and made his stock denial and then got into a taxi and went uptown to tell Odile what had happened. "I'm coming back for Easter," he told the reporters as he pulled away.

The following day, Murray Kempton reviled Rubi in his *New York Post* column as "the first house guest of the President of the U.S. ever to refuse to sign a waiver of immunity before a New York grand jury." But like Hogan and his men, all Kempton could do was snipe.

He would, in fact, never again be questioned by American authorities. J. Edgar Hoover never gave FBI agents permission to interview Rubi, and the New York County DA stopped investigating him, in part because both organizations felt that coming on too strong with him would result in embarrassment—for *them:* Imagine the American government being publically snubbed by the likes of Rubirosa! "It is firmly believed," Hoover wrote in a memo that spring that took note of Rubi's connection to Igor Cassini and his Cholly Knickerbocker column, "that any interview of Rubirosa would be subsequently reflected in some fashion in that column." They kept watching his comings and goings and phone calls and business dealings, but from a distance.*

═══════

Rubi gave them ample opportunity in the coming years to watch him, flitting in and out of the United States several times each year seeking business opportunities. He spent the end of 1962 and the dawn of the following year in the United States and Mexico, with neither an heiress nor a dictator looking out for him, hoping to put some business deals together and enjoying the camaraderie and generosity of friends. On January 3, he and Odile flew from Acapulco to San Diego with Frank Sinatra on the singer's private jet and then visited his Palm Springs home alongside a fairway of the Tamarisk golf club.

That spring, the seed of that visit nearly came to fruit in the form of a connection between Rubi and Sam Giancana, the Chicago mob boss whose friendship with Sinatra had driven a wedge between the singer and the White House. The mob had never gotten over the loss of its lucrative Havana operations to Castro and had always resented the Kennedy administration for its failure to rid the Caribbean of the Communists and get those glittering casinos back into the rightful, crooked hands. They had, however, realistically accepted the fact that they would have to seek new pastures, and they turned their collective sight on the Dominican Republic. Trujillo had never been averse to doing business with American gangsters;** perhaps the people who ran the country in his wake would see the wisdom of the same.

* Nor could the Dominican government get its mitts on him. In February 1962, the new authorities in Santo Domingo requested that the French government extradite Rubi, Ramfis, and some of Ramfis's coterie; a blank refusal followed.
** One long-brewing rumor suggested that a New Jersey mobster named Joe Zicarelli had sold arms to Trujillo and had arranged the assassination of Andreas Requena and the kidnapping of Jesús de Galíndez.

In June 1963, an FBI wiretap captured Giancana stating that he would soon be traveling to Paris to see Rubi about the possibility of a casino business in the Dominican Republic. This so alarmed the Justice Department that it ordered an unprecedented surveillance of the mob boss: FBI agents literally began lock-stepping him, following his every move from just a step or two behind him—even when he entered men's rooms or hit the golf course. The routine of G-men using tee-boxes and urinals beside him so infuriated that Giancana had no time or energy to think about a new Caribbean venture, and the idea—and Rubi's chance to turn a profit off it—died unhatched.

Rubi was back at Sinatra's Palm Springs digs the following September, and this time Sinatra managed to coax his Dominican chum into doing something he'd never done before—swing a golf club. Famed attorney Louis Nizer was a witness: "Rubirosa, poor man, thought he could transfer his athletic skill to golf. If he could hit a speeding ball with a mallet while riding full speed on a pony, plunging against other ponies, how ridiculously easy it would be to strike a stationary ball from a standing position while no one harassed him. He couldn't believe it when he failed to make contact at all, swinging right over the mocking ball." Before long, Rubi was hitting balls into ponds and woods and patches of desert and exploding semiregularly in a white fury. "He was jumping up and down and screaming in exasperation," Nizer recalled. (Sinatra, to be fair, was no better.)

Nizer was on hand to take a deposition from Rubi in an astounding case that had resulted from the botched efforts of Rubi and Cassini to recover the Dominican Republic's good standing with Washington. Journalists had learned about Robert Murphy's secret missions and the role of the playboy-diplomat and the gossip columnist in them, and they had further connected Cassini to the PR contracts that his subsidiary firm had signed with Ramfis and the interim government. When word of this backroom maneuvering made its way to Attorney General Robert Kennedy, he exploded: In his view, Cassini had lied to the president and his father about his connections in Ciudad Trujillo and profited from the falsehoods. When he learned that neither Cassini nor his subsidiary company had officially registered to do business in the United

State as agents of the Dominican government, Kennedy filed a four-count indictment against them in February 1963.

The prosecution didn't have much of a case: No money passed to Cassini or Martial & Company as a result of the Dominican contract with the subsidiary; neither Cassini nor his office did any lobbying or publicity for the Dominican Republic; and the status of the Dominican Republic as an ally of strategic importance meant that its agents didn't have to register themselves. But Bobby was furious at what he perceived as Cassini's cheek, and he was determined to press on. The publicity surrounding the indictment crushed Cassini. He resigned from his post as Cholly Knickerbocker, and one by one his public relations clients slinked away. His wife, who had once nearly become engaged to Jack Kennedy, wrote a pleading letter to her former beau seeking leniency and, indeed, pardon for what even the Justice Department was acknowledging to Cassini's lawyer, Nizer, was at worst a failure to comply with a technicality. But she was too anxious to wait for a reply: She had recently lost her mother and had developed an addiction to painkillers in the aftermath of a skiing accident. The president was appropriately moved by her plea and wanted to do something to mitigate the situation, but he took too much time: On April 8, 1963, she begged out of a social engagement, sending Igor along; then she swallowed an entire bottle of sleeping pills and died of heart failure.

Nizer worked the case doggedly, procuring exculpatory testimony from the likes of Rubi, who went on the record to say that neither Cassini nor Martial worked for or profited from the Dominican Republic. The Justice Department insisted that a single, technical count remain in place, though, and in November Cassini stood before the court a broken man and pled nolo contendere to it. He was sentenced to a $10,000 fine and two years' probation, after which he left the United States to work in Italy for his brother's fashion house.

═══

In Paris, his world shrunken, Rubi puttered.

For so long an icon of the night life, of the never-ending party, of the gay old time, he grew fond of staying in Marnes-la-Coquette, tending to the grounds, reading, playing with his Chihuahua. He spread his nights out more judiciously, giving himself a chance to recuperate from his *parrandas*. Daytime hours were still given over to polo and polo practice, and sometimes in the afternoon there would be a visit to the discreet brothel run by Madame Claude above a bank near the Champs-Élysées, but in the main he was more settled, more staid than ever before.

"I have at last discovered my vocation," he declared to a friend, "the regular, bourgeois life."

"I like home life," he told a journalist. "I like setting up a home and arranging the garden, and I like helping my wife to choose furniture."

Odile wasn't overly fond of the change that had come over him. Now in her mid-twenties, she was worldly and energetic enough to have her own impulse to party and travel. The society dinners of the polo set weren't nearly fast enough for her. But she suggested that she was trapped in his world.

"Rubi never let me make a decision," she said. "He was the master. He would always ask me to be on time, be beautiful and charming. I never had friends of my own. I never made a decision on my own for dinner or anything. I never made out a check. He always gave me cash. I knew nothing about life."

His eye for women's fashion, noted by Zsa Zsa years earlier as one of his most remarkable attributes, became for his young wife a kind of straitjacket. "He counseled me on my hair (he loves chignons)," she said, "on which jewelry I should wear (he prefers simple), on my outfits (these are very important to him). Since we began our romance, I haven't bought a suit, an outfit, a coat in which he hasn't accompanied me to counsel me and give me his judgment." Specifically, she felt, she was being coached into being the anti–Zsa Zsa, more natural than put-together. "He would put me under the shower if my hair was too lacquered."

But she found ways around his conservative tastes, such as going without underwear beneath her couture outfits. And for all her complaining, most of their mutual friends assumed that she managed to skip around his watchfulness just as he had hers. Observers of their fast-moving Paris set wondered openly about Rubi's ability to control his young wife.

Oleg Cassini, was among those who noticed. "Odile had the power over him that he had, all his life, wielded over others," the fashion designer remembered. "She exhausted him and made him jealous." He claimed that Rubi admitted in a weak moment, "All my life I have controlled women—every woman I've ever met, except this one. She is under my skin." His confusion over her was noted by other observers. Zsa Zsa, who had a stake in making Rubi's marriage look a sham, acknowledged that Odile was "a clever little thing," but insisted that Rubi "was very unhappy. Odile ruined his life." And there were hints that the marriage may have been on thin ice. "There were big rumors that Rubi was going to spring another surprise and marry Pat Lawford," remembered Taki Theodoracopulos. "But he was very secretive."*

The fact that his Parisian friends were settling into middle age actually served to keep Rubi and Odile together. Increasingly, he grew irritated with the lack of freedom that kept his chums, with their responsibilities to their families and workplaces, from palling around with him. "Are my friends all of a sudden *ouvriers* ['laborers']," he thundered to Odile after being frustrated in an effort to get some afternoon liveliness together. As a result, he was more drawn to a younger set of playmates—Taki, Juan Capuro, Gunther Sachs: men who idolized Rubi for his notoriety, his way of life, his unapologetic hedonism, his brilliant style.

Running with these young men, he was still taken as a symbol of pleasure-seeking, a label that he actually defended in the press. "What's wrong with pleasure?" he snapped at a reporter. "Why can't you go out at night and twist and get drunk and still do your job properly? What's wrong with marrying rich women? Those little bastards who criticize me don't understand. Imagine what they would have done if they'd been married to such wives. I took them simply as women. And what's wrong with taking presents from a woman? I give them, too, even though I give a ring and she gives a bomber. So what? An airplane is not the moon. It's a toy. If you can have a little Austin, you have it. If

* The Kennedy sister was separated from actor Peter Lawford and would divorce him at the beginning of 1966. Rubi was also rumored to be interested in Mellon heiress Peggy Hitchcock, who proved her swinging 1960s bona fides by providing Timothy Leary with a Milbrook, N.Y., haven for his psychedelic studies.

you can have a bomber, you have it. So what? I have never broken up a marriage, never talked about my affairs, and never quarreled with a woman." (That wasn't entirely true, and he wasn't always so defensive; answering a similar query another time, he smiled and said enigmatically. "The difference between a gigolo and me is that all of the rich women I have married have been even richer when we parted.")

What young man making his way in Parisian society wouldn't be drawn to such a daring character? Taki was sharing a Paris flat with two Argentine polo players when he fell under Rubi's tutelage. The two had met years before in Palm Beach when Taki was a kid and Rubi the king of the world who nevertheless took an interest in a younger man. Now, meeting each other again on the pitch at the Bagatelle, they were more truly equals, and Rubi embraced him fully, introducing him to his favorite nighttime haunts such as New Jimmy's and Le Calvados and to Madame Claude's, to which he sent him with the brotherly warning against rowdiness, *"Ce n'est pas un bordel, mon vieux"* ("It isn't a bordello, old man").

Taki was one of the few in Rubi's crowd who didn't succumb to the modern fashion of actually having a career. All around, perfectly wealthy men felt the need to do something; not Rubi, and not Taki. "As the '60s came on and more people were working, one of the few friends Rubi had who didn't work was me," Taki recalled, "and we became closer and closer. He was an interesting man to have as a mentor because he had a lot of style and great charm, and I learned a lot from the way he handled women—very gentlemanlike and no Hollywood bullshit."

The two bonded especially over sports. "We'd work the polo ponies," Taki remembered, "and we'd box. I wasn't allowed to hit him in the face, and I'd say, 'For God's sake, where can I hit you?' And he said, 'In the shoulder.' And he was mad about *boule*—he had a gravel pitch in his garden for it and we would play all day." At times, Taki actually lived with Rubi and Odile, even after he eloped with Cristina de Caraman, the daughter of a French duke who disinherited her for marrying this roguish Greek with no special standing. (After the wedding, Taki and Rubi continued to visit Madame Claude's; "Rubi insisted these visits made for a happy married life," Taki remembered. "The contrast was invigorating. It was like stepping into a sauna after a cold shower.")

An even more unlikely party pal at the time was Sammy Davis Jr., who spent a month in Paris in 1964 appearing at the Olympia Theatre in a one-man show. He had met Rubi through their mutual buddy Frank Sinatra and found in him a perfect tour guide to Parisian society and night life. "He could put a reading on anyone," Sammy recalled. "He would just trim the fat off everything. People would come in and he'd go, 'bullshit artist.' He had unerring instinct." Rubi steered Sammy toward the right people—who included Romy Schneider, with whom Sammy had a passionate, drunken affair—and away from the less desirable fawners and hangers-on who were drawn to his celebrity. He taught him how to kiss a woman on the hand with the proper Continental touch: "It is done more with the eyes than with the lips."

In particular, Rubi deeply impressed Sammy, who always sought to fashion a gentleman of himself, with his sartorial sense. "I have always cared about clothes, and I will go to any length to look good," Sammy confessed. "But the way Rubirosa dressed made me feel as if I'd fallen off the garbage truck." And he took him out on *parrandas* that even Sammy, whose drinking mates included such heroic tipplers as Dean Martin and Frank Sinatra, couldn't handle. Sammy recalled with a grimace a night of drinking whiskey with Rubi and the Spanish playboy Don Jaime de Mora y Aragon that ended at dawn with the American entertainer staggering, swearing, and spinning; that afternoon, Rubi called on Sammy at his hotel to bring him to a lunch date, and the singer could barely dress himself and crawl to their rendezvous point. "I struggled to get myself together," Sammy remembered, "and when I got downstairs he was standing at the bar sipping a Ramos gin fizz like he'd gone to bed before the evening news." Sammy had to know the secret. "Hanging from the bar to support myself, I implored, 'How do you do it?' He explained reasonably: 'Your profession is being an entertainer, mine is being a playboy.' "

Gunther Sachs was less a running mate of Rubi's than an acolyte, the inheritor of a fortune—his full name was Gunther Sachs von Opel, as in the German automobile company—who skied with Rubi in St.-Moritz and, like Rubi, tooled about in high-end sports cars, although he never actually raced them. Sachs would go on to marry Brigitte Bardot, a triumph of the skirt-chaser's craft that endured three years. His hero-worship led him into at least one sticky misunderstanding with his idol: Rubi had an idea for a business and was hoping for seed money from Sachs. The scheme was for a perfume with the ungainly name *Mic Mac* (the question of why he didn't choose, say, *Rubi,* would go unanswered). It wasn't as lunatic a notion as selling dried fish to starving Africans or diving for treasure in the Caribbean, but without the capital from Sachs, which never materialized, the concept died.

Indeed, even as he claimed to have an income of as much as $5,000 a month,* Rubi was clearly living on his uppers. "Most men's ambition is to make money," he liked to joke. "Mine is to spend it!" That, though, was the boast of an earlier time. By 1965, things were different. "He was rather depressed," Taki recalled. "He was running out of money."

He and Odile quietly sold off the antiques and works of art with which Doris Duke had filled the house on Rue de Bellechasse as a means of paying for their jet-set lifestyle: the Cannes–New York–Palm Beach–Deauville circuit on which they still traveled. He hit on a few moneymaking schemes, which failed to come to fruition: buying an interest in a hotel in San Juan, Puerto Rico (his partner would have been, of all people, Felix Benítez Rexach, his old rival in the dredging of the harbor in Ciudad Trujillo), and appearing in a film alongside tough guy actor Eddie Constantine. But he was, and he knew it, an awful businessman, with no patience for the sort of details on which moguls thrived. When the Cassini brothers were planning their Sugarbush ski resort, Oleg took Rubi to a Chinese restaurant in New York to tell him the idea and allow him in on the ground floor; Rubi listened dutifully for a while and then brought the talk to an abrupt end: "Stop, Oleg, stop! I have a headache. This business talk is killing me!"

The most visible effort he made to earn a living was the publication of his memoirs, which were serialized in a French magazine in 1964. While hundreds of women might have shuddered at the thought of what he would spill, he was rather chaste and tasteful—to the frank detriment of the work. Rubi spoke kindly of all his wives, including Barbara

* About $360,000 a year in 2005 terms.

Hutton, never mentioned Zsa Zsa by name, allowed Odile an installment of her own, and generally bored where he ought to have titillated; as a result, no book publisher or movie producer came calling for the rights.

Good thing he'd never had to rely on his business sense . . .

———

Don Pedro Rubirosa had dreamed of stability in his homeland, and his dream had come to life in the nightmarish figure of Trujillo. For thirty years, the Dominican people feared Trujillo as a fifth horseman of the apocalypse—but they enjoyed peace, more or less, within their borders. During the four years since the Benefactor was gunned down, though, a sense of foreboding had hung in the air—and things were getting worse.

After Ramfis fled the country at the end of 1961, a military authority was established with the promise of free elections in a year. Those were held—in December 1962—but Juan Bosch, the new president, took his reform movement too far for some tastes; in September 1963, he was overthrown in a coup by a military junta. A period of intense plotting followed, with Bosch, Trujillo's puppet vice president Joaquin Balaguer, and some others jockeying to take control of the country. The United States—as it did in Don Pedro's day—kept active watch on the situation. With Cuba right next door and Vietnam heating up, they would not lose the Dominican Republic.

In 1965, leftist rebels hoping to topple the junta took over the national media and declared outright revolution against military rule, and the Yankees felt sufficiently provoked to land troops on Dominican soil for the first time since before Trujillo's reign. Outright battles raged in the streets of Santo Domingo.* American interests were threatened— not only in the geopolitical scheme but in the flesh-and-blood-people-on-the-ground sense. On April 28, President Lyndon Johnson sent in the first 1,000 of what would eventually be a force of 30,000 U.S. marines. For the next four months, the Dominican Republic was a tinderbox, with skirmishes likely to break out at the least provocation and

* The capital had regained its traditional name in 1962 after the Trujillos fled.

no clear impression of what shape an eventual government might take—if one ever managed to hold on to the country.

Nobody in the American press thought to call Paris and ask Rubi about a situation that would have made his father heartsick. He had been a civilian for more than three years, but since his dismissal by the interim government in 1962, he had turned his back on his country. Indeed, he may have, in some way, thought of himself as more French than Dominican: He had lived only ten or so of his fifty-six years in his homeland, after all, and only the first of his five wives had been a compatriot.

The spring that found his country enmeshed in warfare was, for him, another lark. He and Odile cruised on Stavros Niarchos's massive yacht; to give an impression of just how big the boat was, consider that the voyage served as well as the honeymoon for Taki and Cristina. In one of the more memorable episodes of the trip, the partiers decided to make their own parodic version of the hit film *Goldfinger*, with Rubi playing James Bond, Niarchos playing the titular tycoon, Taki as Oddjob, Odile as Pussy Galore, and Gunther Sachs as cinematographer; it was a drunken pastiche—nobody remembered lines and the camera failed to work—best remembered as an afternoon's hijinks.

And spring was, too, the start of the French polo season.

July especially was big: the annual Coupe de France tournament at his home pitch, the Bagatelle in the Bois du Boulogne. Rubi and his Cibao–La Pampa teammates had enjoyed particular success in the Coupe de France in the mid-1950s, when he had the dough to bankroll a top-flight team: They won it three years running at one point. He was no longer up to that standard, quite, but he was still a hale player, if less adventurous than formerly. And it was one of the great social events of his summer.

His new team—including two Frenchman and an Argentine—made a fine showing. In red jerseys with a broad white horizontal stripe across the breast, Cibao–La Pampa tore a path straight through to the final, where, on Sunday, July 4, they faced Laversine, another Paris-based team with Baron Elie de Rothschild as its captain. It was a bright afternoon and a lucky one for Rubi; in a closely contested final, Cibao–La

Pampa won by a score of 2½ to 2. A worn-out Rubi stood beside his teammates with a small smile during the award ceremony, one hand holding the bridle of his horse, the other dangling his red polo helmet.

Rubi had maintained pretty good discipline during the tournament, but this called for a celebration. "Rubi used to like to go, as he would say, '*todo líquido*'—all liquid, all drinking, nothing to eat," as Taki remembered: a good old-fashioned *parranda.* And the night of this unexpected victory would be one of those *todo líquido* nights. In the spirit of sportsmanship, Elie de Rothschild organized a party at New Jimmy's to mark Rubi's triumph. Both teams were present, as were the wives and many friends from all the worlds Rubi had managed to touch in his decades in Paris: restaurateurs, diplomats, young playboys, some minor royals. It was one of those evenings that more people claim to have attended than the place could have managed: Everyone who knew Rubi in Paris at the time seems to recall being there.

Rubi and Odile had arrived in separate cars, she in the Austin, he in the Ferrari he bought in Belgium, and seemed not to be getting on in perfect harmony: not unusual at the time. The party raged on into the early morning hours and little by little the throng thinned—Rubi's *"ouvrier"* buddies heeding the impending call to their posts the next morning. By 5 A.M., Odile had left for home, tired or bored or maybe just getting ready for a trip they would be making later in the day to Cap d'Antibes with some Brazilian friends. Soon after that, New Jimmy's closed.

Rubi wasn't done, though. With a pair of Argentine polo buddies, he made for Le Calvados, the Spanish-themed nightspot near the Champs-Élysées; Rubi was fond of the musicians there and liked to finish his up nights listening to them and chasing a sandwich with a beer.

The trio got there at nearly 6 A.M. and found that there was already a party in progress: some Americans celebrating a birthday. Rubi and his chums joined in the festivities, singing Brazilian songs; Rubi got high marks for his comic impersonation of a rooster.

He called home and got no answer.

His friends left.

He sat with a ham sandwich and an Amstel and floated on the gentle swell of the music.

Sometime after seven, the headwaiter, Palomba, came over to him: "Rubi, don't you want to go to bed?"

"I'm fine here," he answered. "There's nice, soft music, I have my glass of beer. Why stir things up?"

(He used to brag about *always* wanting to stir things up.)

Then Palomba stopped to chat with Dany the waiter, and when he looked back Rubi was gone.

Yves Ricourt was an engineer from Viroflay, near Versailles. He was in the habit of driving his white BMW into the Bois de Boulogne and sitting on a bench to read the newspaper before reporting to work. He found himself a perfect spot that morning on the Allée de la Reine Marguerite, about two hundred yards north of the Avenue de Hippodrome. By 8 A.M. of what was shaping up as a warm, dry summer day, he was immersed in his paper.

Someone else was nearby: a bicyclist, heading north in the Allée de la Reine Marguerite.

And then a third party came suddenly upon them.

First to notice him was the bicyclist, who had just ridden past Ricourt's BMW, which was parked on the right side of the road. Then he heard a metallic scrape behind him and turned to see a silver Ferrari with a black convertible top hurtling toward him at some eighty miles an hour; prudently, he bailed off his bike onto the bridle path.

He didn't see as the Ferrari careered another fifty yards or so down the road. He didn't see as it hit a chestnut tree head-on.

Ricourt missed the first sound—his car being clipped by the Ferrari and pushed onto the bridle path. But he heard the second—"a brutal crash"—and he looked around to see the dazed bicyclist picking himself up off the ground. "The Ferrari came by like an arrow a few centimeters from his bike before crashing into the tree," Ricourt later explained.

The two raced to the wreck to see if they could help the driver. The rear of the car was still in the roadway. The front end had struck the tree just right of center. The grill was crumpled; the hood had been forced up from its hinges and backward toward the passenger compartment.

Ricourt and the cyclist approached the wreck to see if they could extricate the driver. Inside, a bloody mess: The fellow hadn't been wearing a seat belt; he was crumpled over the steering wheel, which had been bent forward above and below the hub by the thrust of his body; half his scalp was gone; he was covered in glass from the windshield, which had shattered; he was moaning; he was wedged in.

They dared not wrestle him out of the car. They dithered: What to do?

After a few minutes, a miracle: An ambulance came down the road, transporting a sick man to—would you believe it?—Hospital Marmottan, the very place where Rubi was taken the night he was shot beside Danielle Darrieux. The witnesses flagged the ambulance down, and the driver got out to help them rescue the injured man.

"It was difficult to extricate him," the ambulance man, Georges Bosquet, said. "He was jammed between the seat and the instrument panel." Barely conscious, he could do nothing to help himself.

"He was alive when we arrived to pry him from between the seat and the steering wheel," Bosquet remembered. "At one point I saw his lips move and I leaned forward. I heard him murmur a name. He said something like, 'Odile, Odile, where are you?' There was a look of pain on his face. When we placed him in the ambulance he lapsed into unconsciousness."

Bosquet secured him on a gurney and drove off. Ricourt stayed to see to his car and talk to the police and reporters. The bicyclist rode away without leaving his name.

And by the time the ambulance got to Marmottan, barely a mile away, it was too late.

=====

Should he have withered? Developed a cancer? Grown old? Unthinkable.

A flash of steel and rubber and noise and he was gone, just like that: Had he given a thought to his mortality, he would have wished for precisely such a finale.

He was identified at the hospital and Odile was phoned. She raced to Marmottan with her Brazilian friends at her side.

Soon word spread out of the hospital. A newspaperman called the house in Marnes-la-Coquette and spoke to the maid, Luisa. "Madame has left for the hospital," she said. "Monsieur has had an accident. I don't know anything. Everyone is calling for news. Just now it was Regine, you know, from the nightclub. But I don't know anything." Soon Regine came out to the house to relieve Luisa, answering the phone and meeting whoever showed up.

Manuel Pastoriza, a Dominican diplomat and friend of Rubi's, was alerted to the calamity by a journalist, and he sent his wife to fetch a priest to meet Odile at the hospital. It was no easy task to find a clergyman willing to attend to such an unrepentant sinner, and in the coming days Rubi's friends would fail to successfully negotiate for a funeral mass, settling instead for a simple, nonreligious remembrance.

Another journalist managed that afternoon to get Odile to share a few thoughts with the Hearst news syndicate, which had always been kind to Rubi:

> It is better that it happened this way. A clean break with the life he loved. Neither he nor I could have endured the spectacle of him lingering on, a cripple, unable to dance, play polo or drive his car.
>
> If Rubi could have chosen the way he died, this is the way he would have gone. In his car, in the dawn, going fast as he loved to do. He loved speed. But he loved life even more.
>
> I remember when Aly Khan died. Rubi grieved for Aly, whom he considered one of his closest friends. Then he remarked to me, 'If I must die this is the way I would like to finish—quickly, without pain.'
>
> Now I wish I had been with him. Perhaps I should have stayed with him. Perhaps he would have been more careful with me by his side. But even if he had driven as he always did, at Le Mans, at Sebring, anywhere, I would have liked to be beside him, even in death.

"It was fate," she told another journalist on the phone. "He believed in fate and I do too. Maybe it was better it ended this way than in some other more painful way."

═══

His death made headlines all over the world: a front-page story in many American newspapers and the better part of a full page each in *Time* and *Newsweek*. Predictably, all the juicy yarns from his past were rehashed, and photos of all five of his wives—plus Zsa Zsa—were dug out. Only one of his exes, Danielle, gave a statement to the press: "He died as he lived and would have wished—fast and furiously." There were testimonies to his sporting life, his *joie de vivre*, his personal magnetism and charm, his escapades as an international man of mystery and tiger of the boudoir seen, in retrospect, as harmless. It was often remarked that he wasn't wearing a seat belt at the time of his death, and it was always laughed off as an impossible thought. "A Rubirosa wearing a safety belt to cross the Bois de Boulogne," scoffed a friend. "That would have been perfectly ridiculous!"

Virtually none of the obituaries made a connection between Rubi's life and the contemporary crisis in the Dominican Republic, though the French left-wing newspaper *L'Humanité* managed to get off a potshot: "It wasn't only a playboy of merry escapades and sensational days who died yesterday, but also the right-hand man of a tyrannical regime that profited him and which the Americans would like to restore today in Santo Domingo in the name of 'liberty.' "

But much was made about the similarity to the Aly Khan tragedy of just over five years earlier (a few reports also invoked Portago). There were crucial differences between the deaths, though, that revealed something about each man. Aly had been driving with his sweetheart and a chauffeur and had been killed on his way to dinner in the suburbs, about a mile west of the Bois du Boulogne; Rubi's accident involved only him and could be laid to the fact that at fifty-six and after a night of *todo líquido* he was simply exhausted and shouldn't have been at the wheel. What was more, Aly had died in a Lancia sedan, not a proper sports car; for Rubi, however, it had long been a point of pride to drive a car very like the ones he had raced. "When I die, it won't be in a Lancia Flaminia like Aly," he told a friend once. "It would have to be at least a Maserati or a Ferrari."

Among the people who talked about such things, there were other whispers, about the coincidence of Rubi's death with that of Nina Dyer, an English model and onetime wife of Aly's brother, Sadruddin. Nina was found that same weekend in her house near Rubi's outside Paris, dead of an overdose of pills that may or may not have been accidental. She was only thirty-five and had once been married to Baron Heinie von Thyssen, another of the world's richest men; for surviving that contentious ten-month union, she was awarded an island in the Antilles, two luxury cars, a fortune in jewels (among them a famous set of black pearls said to have a curse on them), and a private menagerie including a panther and a leopard. During her marriage to von Thyssen she had attended a party hosted by Aly Khan and then met his brother; two years later, they were wed in a grand ceremony befitting his princely status, and it lasted nearly five years—they divorced in 1962. Since, she had retreated into seclusion. Whisperers tried to connect the two deaths: Had Rubi been grieving for Nina, or she for him, to the point of suicide? Were the legendary black pearls somehow involved? Daffy, but the stuff of society gossip nonetheless.

The idea that Rubi was a suicide had currency in more sober speculation as well. Fifty-six, out of work, married to a bored, frisky girl half his age, with no prospect of a new matrimonial payday, high on an upset polo victory, dressed in impeccable nightclubbing clothes, living amid suspicions that you were broke: Why not put your foot to the floor and aim at something solid? It seemed out of character—who else had such a zest for pleasure?—but there were hints from old chums like Claude Terrail and Regine that Rubi had slipped into a morose moment every now and again. Odile hadn't noticed—or hadn't, after he was gone, wanted to admit to noticing.

And nobody was really digging: It was, in the words of the *Times* of London, "the mundane death of a minor diplomat from a tiny country," another feckless playboy who pushed his luck once too often. In some senses, his death was a relief to those close to him: They could stop wondering what would become of him in another ten, twenty years. "We figured Rubi had about two years before his money ran completely out," said a friend, "and he would have been very miserable living the life of a pauper. He knew how to live life and how to die."

And it freed Odile, who was far worldlier at twenty-eight than she had been a decade earlier and who suddenly seemed a catch. Her future began even before Rubi was buried. "Jean Smith and Pat Kennedy [the sisters of the dead American president] arrived," Taki remembered. "It was simply awful. They have this tradition of Irish wakes, but the Latin Americans who were there practiced this sort of vigil and were very angry with them. They arrived and one of them said, 'Oh, God, Odile! Now you're ready for Teddy!' "

On July 9, the day of the funeral, though, she wasn't thinking of her future but her past. Heartbreakingly young to be the center of such an event, she watched the funeral from behind a black veil, her eyes weary from crying, her gaze half-empty. She was escorted through the day by Rubi's nephew Gilberto, and an escort was called for, not only because the widow was so staggered but because the steady rain meant somebody would need to hold an umbrella over her head. The cemetery was almost right next door to their house; they could have walked if the weather had been fair.

There was no mass, nor was there a graveside prayer. At 10 A.M., some 150 people gathered on the uninviting morning to hear Gunther Sachs and Pierre Leygonie deliver brief eulogies—the usual assortment of royalty, poloists, socialites, playboys, club owners, and celebrities, plus a liberal sprinkling of Dominicans with the means to live abroad. There were others, as well, nonboldface names: "Rubi had a lot of French friends who weren't in the jet set," said Taki. "I'd never seen them before: very bourgeois, solid, with good war records." People took note, of course, of all the women. "This could be a sultan's funeral," said one wag on the scene, "practically every woman present has shared his bed at some time." None of his previous wives was there, but the two Kennedy sisters were, and Claude Terrail and Regine, and Genevieve Fath and Helene Rochas, and the director Serge Marquand, and the actress Dany Robin, and the industrialist Paul-Louis Weiller, and Baron Elie de Rothschild, and the Dominican ambassador, Jose Puig. There was a huge bouquet of lilies from his Cibao–La Pampa teammates, and there were two hearses full of wreaths. By eleven-thirty everyone had filtered away.

Nobody wanted Odile to sit in the house in Marnes-la-Coquette and grieve. "My friends decided that the best thing for me to do was to leave my house in the country and go somewhere very far so I could forget about the whole thing," she remembered.

She went to the Kennedy compound on Hyannis Port, urged on by Patricia Lawford and Jean Smith, who took on, briefly, the roles of surrogate big sisters.

She needed their help more than she knew. "I went out to the airport and tried to cash a check," Odile said of her journey to Massachusetts. "Pat asked me where my checkbook was. I told her that I never had a checkbook. It was very embarrassing."

That she had only previously visited Hyannis Port in Rubi's company seemed not to weigh on her. Bobby's family was there, the sisters, Teddy, Rose, and old Joe. She sat amid the bustle of a Kennedy summer—sailing, touch football, tennis, movies, noisy meals, high spirits—and she felt better. "It was very good for me," she said. "I was so lost because Rubi was my husband and my love. He was a very good lover, as everybody knows. Everybody says that I was the great love of his life. So for me, I lost everything."

Other friends looked in on her and tried to divert her from her grief. "Gunther Sachs and Gerard de Clery came and spent the last weekend with me in Hyannis Port," she said. "We then went to New York. They both took me back to Europe on a cruise. We went to the Greek islands."

Finally, she put it behind her—"it took me about a year"—and moved on to Italy, to Brazil, to another playboy husband, Paulo Marinho. She was a familiar face at discos in New York, Rio, and Paris in the 1970s. Twenty years after that, she was living in New England, with an American husband, reluctant to remember her sensational first marriage.

Rubi had happened to her, as he had to so many other women, a whirlwind, a tidal wave, a flush, and then her life had gone on.

The long good-bye had never been his trademark.

SEVENTEEN

RIPPLES

The day after the funeral, the myth of Rubirosa began at once to fix itself and evanesce.

In Santo Domingo, where civil war was still raging, there were no obituaries: All of the daily newspapers had ceased publication during the hostilities. In their place were little partisan handbills and pamphlets, which carried spotty doses of news and rabid opinion—particularly the latter. On July 9, one of these, the right wing *La Patria,* carried this stirring notice:

We lament the death of Porfirio Rubirosa, and we lament his death because in Cuba, when the bandits of July 26 seized power and the Fidelist scourge began to persecute Cubans with criminal rage, this noted Dominican saved many lives by offering asylum in the embassy. Among those Cubans saved from falling into the hands of the red rabble was our brother Alberto Rodriguez.

To be grateful is a virtue of the well-born. For that reason, we are pained by the death of a friend who knew how to return friendship.

Rest in peace, Rubi, envied by many, a man in every sense of the word.

Rubi as political hero!

═══════

That same day, in the *New York Post*—then an oasis of liberal views—the poet Langston Hughes offered a commentary entitled "Playboys." He began by remembering an autumn day when he saw a crowd milling about an elegant Manhattan town house. A door opened. "Down the steps to the street in a straight back topcoat, with a discreetly gay scarf at his throat, came a handsome suede-gloved very well groomed young colored man. He was Porfirio Rubirosa. . . . A front-page face out of international news, one of the famous playboys of the Western World. And not white!"

To Hughes, mainstay of the Harlem Renaissance, it was obvious that Rubi was of mixed blood—a fact that no mainstream obituary mentioned and that was, indeed, never really discussed in his years of marrying rich and famous white women and running in the most elite circles in England, France, and the United States. For Hughes, his race made Rubi something of a wonder, an instance of a culture free of racial divides who managed to carry his birthright liberty into any world in which he circulated:

> In his youth Rubirosa was a handsome colored boy. In middle age he was still good-looking, dashing and dynamic. He must have possessed the same sort of personality attraction for women as does our Congressman from Harlem Adam Clayton Powell, who, although Negro, is several shades lighter in complexion than was Rubirosa. Mulatto Latins, however, in their own Caribbean or South American lands, are not classed as Negro in the U.S.A. sense of the term, especially if their tongue is Spanish. . . . Had he been an American

citizen by birth, the headlines would probably have read: NEGRO PLAYBOY DIES.

Rubi was, Hughes concluded, a breath of fresh—and racially liberated—air: "I am all for colorful gentlemen of color adding color and excitement, romance and the light touch to this rather grim world of wars, poverty and racism in which we live."

Rubi as civil rights icon! Rubi as hedonist liberator!

He was barely dead a year when he—or, rather, a barely fictionalized version of him—appeared as the hero of a door-stopping novel by Harold Robbins. *The Adventurers* was the story of Dax Xenos, son of a morally upright lawyer/soldier from Corteguay, a fictional Latin American country that had been taken over by a ruthless mercenary who slaughtered everyone who dared oppose his cult of personality. Dax was raised in Europe, where he played polo, drove sports cars too fast, and bedded countless women: society girls, rich men's wives, and, finally, the world's wealthiest girl, whom he married. His one true love, though, was the dictator's daughter. Among his decadent European friends was a White Russian fashion designer. Dax's was a world of incalculable wealth, depravity, and boredom. But when his father mysteriously died back home, he determined to rid Corteguay of its evil leader.

The book was, predictably, overheated and a drag—an endless eight hundred or so pages of pulp sensation. Naturally, it was a massive hit. And, naturally, Hollywood came calling. In 1970, a megabuck version of *The Adventurers* starring an international all-star cast was released to universally derisive reviews. Ernest Borgnine; Candace Bergen; John Ireland; Olivia de Havilland; Rossano Brazzi; Fernando Rey; Anna Moffo; Charles Aznavour; Peter Graves; Jaclyn Smith: They all dirtied their hems in director Lewis Gilbert's hilariously off-kilter, sprawling mess of a movie. Most sullied, though, was Bekim Fehmiu, the thirtysomething Yugoslavian heartthrob cast in the role of Dax. With thick lips and protruding brows, he looked a degenerate cross of

Ringo Starr and Jean-Paul Belmondo—and without the acting chops of either. The endless three-hour film was sexually explicit—chunks of Gilbert's clumsy flesh-flashing had to be cut for the U.S. release—and explicitly awful: strictly for Bekim Fehmiu completists.

Rubi as turkey!

=====

In Mexico in 1972, the editors of the comic book *¡Asombro!* ("Amazement!") saw fit to publish an entire issue telling the life story of *"El Famoso 'Play Boy'"* Rubirosa. It began with the *"conquista"* of Flor de Oro Trujillo (the two were illustrated as if almost middle-aged), continued with his marriage to Danielle Darrieux (drawn as a platinum blonde), introduced Zsa Zsa as a lover during the Doris Duke years, depicted him as a great poker player and master bullfighter (and breeder of fighting cocks, complete with full Mexican costume), credited him with winning an auto race that he lost, and had him happily honeymooning with Barbara Hutton in Spain and Venice. At the same time, it entirely ignored his life as a diplomat, his activities during World War II, his service in Argentina and Cuba, his relationship to Trujillo's tyranny, and all the potentially nasty business he engaged in throughout his life. Whether it was adhering to conventions of Mexican comic books or was just a quick piece of hackery, it was a magnificently bizarre simulacrum of his life.

"You are the most agile journalist I've ever known," he tells Doris over dinner at Maxim's. When he first kisses Zsa Zsa, he thinks to himself, "She doesn't kiss badly, but she could improve with me," and then he watches appreciatively as she performs a drunken striptease on a nightclub table. He encourages Barbara to drink the freshly spilled blood of a goose at the Tour d'Argent restaurant, which has been relocated to the French countryside.

Rubi as opium dream!

=====

And then he truly did begin to fade.

A decade and more after his death, his name ceased circulating other than when people he knew died or places and pastimes associated with him came to an end. When Ramfis Trujillo wrecked his car in Spain in 1967, killing his female passenger, Rubi's name was inevitably mentioned. Ditto three years later when, again in Spain, Ramfis drove headfirst into a Jaguar driven by the duchess of Albuquerque; the duchess died at the scene; Ramfis lingered for a week before his injuries took him. When Doris Duke died in 1993, ghostly and weird and gulled by a bullying butler who made off with her fortune far more ruthlessly than Rubi had dipped into it, she was said still to have a photo of her second (and last) husband by her bedside; she had tried to contact him through mediums, and she'd never parted with the ruby-encrusted jewelry he'd given her.

In Florence, Italy, some enterprising lads opened a successful night spot and called it Porfirio Rubirosa; it was popular for years. In Washington Heights, the Dominican neighborhood north of Harlem, some equally enterprising lads opened a men's boutique called Rubirosa that didn't last. Hugo Boss designed a line of suits and called it Rubirosa; a Dominican cigar concern called itself the same.

His name popped up in works of fiction: Philip Roth's alter ego Nathan Zuckerman, regarding himself in the mirror before going out, decided he was "neatly attired, but no Rubirosa"; in press materials promoting the film of Brett Easton Ellis's *American Psycho,* homicidal yuppie Patrick Bateman was said to own a rose gold Rolex that was once Rubi's; Rubi made a cameo in the thoughts of the aged Trujillo in Mario Vargas Llosa's *The Feast of the Goat,* while his penis made a cameo in Truman Capote's *Answered Prayers.* Russell Baker and Groucho Marx got laughs by dropping his name, the latter with an almost pathological frequency. Auto sports enthusiasts collected expensive little scale-models of some of the Ferraris he raced.

Always there was talk of a movie: In the 1980s, Julius Epstein, one of the twin brothers who wrote *Casablanca,* produced a massive, sprawling, and largely incoherent version of his life; a Dominican company persisted into the 2000s on their own effort. There was a radio play, a "mock-heroic epic comedy" entitled *The Splendor and Death of Porfirio Rubirosa,* and a musical entitled, yes, *Rubirosa! The Musical.*

The one time he did appear in a film as a character was in *Too Rich,* a TV miniseries about Doris Duke; he was played with oily iciness by Michael Nouri, who had something of Rubi's dark mystery.

In 1984 in a stark bedroom at the Betty Ford Clinic in Rancho Mirage, Peter Lawford, months away from death, submitted to one of the mandatory steps in his recovery from drug-and-alcohol addiction: writing letters expressing his remorse to people who were gone from his life. Among these was a note to his former brother-in-law, John F. Kennedy. First he told the dead president about himself, about contemporary politics, about the state of his health and the condition of their families. And then he turned his attention to JFK and what his existence in the afterlife must have been like: "Are you Pres. of anything? A garden club or bowling team perhaps! You must be running something. . . . How are Marilyn, Bobby, Rubirosa? Give them my love. If you should run into Steve McQueen or Vic Morrow, give them my love. . . ." A glorious, debauched party in heaven and—drat the luck!—Lawford not yet able to attend.

Zsa Zsa, who would be seriously injured in her own catastrophic car wreck in 2002, was always keen to talk about him. She claimed that his last words were "Zsa Zsa" (when, of course, he had mumbled "Odile"). And she claimed to have paid to keep flowers on his grave at Père Lachaise Cemetery (where, of course, he wasn't buried). Too, she always insisted that she wasn't as stuck on him as he on her; asked if he was the great love of her life, she had a stock response that always got a laugh out of Merv, Johnny, and the studio audience: "No, but I was the great love of his."

Back home in the Dominican Republic, Rubi not only faded from memory but was actively hidden away. The occasional Dominican polo player might still wear a red helmet as a tribute to him, but others saw him as an embarrassment, an aberration, and, worst, a throwback to the era of Trujillo, which people still shuddered to discuss. In 2003, a little war was waged in the opinion pages of *Listín Diario* over Rubi's legacy, with one writer declaring starkly his resentment of the fact that foreigners still remembered one Dominican figure over all the others: *"No, señor, yo no soy del país de Rubirosa"* ("No, sir, I am not from the land of Rubirosa"). Letter writers shouted the fellow down for days. Absent children, absent a fortune, absent great works, absent a plaque marking the scenes of his birth, a vainglorious little gesture of sportsmen and a petty quarrel on the op-ed pages stood as his only legacies in his homeland.

A figure of fleeting fascination in life, he remained elusive in death.

He had given himself over to sensations, he created sensations, he ended in sensation, and, predictably, as those sensations faded, so did memory of him. People who knew him aged and died; those left remembered the stuff of the legend and not the man.

He had surpassed all expectations that he might have had for himself—a superstar from a backwater, a rich man with no career or inheritance, a cagey diplomat and schemer with no advanced education, a man more worldly, celebrated, and experienced than either Pedro Rubirosa or Rafael Trujillo—his physical and spiritual daddies—could ever have imagined.

He had epitomized the eras he lived in—Paris before and after World War II, Argentina in its Perónist heyday, Hollywood and Palm Beach in their postwar glow, Havana on the eve of revolution. And he had died at just the right time: Nothing would have been more ridiculous than a Rubirosa, all swank and elegant and bubbling with romantic innuendo, in the hippie era of free love and antifashion.

In leaving behind only a thin spoor, he was himself utterly—a man of moments, brief passions, and slight mysteries, a phantom of sorts, passing flimsily through an easily distracted public ken.

Could he have been more? He had the tools: the native cunning, the daring, the reflexes, the style. He might have been the salvation of his nation or an important international sporting or diplomatic figure.

But his ambition was not so much to *do* good as to *feel* it. He was, in the crudest sense, selfish—not greedy exactly, but rather intent on pleasures that could only be his own. The world was there for him, not vice versa.

He died in Paris, and best serve his spirit by remembering him as a Dominican boy arriving in that city in a kidskin coat, staring up at bombers, frightened by movies, dazzled by soldiers and fancy ladies, his tongue hanging out to visit a nightclub. That boy did everything he ever wanted, everything he could imagine, things he'd never heard of but knew he'd like; that boy and the man he became were closer than anyone ever imagined.

For forty years he gave himself over to his simplest urges. And the urge to do or mean more than that simply never struck him. He wanted the world only for moments. And the world—and why not?—returned the favor.

Look around for a trace of him: vanished: perfect.

INSPIRATIONS, SOURCES,

AND DEBTS

Dominican playboy Porfirio Rubirosa. . . .

I came across that phrase for the first time in 1994 or '95 when I was at work on a biography of Jerry Lewis and writing about *Three Ring Circus,* one of the last films he made with Dean Martin. Somebody named Porfirio Rubirosa had made some headlines by visiting Zsa Zsa Gabor on the Arizona set of the film.

I had no clue who Rubirosa was or why his visit was so notable or any other details of his life. I was simply taken with that phrase, the sound of it: *Dominican playboy Porfirio Rubirosa,* like a Stan Getz riff—I had to put it in the book.

Two years or so later, as I was writing a book about Frank Sinatra and the Rat Pack, there he was again: Dominican playboy Porfirio Rubirosa, sailing off Hyannis Port with Ted Kennedy and Sinatra, cruising the Mediterranean with Frank and Dean and Peter Lawford and old Joe Kennedy. Again, I dropped the irresistible phrase into a couple of sentences.

By then there was such a thing as the World Wide Web, and I was able to troll for more information about this mystery man with the musical name. I learned he'd been married to both Doris Duke and Barbara Hutton, and I went to the library to find biographies of them. There were several, and in every case the author had stopped his or her book to tell a version of the story of the amazing Señor Rubirosa. I couldn't believe what I was reading; I was hooked. It was 1997, and I knew I had to write about this guy.

Encouraged by my agent, Richard Pine, and my friend and editor Bill Thomas, I began research in New York, Los Angeles, Paris, and my own home city, Portland, Oregon. The book I had hoped to write didn't, alas, find a home, but I never let go of what I knew was a swell idea; I kept doing research on Rubi even while writing a completely unrelated book into which I couldn't even drop his name. When that project was behind me, my editors asked what I wanted to do next. I had yet another idea, but Rubi still stuck with me and I hit these foster folks with a brief version of his life. They got it—and, more important, they gave me the green light to go ahead and write it.

Et voilà. . . .

=====

I'm not the first person to tell this story. Rubi left the world a slender memoir, published serially in a French newspaper and then in like form in Spanish in the Dominican Republic. (Many of the direct quotes in this book are taken from my own translation of his words.) Two Dominican authors have written biographies of him—Lipe Collado and Pablo Clase Hijo—as have a German writer, Andreas Zielcke, a French writer, Pierre Delannoy, and a Dominican-American novelist, Victor Peña-Rivera. In English, Rubi appears at length among the playboys depicted in a singular book by Alice-Leone Moats. And there have been many, many magazine and newspaper portraits of him, from obituaries to retrospective features to contemporary accounts of this or that wild episode.

Inevitably, other people's stories factored into the telling of Rubi's. The Trujillo family and the Trujillo Era of Dominican history are covered by dozens of books, most notably those of Robert Crassweller, who wrote the definitive biography of the Benefactor, and Bernardo Vega, who has published the family's letters and uncovered detailed accounts of Ramfis Trujillo's medical history. As I learned early on, the lives of Doris Duke and Barbara Hutton have been the subject of perhaps a half-dozen books each, none better than those by Stephanie Mansfield and C. David Heymann, respectively. Flor de Oro Trujillo published a lengthy memoir in serial form in *Look* magazine in the mid-1960s and then gave no other interviews concerning Rubi until her death. And Zsa Zsa Gabor, unique among Rubi's long-term loves, told her own story not once, not twice, but three times—and some details actually remained consistent throughout: well done!

Two of Rubi's wives—both French actresses—were still alive when I was at work. Danielle Darrieux, through her agent, refused comment, as she has refused all comment on Rubi for more than a half century. The former Odile Rodin and her current husband thought about contributing their memories and then chose not to participate; I thank them just the same for their gracious consideration. Several other acquaintances of Rubi's spoke to me but asked not to be named: I thank them all now in the fashion they preferred.

Quite a bit of the material I used to construct this story—in balance, the majority—comes from two types of written sources: governmental documents from the United States and the Dominican Republic and contemporary newspaper and magazine accounts from those two countries as well as Great Britain and France.

Through Freedom of Information Act requests, I received literally thousands of pages concerning the activities of Rubi, Rafael Trujillo, Ramfis Trujillo, and various other personages who populate this story from the Federal Bureau of Investigation, the Central Intelligence Agency, the Department of State, and the Department of Homeland Security. I am grateful to those bodies for their assistance and especially to Marvin Russell of the United States National Archives and Records Administration for tracking down a trove of helpful documents at the NARA facility in College Park, Maryland. I received additional assistance from Ken Cobb at the Municipal Archives of the City of New York. And I was greeted with warmth, patience, and openness by Julio Campos, Eddy Jaquez, and the staff of the Archivo General de la Nación in Santo Domingo.

Inevitably, I worked long and often at libraries, where I found not only rare books but newspaper and magazine clippings, public documents, maps, sound and video recordings, and so on. I wish to acknowledge the facilities of the Library of Congress, the Margaret Herrick Library of the Academy of Motion Picture Arts and Sciences, the New York Public Library (both the Humanities and Social Science Library and the Library for the Performing Arts), and, especially, the Multnomah County Library in Portland, not only for its indispensable permanent collections but for the assistance of its interlibrary loan staff, who saved my bacon more than once. Overseas, I worked in the British Library Newspaper Reading Room at Colindale, the library of the British Film Institute, and two branches of the Bibliothèque National de France (the space-age François Mitterrand and the lush Richelieu). In particular, I wish to acknowledge the impeccable professionalism and grace extended me by M. E. Diaz and the staff of the Biblioteca Nacional Pedro Henríquez Ureña in Santo Domingo.

I relied on literally thousands of newspaper and magazine articles in three languages covering more than seventy years of history (you should see my collection of 1950s gossip rags!). I'd like to acknowledge, if only with a broad sweep of my arm, all the work that went into those invaluable documents by all the writers and editors who produced them. In particular I want to extend special thanks to two colleagues who shared some essential leads and insights. Gary Cohen, who wrote a lively account of Rubi's life for *Vanity Fair* in 2002, had every reason to be chary of me and did just the opposite; responding to my inquiries with courtesy and speed, he was a consummate gentleman and professional in every respect. And Stephanie Mansfield probably doesn't even remember the help and encouragement she gave me back in 1997 when I contacted her with the first thoughts I had about writing this book.

For photographic assistance, I thank the staffs of Corbis, Getty Images, and, especially the gracious folks at Photofest and the generous staff of Editora Cole of Santo Domingo. I'd like as well to acknowledge the dozens of Web sites where I learned this or that odd detail about auto racing, fashion, night life, polo, Dominican history, or the lives of a number of the curious folks who are touched on in these pages: I can neither recall nor thank all the people who have built those amazing resources, but big-up yourselves.

And there were other people—almost all of them strangers to me when I interrupted their lives—who unstintingly shared memories, ideas, clues, books, information, and wise counsel. They include Cindy Adams, Paul Austerlitz, Diogenes Reyna Brito, David Patrick Columbia, Tom D'Antoni, Robin Derby, Christian Doumit, Leo Hollis, Patrick Jucaud, Douglas W. Keeney, Jim Long, Pete Lowery, Andy Miller, Jim Mitchell, Ed Morales, Raphael Pallais, Jeffrey D. Rowe, Jean-Claude Sauer, Liz Smith, Claude Terrail, Taki Theodoracopulos, Bernardo Vega, and Thomas Vincent. I am in debt to them all.

Finally, because, in a moment of goal-and-beer-induced merriment, I said I would, thank you to the Portland Timbers Football Club and, especially, the Timbers Army, for providing the release that a shut-in desperately needed to survive a grueling spring and summer of writing.

───

In the time I worked on this project I did some writing for *The Guardian* and *Movieline's Hollywood Life,* and I appreciate the confidence of the editors of those publications in my ability to juggle assignments on deadline.

At *The Oregonian* I have long enjoyed the most heartening support network imaginable. The ability to take time away from film reviewing to write this book was granted me by a generous management team including Fred Stickel, Patrick Stickel, Sandra Mims Rowe, Peter Bhatia, and Tom Whitehouse. Closer to my desk, I could not have taken the first step on this project without the help and support of Jolene Krawczak and Karen Brooks. And the editors with whom I work on a daily basis— Grant Butler, Barry Johnson, and Shawn Vitt—were stupendous, as ever, offering encouragement, liberty, and, most important, friendship; I can't imagine what I'd do without them. Lastly, as I wrenched these pages out of my head, my bosom pals Karen Karbo, Marc Mohan, and Michael Russell did an epic job of keeping the good readers of our newspaper abreast of all the film news that was fit to print. It was a treat to read them—and a comfort.

At Fourth Estate, Rachel Safko served the office of traffic cop genially. David Falk was equally genteel in his copyedit. Crucial early encouragement was offered by Matthew Hamilton, Clive Priddle, and Nick Davies, all of whom have moved on. Courtney Hodell, who found this project in her sure hands when the game of hot potato ended, proved not only a tremendous advocate but a wonderfully perceptive line editor and a boon chum to boot: my humble, grateful thanks.

At Inkwell Management (which will always be Arthur Pine Associates to me, sorry . . .), I am in the perennial debt of Richard Pine and Lori Andiman, my longtime partners in genteel crime.

At home, I have yet again been encouraged, humored, tolerated, and even coddled while I put myself—and, too often, those around me—through the wringer. To Mickie Levy, Jennifer Levy, and Lucretia Thornton, my love and thanks. To Vincent, Anthony, and Paula Levy, ditto, and more, with ice cream on top. And to Mary Bartholemy, well, let me just say simply that I owe her everything.

WORKS CONSULTED

Aherne, Brian. *A Dreadful Man: The Story of Hollywood's Most Original Cad, George Sanders*. New York: Berkley Books, 1981.

Alleged Assassination Plots Involving Foreign Leaders: An Interim Report of the Select Committee to Study Governmental Operations with Respect to Intelligence Activities, United States Senate. Washington, D.C.: U.S. Government Printing Office, 1975.

Arzeno Rodgriguez, Luis. *Trujillo . . . Chapita No!* Santo Domingo: 1997.

Balaguer, Joaquin. *Memorias de un Cortesano de la Era de Trujillo*. Santo Domingo: Editora Corripio, 1989.

Beezley, William H., and Linda A. Curcio-Nagy, eds. *Latin American Popular Culture: An Introduction*. Wilmington, Del.: Scholarly Resources, 2000.

Brashler, William. *The Don: The Life and Death of Sam Giancana*. New York: Harper & Row, 1977.

Breuer, William B. *Vendetta! Castro and the Kennedy Brothers*. New York: John Wiley & Sons, 1997.

Brown, Peter H. *Kim Novak: Reluctant Goddess*. New York: St. Martin's Press, 1986.

———. *Such Devoted Sisters: Those Fabulous Gabors*. New York: St. Martin's Press, 1985.

Bruno, Michael. *Venus in Hollywood: The Continental Enchantress from Garbo to Loren*. Secaucus, N.J.: Lyle Stuart, 1970.

Capote, Truman. *Answered Prayers*. New York: Random House, 1987.

Casanova, Giacomo. *The Story of My Life*. Trans. Stephen Sartarelli and Sophie Hawkes. New York: Marsilio Publishers, 2000.

Cassini, Igor. *I'd Do It All Over Again: The Life and Times of Igor Cassini*. New York: G.P. Putnam's Sons, 1977.

Cassini, Oleg. *In My Own Fashion: An Autobiography.* New York: Simon and Schuster, 1987.

Cirules, Enrique. *El Imperio de la Habana.* Havana: Editorial Letras Cubanas, 1999.

Clase Hijo, Pablo. *Porfirio Rubirosa: El Primer Playboy del Mundo.* Santo Domingo: Biblioteca Taller, 1978.

Collado, Lipe. *Anécdotas y Crueldades de Trujillo.* Santo Domingo: Editora Collado, 2002.

———. *El Foro Público en la Era de Trujillo.* Santo Domingo: Editora Collado, 2000.

———. *Porfirio Rubirosa: La Impresionante Vida de un Seductor.* Santo Domingo: Editora Collado, 2002.

———. *El Tíguere Dominicano.* Santo Domingo: Editora Collado, 2002.

Collins, Joan. *Past Imperfect: An Autobiography.* New York: Berkley Books, 1985.

Crassweller, Robert D. *Trujillo: The Life and Times of a Caribbean Dictator.* New York: Macmillan, 1966.

Darrieux, Danielle, with Jean-Pierre Ferrière. *Filmographie Commentée par Elle-Même.* Paris: Ramsay Cinema, 1995.

Davis, Sammy, Jr., with Jane and Burt Boyar. *Why Me? The Sammy Davis, Jr. Story.* New York: Warner Books, 1989.

Delanney, Charles, *Django Reinhardt.* Trans. Michael James, New York: Da Capo Press, 1961.

Delannoy, Pierre. *"Just a Gigolo": Rubirosa, Le Dernier des Play-Boys.* Paris; Olivier Orban, 1987.

Demaris, Ovid. *The Last Mafioso: The Treacherous World of Jimmy Fratianno.* New York: New York Times Books, 1981.

Derby, Lauren H. *The Magic of Modernity: Dictatorship and Civic Culture in the Dominican Republic, 1916–1962.* Chicago: University of Chicago dissertation, 1998.

Diederich, Bernard. *Trujillo: The Death of the Goat.* Boston: Little, Brown and Company, 1978.

Dold, Gaylord. *Dominican Republic Handbook.* Chico, Calif.: Moon Travel Handbooks, 1997.

Duke, Pony, and Jason Thomas. *Too Rich: The Family Secrets of Doris Duke.* New York: HarperCollins, 1996.

Enciclopedia Dominicana, Santo Domingo: Enciclopedia Dominicana, 1978.

Epstein, Edward Z. *Notorious Divorces*, Secaucus, N. J.: Lyle Stuart, 1976.

Espaillat, General Arturo, *Trujillo: The Last Caesar.* Chicago: Henry Regnery Company, 1963.

Estévez, Luis José León. *Yo, Ramfis Trujillo.* Santo Domingo: Editorial Letra Gráfica, 2002.

Gabor, Eva. *Orchids and Salami.* Garden City, N.Y.: Doubleday, 1954.

Gabor, Jolie (as told to Cindy Adams). *Jolie Gabor.* New York: Mason/Charter, 1975.

Gabor, Zsa Zsa. *How to Catch a Man, How to Keep a Man. How to Get Rid of a Man.* Garden City, N.Y.: Doubleday, 1970.

———. *My Story, Written for Me by Gerold Frank.* Cleveland: World Publishing Co., 1960.

———, with Wendy Leigh. *One Lifetime Is Not Enough.* New York: Delacorte, 1991.

Galíndez, Jesus de. *The Era of Trujillo.* Ed. Russell H. Fitzgibbon. Tuscon: University of Arizona Press, 1973.

Graham, Sheilah, *How to Marry Super Rich, or Love, Money, and the Morning After.* New York: Ballantine, 1974.

Granger, Stewart. *Sparks Fly Upward.* New York: G. P. Putnam's Sons, 1991.

Harvey, Sean. *The Rough Guide to the Dominican Republic.* London: Rough Guides, 2002.

Hersh, Seymour M. *The Dark Side of Camelot.* New York: Little, Brown and Company, 1997.

Heymann, C. David. *Poor Little Rich Girl: The Life and Legend of Barbara Hutton.* New York: Random House, 1983.

Howard, David. *Dominican Republic: A Guide to the People, Politics and Culture.* New York: Interlink, 1999.

Jennings, Dean. *Barbara Hutton: A Candid Biography of the Richest Woman in the World.* London: W. H. Allen, 1968.

Kelley, Kitty. *His Way: The Unauthorized Biography of Frank Sinatra.* New York: Bantam, 1986.

Kitt, Eartha. *Confessions of a Sex Kitten.* New York: Barricade Books, 1989.

Malossi, Giannino, ed. *Latin Lover: The Passionate South.* Milan: Edizione Charta, 1996.

Manchester, William. *Portrait of a President: John F. Kennedy in Profile.* Boston: Little, Brown & Co., 1962.

Mansfield, Stephanie. *The Richest Girl in the World: The Extravagant Life and Times of Doris Duke.* New York: G. P. Putnam's Sons, 1992.

Moats, Alice-Leone. *The Million Dollar Studs.* New York: Delacorte Press, 1977.

Morales, Ed. *The Latin Beat: The Rhythms and Roots of Latin Music from Bossa Nova to Salsa and Beyond.* New York: Da Capo Press, 2003.

Nicholas, Margaret. *The World's Greatest Lovers*. London: Octopus Books, 1985.

Nizer, Louis. *Reflections Without Mirrors: An Autobiography of the Mind*. Garden City, N.Y.: Doubleday, 1978.

Ornes, German E. *Trujillo: Little Casear of the Caribbean*. New York: Thomas Nelson & Sons, 1958.

Osorio Lizarazo, J. A. *Portrait of Trujillo*, Santo Domingo: 1958.

Peña–Rivera, Victor A. *El Playboy Porfirio Rubirosa: Su Vida y Sus Tiempos*. Miami: Victoria Press, 1991.

Robbins, Harold. *The Adventurers*. New York: Trident Press, 1966.

Roemer, William F. Jr. *Man Against the Mob*. New York: Ivy Books, 1989.

Rubirosa, Porfirio. *Mis Memorias*. Santo Domingo: Editorial Letra Gráfica, 2000.

Saillant Valverde, Cesar A. *Disclose to Sanchez Cabral: Ramfis Trujillo's Role in the Murder of the Heroes of May 30, 1961*. Santo Domingo: Editorial del Caribe, 1962.

Sanders, George. *Memoirs of a Professional Cad*. (New York: G. P. Putnam's Sons, 1960.

Shack, William A. *Harlem in Montmartre: A Paris Jazz Story Between the Great Wars*. Berkeley: University of California Press, 2001.

Slater, Leonard. *Aly: A Biography*. New York: Random House, 1965.

Smith, Liz. *Natural Blonde: A Memoir*. New York: Hyperion, 2000.

Stern, Michael. *No Innocence Abroad*. New York: Random House, 1953.

Szulc, Tad. *Dominican Diary*. New York: Dell, 1965.

Theodoracopulos, Taki. *High Life*. London: Penguin, 1989.

———. *Princes, Playboys and High-Class Tarts*. Princeton: Karz-Cohl Publishing, 1984.

Turtu, Anthony, and Donald F. Reuter. *Gaborabilia: An Illustrated Celebration of the Fabulous, Legendary Gabor Sisters*. New York: Three Rivers Press, 2001.

Ulmann, Alec. *The Sebring Story*. Philadelphia: Chilton, 1969.

Unanue, Manuel de Dios. *El Caso Galíndez*. New York: Editorial Cupre, 1988.

Valenti, Peter. *Errol Flynn: A Bio-bibliography*. Westport, Conn.: Greenwood Press, 1984.

Valentine, Tom, and Patrick Mahn. *Daddy's Duchess: An Unauthorized Biography of Doris Duke*. Secaucus, N.J.: Lyle Stuart, 1987.

Van Rensselaer, Philip. *Million Dollar Baby: An Intimate Portrait of Barbara Hutton*. New York: G. P. Putnam's Sons, 1979.

Vargas Llosa, Mario. *The Feast of the Goat.* Trans. Edith Grossman. New York: Farrar, Straus & Giroux, 2001.

Vega, Bernardo. *Los Estados Unidos Y Trujillo, Año 1930.* Santo Domingo: Fundación Cultural Dominicana, 1986.

———. *Los Estados Unidos Y Trujillo, Año 1947.* Santo Domingo: Fundación Cultural Dominicana, 1984.

———. *Los Estados Unidos Y Trujillo, Los Días Finales: 1960–61.* Santo Domingo: Fundación Cultural Dominicana, 1999.

———. *Los Trujillos Se Escriben.* Santo Domingo: Fundación Cultural Dominicana, 1987.

Vilallonga, José Luis de. *Á Pleines Dents.* Paris: Éditions J'ai Lu, 1974.

———. *Gold Gotha.* Paris: éditions de Seuil, 1972.

Vorshim, Alfredo F. *From Hitler to Trujillo: In Search of a Homeland.* Raleigh, N.C.: Boson Books, 2000.

Wiese Delgado, Dr. Hans Paul. *Trujillo: Amado por Muchos, Odiado por Otros, Temido por Todos.* Santo Domingo: Editorial Letra Gráfica, 1983.

Wilson, Christopher. *Dancing with the Devil: The Windsors and Jimmy Donohue.* New York: St. Martin's Press, 2001.

Wright, William. *Heiress: The Rich Life of Marjorie Merriwether Post.* Washington, D.C.: New Republic Books, 1978.

Zielcke, Andreas. *Der Letzte Playboy: Das Leben des Porfirio Rubirosa.* Göttingen: Steidl Verlag, 1992.

INDEX

Rubirosa, Pedro Maria "Don Pedro,"
      5–6, 9–11, 23, 46, 55, 74, 308
   birth of, 9
   death of, 26, 35, 36, 37
   diplomatic career of, 13, 16–21, 22,
      57
   ill health of, 24, 26–27
   as lover of women, 10–11
   marital infidelity of, 11, 12–13
   as military general, 9, 12, 26
   Rubi's relationship with, 21, 22,
      23–24
   studies of, 18
   tíguerismo of, 10, 18
   Trujillo and, 27, 33, 36–37
Rubirosa Ariza, Porfirio "Rubi":
   appearance of, 21, 25, 39, 46, 62,
      91, 122, 134, 178, 203, 225,
      270, 271, 320
   attempted assassination of, 98–102
   attentive attitude of, 123
   auto accidents of, 40, 311–12, 314
   baccalaureate failed by, 22–23
   birth of, 11
   bourgeois lifestyle enjoyed by, 302–3
   boxing skills of, 21–22, 26, 49, 265,
      305
   business ventures of, 50, 51–54, 59,
      155–59, 264, 267, 300–1,
      307–8
   charm of, 122–24, 223–24, 240,
      271–72
   childhood of, 5–6
   childlessness of, 60*n*, 127
   clothing style of, 132, 224–25, 306
   comic book biography of, 322
   courting technique of, 166–68,
      223–24, 237–38, 240–41
   Creole heritage of, 62, 122, 131,
      320–21
   death of, 311–17, 325
   diplomatic career of, 46, 49–50,
      56–57, 61–69, 71–72, 74,
      79–82, 91–92, 103, 104, 113,
      131, 137, 138–40, 149,
      154–55, 163, 262–67, 268,
      272, 274–75, 295, 297–98, 322

   as divorce correspondent, 161–63,
      187, 195, 200
   in Dominican army, 37–40, 42–44,
      51, 54
   education of, 18–19, 21–23, 24, 27
   extended family of, 44–45, 50, 55
   fame of, 214, 223–29, 231, 233,
      236–37, 245, 263, 265, 288,
      304, 319–26
   in fiction, 321–22, 323
   financial resources of, 143, 150,
      154–55, 200, 214, 236–37,
      262, 270, 288, 291, 294,
      307–8, 315
   fortune-teller's prediction for, 101
   funeral of, 313, 316
   genital endowment of, 124–28, 130,
      141
   golf attempted by, 301
   government investigations of,
      290–91, 297–302
   height of, 225
   homosexuals' attraction to, 276–77
   knee injury of, 40
   last words of, 312, 324
   legal studies of, 24, 36
   as legendary lover, 48, 159–63, 276,
      280, 317
   memoirs of, 307–8
   movie biographies of, 323–24
   naming of, 11–12
   obituaries of, 313–14, 315, 319–20
   parrandas of, 50–51, 61, 73, 134,
      209, 283, 303, 306, 310–11
   pato played by, 140, 141
   perfume scheme of, 307
   personality of, 38, 74, 122–28, 140,
      159, 177, 178, 191, 225, 239,
      240–41, 263, 271, 304
   playboy qualities of, 115–16, 306
   pleasure pursued by, 19, 22–23,
      50–51, 61, 73–74, 76–77, 88,
      102, 134–35, 140–41, 177,
      209, 271, 274–75, 302, 303,
      304–5, 325–26
   reading habits of, 218
   sexual compulsiveness of, 160–61

Rubirosa-Gabor relationship (*cont'd*)
   Zsa Zsa's black eye in, 196–97,
      200–2, 204, 206, 217
   Zsa Zsa's press conferences in, 201,
      206, 216–17, 221–22
Rubirosa-Hutton relationship, 2–3,
      189–91, 194–97, 199–215,
      224, 242, 276, 240, 307–8, 322
   B-25 airplane in, 208, 214, 304–5
   Barbara's broken ankle in, 207–8
   courtship in, 191, 204
   divorce in, 215
   first meeting in, 181, 189–90
   gifts in, 208, 214, 304–5
   honeymoon in, 207–9, 264
   prenuptial agreement in, 3, 200
   press coverage of, 194, 199, 200,
      202, 203, 204–5, 206, 212–14,
      298
   public interest in, 202–3
   Rubi's clothes shopping in, 191, 207
   Rubi's financial problems in, 195–96
   Rubi's infidelity in, 209, 213–14
   Rubi's profits from, 200, 214
   Rubi's valedictory comments on,
      212–14
   separation in, 209, 212–14
   sex life of, 207
   wedding in, 199–200, 201, 202–6
Rubirosa-Rodin relationship, 238–43,
      284–85, 294, 298, 299, 300,
      305, 308
   courtship in, 239–42
   in Cuba, 264–67
   financial problems in, 307
   honeymoon in, 243
   New York jewel theft in, 269–70
   Odile's self-assertion in, 270–71,
      303–4
   Odile's widowhood and, 312–13,
      315–17
   Rubi's authority in, 270–71, 303,
      317
   Rubi's auto racing in, 263, 276
   sex life of, 317
   social life in, 269–70, 275, 276–77,
      280–81, 291–92, 309, 310

   wedding in, 242–43
   Zsa Zsa Gabor and, 252–53, 304
Rubirosa! The Musical, 323
Rue de Bellechasse Residence,
      133–34, 140, 141, 142, 143,
      144, 241
   luxurious furnishings of, 134, 177,
      307
   sale of, 270
   Zsa Zsa Gabor at, 176–77
Ruiz Trujillo de Berges, Ligia
      "Japonesa," 68
Rusk, Dean, 285

Saborit, Eduardo, 124
Sachs, Gunther, 304, 309, 316, 317
   Rubi's mentoring of, 306–7
Sadruddin Khan, 314, 315
"Saint, The," 171
Salazar, Dr. Joaquin, 199–200, 203,
      205
Salinger, Pierre, 285, 292
Salvador, Henri, 73
Samuel, Henri, 134
Sánchez, Ana Rubirosa, 11, 17, 18, 24,
      132, 141, 241
Sánchez Lustrino, Gilberto, 24, 36, 39,
      141
   in stamp scandal, 66–67
Sánchez Rubirosa, Gilberto, 141, 247,
      250, 251–52, 272, 284,
      293–94, 316
San Cristóbal, 30
Sanders, George, 166, 167, 170–79,
      220
   career of, 166, 171, 172, 252
   marrying wealth advocated by,
      172–73
   personality of, 171
   psychotherapy of, 172, 192
   suicide of, 222*n*
Sanders-Gabor relationship, 166, 167,
      170–76, 178, 201, 222
   divorce in, 192–94, 196, 216, 217
   first meeting in, 170–71
   George's belittling remarks in,
      172–73, 174–75, 176